The High-Concept Massacre:

Genre Screenwriters Tell All!

By Jose Prendes

The High-Concept Massacre
© 2016. Jose Prendes. All rights reserved.

All illustrations are copyright of their respective owners, and are also reproduced here in the spirit of publicity. Whilst we have made every effort to acknowledge specific credits whenever possible, we apologize for any omissions, and will undertake every effort to make any appropriate changes in future editions of this book if necessary.

No part of this book may be reproduced in any form or by any means, electronic, mechanical, digital, photocopying or recording, except for the inclusion in a review, without permission in writing from the publisher.

Published in the USA by:
BearManor Media
P O Box 71426
Albany, Georgia 31708
www.bearmanormedia.com

Printed in the United States of America
ISBN   978-1-59393-940-3 (paperback)
         978-1-59393-941-0 (hardcover)

Book & cover design and layout by Darlene Swanson • www.van-garde.com

Contents

Acknowledgments v

Fade In: An Introduction To Masochism 1

Shane Bitterling 7

Carl Gottlieb 33

Trent Haaga 59

Stephen Johnston 89

Amy Holden Jones 109

C. Courtney Joyner 129

Rolfe Kanefsky 157

Sean Keller 181

William C. Martell 203

John Penney 221

Doug Richardson 245

Chris Watson 269

S.S. Wilson 291

Fade Out: A Re-appraisal of the Typist 317

Acknowledgements

This love letter to the craft of screenwriting could not have been possible without my fellow screenwriters, who willingly shared their time and their stories with me. I would very much like to thank my friends and colleagues, Shane Bitterling, Carl Gottlieb, Trent Haaga, Stephen Johnston, Amy Holden Jones, C. Courtney Joyner, Rolfe Kanefsky, Sean Keller, William C. Martell, John Penney, Doug Richardson, Chris Watson, and S.S. Wilson.

I would further like to thank Chris Watson for putting BearManor Media on my radar with his amazing interview book *Badass Women of Cinema*; to Doug Richardson for putting me in touch with Amy Holden Jones; and to John Penney for putting me in touch with Stephen Johnston and for his continued support. Thank you to fellow screenwriter Scott Alexander, who put me in touch with John Penney. A big thank you goes out to scriptmag.com and the most excellent Jeanne Bowerman for putting me in touch with Doug Richardson and William C. Martell.

Thank you to my publisher, Ben Ohmart, for believing in this book immediately, and Editor Dave Menefee for dotting dots and crossing the crosses. A very big thank you to my first line of defense, and the "light of my life" as Jack Torrance would say, my wife Jessica, who read every word and was crucial in making sure this didn't suck.

I am very grateful to my special guest for the wonderful opening act of this book, and to a special person for putting us together.

And lastly to you, the person who read this, I hope it helped. Now put this on the shelf, it will be here if you need it again, you have some writing to do.

Fade In: An Introduction to Masochism

> *"I could be just a writer very easily. I am not a writer.
> I am a screenwriter, which is half a filmmaker ... but it is
> not an art form, because screenplays are not works of art.
> They are invitations to others to collaborate on a work of art."*
>
> -Paul Schrader, screenwriter

When you ask someone who their favorite actor or director is, they usually have an answer. Even the fellah down the street, the one with no teeth and no feet because of diabetes, the guy with one shirt that's barely that now, and with pants that sag around him from when was fiendishly obese, even he has an answer. Sure, they all might say the same folks: Humphrey Bogart, Marilyn Monroe, Steven Spielberg, or Stanley Kubrick. The point is most of them have an answer. Now, you ask anyone, even someone who isn't necessarily film-literate but goes to the movies every weekend to digest the recent glob of multi-colored fast-moving things, who their favorite screenwriters are, they would be hard-pressed to give you an answer.

The High-Concept Massacre

Why does the lowly screenwriter not get the praise he or she deserves? Why aren't they as lauded by the masses as say Scorsese or Cameron? Why is the act of movie writing such a disposable element in the big, greasy brass cog of the Hollywood dream machine? Why does the scriptwriter have to eke out a living so that others can hog the fortune and glory, like Indiana Jones?

By the way, if you get that reference to *Indiana Jones and the Temple of Doom* (1984), then you know the work of Willard Huyck and Gloria Katz, who wrote that film. In fact, almost every single moment from a movie and almost every single bit of dialogue from a movie came from that nameless writer you failed to think of.

"We're going to need a bigger boat." –*Jaws* (1975), Carl Gottlieb

"Frankly my dear, I don't give a damn." –*Gone With The Wind* (1939), Sidney Howard (among many others uncredited)

"Here's looking at you kid." –*Casablanca* (1942), Julius J. Epstein, Philip G. Epstein, Howard Koch

"Go ahead, make my day." – *Sudden Impact* (1983), Joseph Stinson

Odds are that you, the person whose eyeballs I've managed to get my word hooks into, aren't the no-goodnik who doesn't know their ass from their elbow when it comes to screenwriters. As a matter of fact, I'll wager you picked this book up because you hunger to join the unwashed masses of forgotten typists who spin out lyrical celluloid dreams in the promise of big bucks. I shouldn't have to tell you to be aware of the screenwriter; you should be highly attuned to them already. I shouldn't have to spend pages here convincing you that screenwriters make the actual stuff that dreams are made of; you figured it out on your own that, without words, people like Brad Pitt or Audrey Hepburn are just well-put-together pretty faces.

The people that should be reminded of it, the studios, producers, and whatnot, won't read this, and in a way that's good news. That means I can be subversive, I can be candid, and my interviewees can be candid also. That means that here, within these pages, you hold not only a book of interviews, but a book of cautionary tales from one writer to another and to you.

I lost my parents at an early age. I was adopted and grew up in a new family, feeling always like the outsider. They were good to me, which I am thankful for, but there were times when I just wanted to escape the harsh realities of life and when I fled, I found movies waiting for me. I could dive into any kind of time, any kind of place, and make friends with strangers and survive unheard-of dangers, and come out in one piece, transformed.

I didn't understand that movies were written until I saw *Jaws* (1975), and it left a profound impact on me, not only for its sheer mastery of every element but by the simple way the characters spoke; they were real people to me, not actors. The film that drove the screenwriting nail deeper into my brain was Frank Capra's mind-blowing *It's A Wonderful Life* (1946). Yeah, some call it hokey, but that simple movie wields more power in one scene than almost any movie does with its entire runtime. The idea that a writer could tell a story and at the same time say something, I mean *really* say something, about the human condition moved me to tears, and it still does to this day. Just thinking about either movie fills me with a warmth that reminds me of the power of movies, and that's why both films share the top spot as my favorite films and scripts of all time. I decided one night, wishing on a star as I lay awake thinking of my parents, to dedicate my life to movies and books and as of this writing I have twelve produced screenplays, three published novels, and two published non-fiction books.

I say all that as preamble to explain who I am, since I won't be speaking much in the next few hundred pages, but also as a living example that if you dream it, you can accomplish it. I've brought to you a selection of screenwriters from the tops of the industry to the micro-budget level, because every writer's experience is a valuable learning tool. Not everyone's career is the same, as you will see, but there are striking similarities to the ebb and flow of this business in regards to the wonderful masochists at the keyboards.

Why do I call screenwriters masochists? The definition of a masochist is one who likes pain, and in all honesty writing movies is a very painful process. The thing is that we love movies, and we will do almost anything to make movies. We'll work for peanuts. We'll toss out draft after draft just for the chance of saying we got a movie off the ground. We'll fight for credit. We're masochists because this business treats us like second-class citizens, but if you do ok, you can make a living. If you don't do ok, you have to live in your car, but you still find a way to make movies.

So, here's a warning, against my better judgment as a content maker, this book is going to scare you. It will make you rethink screenwriting as a career. It will turn your stomach and make you apply at the nearest fast food place, where you could be manager in two years. This book will twist and turn your notions on how Hollywood works; it will cause you great pain and sadness upon learning the ungodly odds. This book should be viewed as a giant stop sign for your screenwriting career, where you must pause to reflect. If you're not ready to know the bad, bold realities, then go ahead and put this book down....

Still with me?

Not scared out of your mind by the daunting challenge?

There's hope for you yet, young scribe, because you'll need those guts. Guts make all the difference. The good news is that it isn't all gloom and doom. Settle in and let's chat with some industry pros. There are plenty of great, untold stories within these pages that will either horrify you or make you chuckle, or both at the same time, and when I say these are cautionary tales, I mean it.

~ Jose Prendes, August 2015

Shane Bitterling loses head over screenwriting!
Photo courtesy of Shane Bitterling

Shane Bitterling

Beneath Loch Ness (2001)
Desperate Escape (2009)
Puppet Master X: Axis Rising (2012)
Reel Evil (2012)

Jose: What brought you to screenwriting?

Shane: Actually, I came into it sort of by accident. I was an artist and wanted to get into comics. When I was looking at colleges for art and that type of thing, I just didn't want to hang around with those people, to be frank. And looking at it now, I was stupid. That's exactly who I wanted to hang out with. I was an Indiana Hillbilly, who didn't want to hang around with the art crowd. So, I went into school and wrote my first short script. Got best in class and all that, but really only because I finished the assignment when nobody else did.

Jose: Then you were hooked on a feeling.

Shane: Yeah. I later moved to L.A. and the intention was to direct or whatever. I just wanted to make movies. I had optioned a comic book with a friend and we were going to go and make this movie. But it would have cost $150 million. There was no way we were going to make this thing. The only thing we could do was write. That was free. We stole a download of a writing program from somebody and that's what we used to write our screenplay. We were so proud of it, and it was an absolute piece of crap. It had a lot of good ideas in it, but it wasn't well written. It was horrible.

The High-Concept Massacre

Jose: What was it about?

Shane: It was a comic book called *The Light and Darkness War,* and it was about a Vietnam veteran, who slips into a coma and his wrecked body is here on Earth, but his soul goes to this other planet. It's sort of Valhalla. So, he's a Vietnam vet fighting against knights in shining armor, fighting against World War II veterans, Civil War, Huns, and all that. You know, the good and evil type thing. It had a lot to do with Nikola Tesla, and Leonardo da Vinci was the one creating the weapons, because that's one of the things he actually did in his life. There were so many great, cool things in there. Tom Veitch was the writer on that. We got so much interest on that thing. My friend and I had only been out here eight or nine months, and we did this and got a lot of really great meetings at studios through the help of other people and that type of thing.

Jose: Basically networking your ass off.

Shane: Yeah. It was like "Hey, these two knuckleheads have something really cool, we want to try to help." Everyone wanted to be a part of it. Some people really loved it. They loved the comic book side of it and the idea. A couple people thought, "Wow, you guys are really good writers." Looking at it now, I don't know why they would say that. There was a guy at Village Roadshow that was a big fan of it. Nothing happened there, but we got on their books as writers to look out for. And then we went and talked with these other guys, whose sole purpose of the meeting was to tell us, "This is the biggest piece of shit we've ever read. Don't know why you guys wasted our time. You're killing trees printing it on paper. We just wanted to look at the two fuckups who wrote the worst piece of shit we've read in our life. We have really important things to do, like producing an adaptation of *The Mod Squad.*" So, you know, there was a lot of bad to go with the good.

Jose: Ouch, what a learning experience.

Shane: We came out here and we didn't know you're not supposed to do that. You're not supposed to just call these people on the phone. You're not supposed to do this or that. You have to go through channels. And it's really something that I think Hollywood has beaten out of everybody, the can-do attitude. We came out and didn't know anything or anybody and we weren't a couple of rich kids, but we came here to make movies. Just through necessity and being absolutely broke, we became writers and managed to get the option for the comic book. Tom Veitch was a big name, but we approached him and his manager and said, "Look, we have no money in our pockets at all. Our pockets are sewn shut. But we really want to do this. We really want to try." They appreciated us being flat-out honest. We didn't have any Hollywood bullshit about us, and they gave us a shot. Unfortunately, nothing really ever did happen, but we became close friends with everybody on that side of things, even though we failed. We were real close to a deal, but it came to, "You guys are fired, we have our own writers, go sit in a corner," which we didn't understand at the time and it was unacceptable to us. But then again, no one offered us any money to go sit in the corner, either.

Jose: This was all on your own, without representation?

Shane: Totally without. We learned a ton. There was a big moment when there was a showdown between us and this guy, who was really trying to screw us. We held all the cards, and being dumb and super broke, we could have just rolled over for a chance. He was under the impression that we signed some papers, but we didn't. So, he walked in the room and started screaming at us like we were animals. Pacing back and forth, calling us every name in the book because he thought he had us by the balls. "I own you," and all those bad clichés. I've never heard such a tirade in all my days. My friend, Devin Kelsay, and I looked at each other when the guy took a breath, nodded to each other, stood up, and told him to go fuck himself. We didn't sign the deal. His face hit the floor and we walked out. Gave each other a high-five on the sidewalk. Got in the car and said, "What did we do?" But it was absolutely the right thing to do, this guy was such a piece of shit and it destroyed a lot of relationships. Unless there was an epic death, you don't talk to or treat people like that.

Jose: Was there a day job involved to keep yourself sane?

Shane: I worked for a distribution company that was in the same office as a production company. My side was selling the movies, and the other side was making them, and then the lines kind of crossed and we started developing our own things. I sort of had a knack for story. I think story is sort of ingrained into your head. You can either tell one, or you can't. We had things that came into the office that we were developing. One time, we had the idea to develop a series of movies based on one of the teen magazines, and I was kind of in charge of that. We had this kid in the office that was in some whoop-de-doo writing program, and the guys that I worked for brought him in and said, "Hey, Shane developed this whole thing based around this magazine and we want you to write the script." And he goes, "Great, how much?" They go, "$5,000 bucks." And he went "Ha! You got to be shitting me! That's not even WGA." And it was such an insult to those guys and me. I mean, I'm basically an intern and chewed up my entire savings in six months living in L.A. They screamed at him so bad, he cried and ran out of the office. We never saw him again. I told them I'd totally take that job, but the project just never happened. I went on to do work on some other stuff, and I got no credit, and not even a thank you. I said, "That's enough," and I quit.

Jose: Ok, let's talk about your first actual screen credit, *Beneath Loch Ness*. How did that project materialize?

Shane: A few months went by, and I got a call from one of the guys I'd worked for and they asked about this cryptozoology series. It was supposed to be like *Indiana Jones*, but this one's Bigfoot, this one's the Loch Ness Monster, and the next one was Jersey Devil. It was going to be a series of movies like that. They said, "We want you to write it. This was your idea, we want you to go do it." That was my first sort of thing. It was four years since I'd moved out here and I got my first real, paid writing thing. The movie didn't turn out that well, and there was a whole history as to why that was even made. I was kind of a pawn in the whole thing. I found that out years later. But it was my first paid job and I'm thankful for it.

Jose: Well, now my curiosity is piqued. I want to hear more about these behind the scenes shenanigans.

Shane: The guys that I worked for, they were the distribution/production guys, and we had distributed a whole catalog of movies for another man. I don't know exactly what it was, but his investors didn't feel they were getting the amount of money that they wanted to, and the *Loch Ness* thing was dug up because they wanted to pay these guys and it was sort of a way to clear the slate between all of them. Basically, everyone is getting this amount of money and everybody's friends again. They brought me on because they knew I was really upset, obviously, because I had quit.

Jose: Now, your script idea gets picked to be this slate cleaner, you get the green light, but there's another writer credited alongside you.

Shane: There's another writer. I was working at an Internet company and we were going to launch the website very soon, and we were working sixteen to seventeen hours a day, and they needed the script immediately. I had this writer friend, and I said, "Hey, I'm working all day, can you do the work during the day. Send me what you got and then I'll work all night before I go back to this Internet thing, because it's killing me." He ended up not doing a damn thing. Nothing. I had it all laid out, all the story beats, and he went on the most wild tangents, and he could not follow anything. He did absolutely nothing but create more work for me. Then he went off and did a free rewrite for another producer, while this one was paying. So, I wrote the whole script myself, but since he was already in there, I had to give him credit. I think he should have gotten a story credit, and not screenplay credit, because he didn't do anything. Then after all was said and done, I got the check and paid him half, and then he had the nerve to call those guys, who were my friends, and complain that he didn't get enough money.

Jose: Seems like greed is the overriding force in Hollywood sometimes, but the good news is that they actually went on to make the movie, which doesn't always happen.

Shane: They made the movie. I was sent the script by the main producer with a note saying, "Shane, can you fix this?" This was a $2 million budget movie, and one of the other guys had gone in and rewritten it as a $50 million movie. We can't afford any of this stuff, plus it was all typos and everything. You know, I have the belief that you don't have to be good, people don't have to like your story, they don't have to like your characters, but you have to be professional. I mean, a typo will happen here and there; you just can't avoid it sometimes. But if you clearly don't give a shit and you give this to somebody to read, they're either going to think you're an idiot, or worse, you wasted their time. I mean, writing programs format for you, but people still find a way to mess it up. Spell-check takes ten minutes. Read your script a few times before sending it to people. Show that you care and take the job seriously. It takes you ten minutes to run a spell check. I've had scripts turned down because it wasn't their thing for one reason or another, but I got put on approved writers lists because my scripts are super clean and professional. I agonize over that stuff. I was really pissed off about that, and I had to rewrite it.

Jose: Did you get bombarded with notes from all sides?

Shane: I was getting notes like, "Suspense is free. At this point, have him creeping around the shadows," or "Character is free." One of my favorite notes was, "He needs to be more like a character, you know, like he eats beef jerky." I said, "Ok," and that was his character stuff. I just did whatever I was told, really. I was still learning the process. But somewhere in the middle, all the producers got into a fight. There was going to be no smoothing it over, and the director kept walking off the set. I went up there two days, and it was turmoil. There were so many problems with everybody, but the movie finished. I went to a screening at AFM with a whole bunch of buyers, and the movie started and I said, "Oh my God, what is this?" I mean, it sort of resembled what I wrote, but it just didn't really play how I imagined. And the script wasn't genius, it was a *Jaws* and *Aliens* rip-off, but there were scenes in there that I don't know where they came from, and I get shit about it all the time!

Jose: I haven't seen the film, so you'll have to describe one of these infamous sequences for us.

Shane: There's this scene with Patrick Bergen. When they've decided they're going to go hunt Nessy in her lair, he comes out in *Braveheart* makeup and a spear and he gives this really bad *Braveheart* speech. At this point, during that screening, I looked around at everybody and they were all cocking their eyebrows and giggling, and I just shrunk all the way down to the floor. It was full of stuff like that. But it was pulled away from the director in post, so not even was it not really my script, but the effects aren't done so they're just pre-viz [Author's Note: The term "pre-viz" is short for "Previsualization," in this case the computer-generated effects have been roughed out as an idea of what the final CG image would be], there's no color timing so Scotland is all brown because it was shot in California, and they didn't have a final sound mix. It was an unfinished movie. The guy who directed it, Chuck Comisky, is a great special effects guy. He's James Cameron's right hand man. He developed all the 3D technology for Cameron, but it was pulled away from him.

Jose: And that unfinished version was released?

Shane: That's what was released, and it's on Syfy Channel all the time! It's the only movie I know of that was released totally unfinished and it's been really successful over the years. And it was Miramax/Buena Vista Home Video who put it out. Of all the movies I've made, I got paid really well for it, actually. It wasn't Writer's Guild, but I get the Foreign Levies checks. It's been really good to me. I was really irritated about it for many years, because you want it to be good. I just wanted a cool monster. But that movie won't die. Like Nessy, it just keeps going, and going, and going. People make fun of me for that movie, but for good, bad, or indifferent, it's helped me get other jobs.

Jose: That's similar to my experiences. The interesting thing about screenwriters is that we're the kind of writers that get fucked with the most. In theater, you can't touch a word of a play, even if there's typo. Novelists have the editor coming in and saying their piece, but for the most part the writer is in charge. However, the work of a screenwriter is largely taken for granted.

Shane: Right, everyone thinks that your screenplay is the skeleton, but it's not. It's the body and soul and the brain of the entire thing! But from top to bottom, it doesn't matter if you're the director or if you're the guy who gets coffee for everybody, they all have an idea on how to fix your script. It's really frustrating. A lot of directors and producers don't understand story. But they can demand something that they thought of while taking a shit that morning, and you're forced to put it in there because the writer's the whipping boy. But they don't understand that the little butterfly they mess with has a ripple effect through the entire script. Sometimes, those things don't really matter, but sometimes, that little thing, whatever it is, is the difference between your audiences going along for the ride. I think all ideas should be considered. Some are great until you find out they're not. Some are horrible, but lead to a great one. You have to have what I call a shit-o-meter. Knowing when to give up on an idea or pursue another one. Some people are just pure ego. They force every idea they have on the project because it's the only idea they have. Entire scripts change to make that crappy idea seem not so crappy. Good writers and execs have a well-tuned shit-o-meter. Some people have a broken one.

Jose: Have you ever had that issue with an actor wanting to replace words or throw out whole monologues in favor of their own witticisms?

Shane: If you're an actor, and you have something better, if it's more natural for you to say, by all means do it. I don't bow to every one of my words, like most writers do. If you can improve it, then do it. Most that I work with think they can, but they can't. At all. I have one guy who constantly changes every single word every single time. Nobody thinks he's funnier than he does. He's anti-funny. I've only come across a few actors, who have actually been able to improve something I've put down by leaps and bounds. Those guys are actors who really get into their character, so it all comes out naturally. Sometimes actors don't understand the tone of the scene, they're only concerned with their lines, but then they play with them and screw them all up, which changes the dynamic of the scene. I'm always trying to reign those in. With my career, I don't get to work with your [Robert] De Niros or your [Al] Pacinos, and those type of guys. I got a lot of the other guys. I get the director's or the producer's girlfriend, and it's her first movie. When they're bad, I look bad. Everybody looks bad. They're not actors. They're line readers. But when you get an actor in the moment, it can be totally righteous.

Jose: Absolutely, that's the curse of the screenwriter. But keeping that in mind, is there one of your films that you feel has been the most faithful to your work?

Shane: There hasn't been one where I thought, "That's exactly what was in my head." Maybe *Reel Evil* came close. I wrote a Lifetime Channel movie that I barely even recognized when I saw the movie. There are scenes that are great, and there are occasions where the scene has actually changed a little bit, maybe for money or whatever reason, and that scene came out way better than I thought. But as a whole, for me, the movies have been disappointing, but I'm also my harshest critic. I don't mean any disrespect to the people making the movie. There are so many moving parts and behind-the-scenes weirdness. I'm just extra tough on my work. I always agonize about it. Being the writer, you just sit and grin. Just shut up and wait for the next job to come around. Also, all the movies that I've done have been work-for-hire jobs. My specs have kissed the big time a couple of times, but I haven't had one of my babies produced.

Jose: Yeah, let's talk about your script *Witch Hunters*, which had a bit of traction for a while.

Shane: I wrote that one with another guy. It was seventeenth century witch hunters and it was a big action/adventure/horror thing. It was a fun one, and it ended up being sold because somebody said it was "Witches of the Caribbean." We gave it to his agent, and she took me on as well. We did a couple of small changes for her and literally within a week we had a bidding war going on. We kept hearing from Jerry Bruckheimer's people, "Jerry's really interested, he wants to make an offer." But that offer never came, and we had these other two guys duking it out, but they were losing interest. So, we had to make a decision and we sold it to Fox. It was originally titled *WitchFinders*, but things changed on the first meeting we had. Soon as we walked in the room to meet everybody, one of which was Arnold Kopelson, who we were in awe of, we realized that everyone wanted something totally different. They said, "Oh yeah, we love this, we're going to throw out your script and we're going to start from the bottom up." We joked, "Well, at least we still have the title." And then the next meeting they say, "You know, your title doesn't make any sense, we're changing it." So, we didn't even have that. Basically, what they wanted was the prequel to our script. They wanted to start months or a couple of years before our script. We said, "Oh, ok, we can do that, I guess. We'll do anything."

Jose: Now, you've sold a script to a huge studio, you're playing in the major leagues, and they immediately start telling you how wrong you are?

Shane: We walked in the door on that first meeting, and everyone was so nice. Arnold Kopelson took us into this massive office and said, "I'm going to make you guys millionaire writers!" And there was somebody in the room who just decided she hated us. She wasn't having it; she hated us the second we walked in the door. I don't know what the deal was, but we were never going to win her over. She wasn't the biggest producer in the room, but she was the strongest personality in the room. So, we cooked up this all-new story for this prequel, and went through like twelve different treatments for it. Finally, we hit on something that these people liked, but these people have to go to these people to get it approved. It seemed like everything we did, that one producer wasn't happy and she raised a stink. We were always dressed down in these meetings by her. So, because she was such a strong personality, her ideas sort of took over what everybody else wanted, because they were afraid of her, I don't know. But we had to do what she wanted and we kept getting beat up.

Jose: At some point, you start feeling like a typist instead of a writer. Almost like a stenographer for a madman. But I'm sensing the breaking point coming.

Shane: We were getting calls at two in the morning, "Oh, you have to do this!" or "No, no, let's change this," and it was this mishmash of ideas from all these different people. My writing partner and I talked and I said, "You know what, no matter what we do, we get yelled at. I'm sick of getting yelled at and we know that this story sucks, but this is what they all want. It's too many cooks in the kitchen and the main cook ain't a good cook." So, we

The High-Concept Massacre

made our own thing without telling anyone and we were really excited about it. We have a pitch meeting a few days later and we went over to [20th Century] Fox to pitch the main guy, and we were told that he was busy and we had to wait. While we waited, we acted out our pitch. We were doing voices and all this other stuff to get it nailed down. Anyway, everybody loved it, except for that lady, because we went against everything she said. I mean if she could have killed us, she would have. We made sure to not even look her way, because we were on such a roll. Sanford Panitch, the head of New Regency, loved it and wanted us to turn in the draft in three days, which was impossible, but we were thanking God we finally got it over the mountain. They all said that was the best pitch they'd ever seen in their lives. Except that one producer.

Jose: The gamble pays off. There's a huge lesson there.

Shane: It was that thing of there being so many people telling you what you should do, that you should do what your gut tells you to do, and what you really think you should do. That totally saved us. Cut to us writing the script, all reinvigorated. At this point, this had been a four or five month process of getting beat up. We did our version and then everybody started sticking their fingers in it again. Nobody would show it to Sanford until they had their say, and nobody knew what they wanted. That kind of ruined us again. It got to the point where someone said, "I don't understand why all these women are standing around cauldrons and there're black cats everywhere." It really hit us that these people really had no clue what they bought. They wanted it because other people wanted it, I suppose. Or they just didn't care anymore, which might be the case. We spent months spinning around the same bad ideas. When a good one would come up, it would get drowned out by all the bad ones. It was exhausting and maybe they just got sick of it.

Jose: It's a wonder anything halfway decent gets made nowadays.

Shane: Yeah, it was really, really crazy. But then we turned in that script, which wasn't what we pitched, but we were happy that we made sense of all the ingredients we were given. We somehow made it work. "Here's some Skittles, here's some M&Ms, here's some roast beef, here's some cheese and a couple of pine nuts. Now make it delicious." We did as much as we could and it's actually not bad. Sanford read it and said, "This isn't at all what I wanted." We kept saying that to them, "This is not what Sanford said he wanted. This is not what made him jump out of his chair." Then he says, "Contractually you guys are done. We're bringing in another team." So, they brought in another team, the guys who wrote *Reign of Fire* (2002), Gregg Chabot, Kevin Peterka, and Matt Greenberg. It was months behind schedule, but it got finished. Somebody sneaked us the script and those guys changed maybe ten percent and they said, "These guys actually did a great job," which is amazing for another writer to say. Then they hired another writer, and a director got attached and they started working together. At that point we knew that at most we would get story on it, but I'll take story credit on a $150 million summer tent pole movie, because our lives will change financially and could only get us more work.

Jose: So, when did this house of cards collapse?

Shane: The director and the new writer turned in their thing, and again somebody sneaked us the script. I wanted it to be great, so it would move forward, whatever our involvement would be. I read the first two pages and said, "Ahh, we're screwed. This will never get made." I don't know who this new writer was, but he was supposed to be this big deal, and it was absolutely abysmal, such a misguided direction to take this thing in. I mean it opens up with the moon raping a witch! This is not fun, summer stuff. At this point they're never going to make the movie, but because we sold that script, every other studio bought a witch script. Then those movies started to come out a few years later, and we read those initial drafts of these things, but the final movies clearly showed that they read our script, because there were little parts that were ours that weren't in theirs at first, like the weapons in *Hansel & Gretel: Witch Hunters* (2013). Story points and characters in others. The experience was the epitome of every writer's dream and it was the epitome of every writer's nightmare.

Jose: And this was your biggest project to date, the most financially lucrative, and never materialized into a finished movie.

Shane: It never happened. I made more on that movie that will never get made than I have on any of the other things I've done. At this point, we were already on meetings for other projects and doing another spec. A year or so after all this, we found out a bunch of producers wanted to work with us, but we didn't get those calls. People in the industry talk, so if they called the producer who hated us to find out what we were like, we were screwed. She told who knows how many people that we were unprofessional and difficult to work with. I mean it was absolutely pointless of her to say such things. Totally untrue. She made it her mission to try and destroy us because she was forced to apologize for the way she treated us at one point. It crushed me that somebody would do that. This is my livelihood. This destroys lives. Again, pointless.

Jose: Would you say it was worth it?

Shane: Yeah, yeah, absolutely totally worth it. Most of it. It's not a new Hollywood story that you just get kicked in the teeth, but you hop right back and you do it again. It was a bad experience, but I learned a huge deal from it. The biggest thing was that you just have to trust your gut, and you have to fight for it, especially at those stages. Once they're signed off and they're making the movie, that's their cross to bear. At least I know I got it to that point the way it should be done. You can't just do stuff to please somebody;

you have to really believe in it and sell it. The only way I've had any success is following that gut.

Jose: Speaking of following that gut, how did that lead you to your next movie, *Puppet Master X,* and the clutches of Full Moon Entertainment?

Shane: I had known Charlie Band for quite a while, and everyone I know has worked with him at some point. A friend of mine was writing a lot for him and he died, so I threw a memorial for him and invited Charlie and a lot of people that he worked with. Charlie showed up and gave a nice little eulogy, and then he told me that night that he wanted me to do some writing for him. He contacted me for a bunch of stuff, but I just didn't have time or I was working on other projects or whatever. But I told him, "You let me know whenever a new *Puppet Master* or one of those projects comes around. I'd love to do it." Sure enough, he called me about it. It was a real easy process.

Shane with Charles Band (center) and composer Richard Band.
Photo courtesy of Shane Bitterling

Jose: Did you pitch an idea or did he have something in mind?

Shane: I went to his office, he gave me a stack of all the *Puppet Master* movies, and he said, "Okay, you're going to follow immediately after the last one. The second that one ends, yours starts. There's a puppet in there called Ninja, I hate that thing. I don't want to see it. If you want to kill it, fine. I don't even really want to see it in the movie. Go make it awesome. See you in a couple of weeks." So, that was it. He called me a couple times and said, "I want to have this character in there, or that character in there," and then asked me to come up with four new puppets. I said to him, "Well, I'm following the Nazi thing here, so I want to do Nazi puppets that work for the bad guys," instead of our already established puppets, who in those movies are good for whatever reason. "Do whatever you want," he said, and that was the coolest thing ever just coming up with new puppets. He liked all of them, and every one of them was made. That was one of the more rewarding things in my writing career. I can hold these toys that I created. That was really a cool thing. But there's no money to make these movies and it shows. You watch all these movies in a short time and your brain just melts.

Jose: I'm pretty sure I know which one you'll pick, but do you have a favorite in the series that's the least brain-melty?

Shane: I think the best of the best is part three. C. Courtney Joyner wrote that and David DeCoteau directed it. It's pretty awesome.

Jose: That's what I thought you'd say. That's my hands-down favorite, as well. I think most fans agree on it being the series high point.

Shane: Yeah, they had some money to do it right. It was really low budget at the time, but now it would be considered some decent money. But the script was awesome, the effects were awesome, they had real stunts, and they had a lot of really cool shit going on. None of which you can do now at Full Moon. Nothing.

Jose: Now you're playing in a similar sandbox with *Puppet Master X*. I assume you wanted to rise to the level of the third film to aide in the restoration of the deteriorating series.

Shane: I didn't know really what to do. I wanted to do *Valkyrie* (2008), or *Inglorious Basterds* (2009), but I called it the *Inglorious Masterds*. I wanted the puppets to go kill Hitler, but Charlie didn't want to get anywhere near Hitler. So, I changed it to what it is now. But when he announced that I was doing this, people found me on Facebook. There are super-fans out there, and they know every detail of these movies. Now I know for a fact that starting with part four they don't make any Goddamn sense whatsoever, but these guys have convinced themselves that there's continuity between all nine or ten of those things, because there's one that's kind of an unofficial sequel. These guys started hounding me saying, "Oh, if you don't do this, you've screwed up the entire series." Yeah, because nobody's screwed it up before me. So, I told them, "I'm not going to be beholden to seven or eight movies that make no freaking sense whatsoever, because all I'm going to be doing is connecting dots between stuff, and explaining things. I just need to tell the story that I need to tell. I want it to be a good movie that makes sense and is fun. I don't know that I can do it, but my goal is to make the best one since part three, and you guys will be the judge of that when it's out. But I can't fuss with two decades of horseshit."

Jose: You certainly wouldn't be able to agonize over such details with the schedule you were given to write it.

Shane: It was a quick and dirty thing. I wrote it really fast. Charlie had a few notes, not really a lot, and then they went off and they shot it. But Charlie is really stuck on continuity. Then you watch the movies and there's no continuity, so what is the point of even addressing it. He forces this stuff, but then he ends up not shooting that stuff. It's a weird thing. Charlie is a great guy; he's been very kind to me. Money happens to arrive, or a job materializes when you kind of need it the most. The sets are fun and the crew is kind of like family. And one thing I love is that when Charlie says he's going to make a movie, he makes the movie. Nobody makes any money, but at the end of the day, you have a movie in your hands.

Jose: I credit Full Moon for inspiring me to make films, specifically *Trancers 2* (1991) believe it or not, but nowadays their stuff unfortunately doesn't hold much interest for me.

Shane: I've been on the set of a lot of Full Moon movies and I've watched a lot of Full Moon films that friends made or whatever, and if you're expecting them to be what they were twenty years ago, or if you're expecting them to have a higher level of competency, I guess I'll say, then you've kind of already set yourself up for failure. I mean everybody on set wants to make a good movie. They want to do whatever it is they can do to make the best thing possible, but there's only so much you can do with that little money, and even worse, the time. You just can't have ingenuity if you don't have the time and there's nothing available to you. You try to make the script as good as you can that can be shot, because there's been times when they'll say, "We don't have time for this," and they'll just rip pages out and throw them in the trash.

Jose: You bring up an interesting point about continuity. I've had to write a part three to the not-so-well-known *Mega-Shark* films, *Mega-Shark vs. Mecha-Shark* (2014), which I had a lot of fun with, but the producers never really asked me to pay attention to part two, for example. But that series has fans, which I was happy to discover, however it puts you in a tricky position as a writer, because if the series has already gone off the rails, it shouldn't be our place to fix it.

Shane: I did what I thought I could do on what could be done. Some of the movie is good, but it is a real cheap comparison to what they used to be. The puppets don't really do anything. We watch these things for the puppets and

**Shane with *Puppet Master X* star Stephanie Sanditz as Uschi.
Photo courtesy of Shane Bitterling**

the gore and that stuff just doesn't really exist anymore in those movies. You know David Allen, who did all the stop motion for those things? Well, he's dead, and there's nobody who can do what he did, so the stop-motion stuff is gone. Charlie doesn't do CG characters. He uses it to enhance things or for magic stuff, what have you. So, you're going to get something that's glued down to a table and they kind of move their arms a little bit.

Jose: But they always want you to write broad and grandiose things that you know the production can't necessarily afford or pull of correctly.

Shane: Yeah, we know how to write for that budget, that schedule. If something should take three shots to pull off, I write it as something that can be done in one, because he won't do the other two shots, so you'll lose all that information. I had this really cool ending that I wrote for *Puppet Master X*, and I asked the special effects guy, "Can you do this?" He goes, "Oh, that's really easy," and he'll walk through the whole thing. So, I say, "Okay, tell Charlie that when we're on set." And he doesn't, so what happens is we're sitting there and they schedule the finale on the last part of the last day of schedule and something took too much time earlier in the day and then for some reason they never have time to shoot the finale. I write this ending with all these moving parts to wrap it up, and Charlie comes up and says, "Your ending makes no sense." I go, "What are you talking about? It's the only thing that makes sense." He shook his head and said, "No, no, no, we're going to do this," and he has the camera locked down and has everybody who's in the finale, which includes different groups of people fighting, running in and out of the frame doing their thing, and then somebody gets stabbed. You know, you agonize over an ending with a cool, doable effect, but with these movies it just always ends up with someone being stabbed. He's like, "Dude, that's a better ending!"

Jose: The perils of low-budget filmmaking. Making a movie is like moving a mountain. Moving a mountain with no money is going to cause a few cracks in the quality of your effort.

Shane: On a big-budget movie with action and this and that, they can spend four months shooting five minutes of film, and with these you're lucky to get two hours. That's why there's never any action in these things. There's not a punch and no running, there's none of that stuff. Basically everyone comes and stands in front of the camera. It's so fucking lame, but that's what we have time for.

Jose: But he used to make real films, which is crazy to me. They were all b-grade, but they were films. Do you think it's because Charles Band lost his touch or is it a money issue?

Shane: I think it's a little of both. I watched Full Moon movies and that really solidified what I wanted to do with my life. I wanted to make *Meridian* (1990). I wanted to make *Oblivion* (1994) and *Ghoulies* (1984). They had quite a bit more money to do these things back then, and most of them were shot in Romania when Charlie had a castle. They looked cool, had a real schedule, and real money. Still not a lot of money, but it was gigantic compared to nowadays. But a lot of things changed. They lost that big deal with Paramount and floundered. The worst period was the mid-1990s to the 2000s, I didn't even know Full Moon was still around, and then a friend of mine started writing for him. You know, one of the things is Charlie directs everything now. Full Moon and Empire had so many varying voices filtered through the same portal, which was Charlie's head. Now it's just Charlie's head. I mean, *Evil Bong* (2006) was really the thing that killed his company, but he keeps going back to that same well over and over and over and it's burying him. The numbers don't lie, but when he sees the numbers I think it's delusional in his head. I mean he'll go on social media and announce, "Who's ready for another *Evil Bong*?" and the comments are a never-ending thread of, "Not me. Fuck you! Do something new!" People don't like the puppet stuff anymore. There're a few core fans, but *Puppet Master X* didn't do well at all.

Jose: Speaking of something new, that brings us to your next Full Moon joint, *Reel Evil*, which was definitely a change up from the type of product he was making.

Shane: Yeah, so that happened right after *Puppet Master X*. Charlie had a sweet deal with Redbox and he called me up and said, "Redbox wants a found footage movie like *Blair Witch* and *Paranormal Activity*. Do you know Danny Draven? He's directing. I'm going to put you two in touch, figure it out. You have this amount of money and this amount of days. Go to it." I talked to Danny, we got along immediately and we were excited because it was something current. Something different. No puppets. We talked about what we didn't like about these movies, like the fact that there's never a reason for the guy to still be holding the camera, or a good reason for them to have a camera in the first place. We wanted to address some of that stuff. I said, "Why don't we do a film crew shooting a documentary." So, I went and wrote the script, and I was under the impression that I could just write a thirty-page script and we were just going to wing it, and improv the dialog. Danny goes, "Oh no, I've edited several of these movies and it's the exact opposite. The script has to be longer than a normal script, because we don't have time to improv. Every single scream has to be written, because we have no time to make this movie.

Jose: How many shooting days did you have?

Shane: We had six days! Danny said, "If your script is like ninety pages, that's going to be like a sixty minute movie. It has to be way longer." So, that sucks, and I went and re-wrote it. It turned out to be 120-some pages. Danny loved it, but I never heard anything from Charlie. The line producer we had said, "The script is way too long, and there's no way we can do this in six days." Danny kind of explained, but the guy still said it was impossible. I just went and reformatted it, I never made any cuts.

Jose: With that hurdle conquered, you go into shooting. What was that process like, in terms of working with actors? I assume on a found footage movie, even with scripted stuff, the actors want to make it as organic as possible. Or they should want to do that, I should say.

Shane: I was in that mode that they could riff on this, especially with found footage, because yeah, you want it to sound organic. So, I told them, "You say what comes natural, because that's what's going to sell the character." They always had an issue with some line that they somehow thought was goofy. I'd tell them to change it to something they were comfortable with. But they'd usually just say something equally stupid. I liked the script a lot. There's a lot of stuff in the movie that I'm very happy with, even though I had no time to write that thing and no money. That's often when your best stuff spills out of your head. You don't have time to over think. You just have to do it, and the long hours and computer radiation makes your brain open up and spew things you normally wouldn't. But my not give-a-damn is still better than most people's give-a-damn. No time and no money isn't an excuse to be lousy or unprofessional. It's still your name on it. Danny and I took it very seriously, because it wasn't the normal Full Moon movie and it had a chance to be seen by a wide audience. There's no visual difference between our $60,000 movie shot in six days and *Paranormal Activity*, which was millions and shot over a luxurious bunch of weeks, and that was exciting to us. I didn't have time to agonize over dialog, and I would have changed a few things, but I liked it. Even though it was totally out of the Full Moon wheelhouse, we had nudity and gore, which put it in with what's expected from the company. The other found footage movies don't have that stuff.

Jose: Would you say that *Reel Evil* was your most satisfying production?

Shane: It was Danny and I. We were a team working together, trying to really do something, whereas most of the people I work for are trying to make crap and we didn't intend to make crap. We wanted to give it the best shot, and it was the closest to what I intended it to be in the script, as a whole; the tone and such. But we didn't have time to do a lot of cool things and there's some weird CG that I have no idea why it's in there. But it was overall pretty satisfying. It was the most fun I ever had on a set, and most of the crew still say that, also. I never had a note from Charlie, ever. I don't even know if he read the thing. But we didn't screw it up. We did what little we could with what we had. Also, the post was sped up. [Author's Note: The term "post" refers to all the work done on a movie (editing, adding music, etc.) that is done after or *post*-filming it.] We thought we had a month and half more, but

The High-Concept Massacre

(from left) **Kaiwi Lyman, Jessica Morris, Shane, Jeff Adler,** and *Reel Evil* director **Danny Draven.** Photo courtesy of Shane Bitterling

ended up with a month less than we thought. Look, either you like found footage or you don't, but there's some really good stuff in it.

Jose: So, after all these tears and triumphs and heartache, why do you continue screenwriting?

Shane: I don't know what else to do. I don't have any other skills. I found out I was pretty good with words, and I kind of fell in love with that. It came naturally and I stuck with it. It's what I do. I'm a writer and I write. It's who I am. It's really satisfying to pluck puzzle pieces from the ether and find the perfect place for them; even better when somebody pays for them. I would love to have a little more control, but I'm the writer, which means everybody on set pisses on me. But I stick with it because it's what I do. I work hard for no security whatsoever, which sucks. I'm stressed most of the time because I don't know if anybody will like what I do. But it's what I do.

Jose: Let's say someone wants to get pissed on because they feel they have no other skills, what advice would you give a future screenwriter?

Shane: You have to sit down and show up for the job. In Hollywood, everybody's a writer. Everybody thinks it's so easy. It's not. It's long, tedious hours with cramps and back pain. Stronger vision prescriptions. It's difficult. But you have to show up and do it. It doesn't happen overnight. It's not just being able to tell a story. It's structure and format and most importantly, characters you want to hang with. You know, get to the end and hopefully somebody will be excited to take a look at it. But you can't be at Starbucks talking about it. Lock yourself in a dark room, turn your computer on, put your ass in a seat, and write something. Anything. When I sold *WitchFinders*, I got tons of calls from people who could barely write their name. All of them are writers now because I sold something. One guy had it all figured out. He was going to write six scripts a year and sell them for $500,000 each then retire early. I don't think he's retired yet. As any kind of an artist, the thing that is most damaging is being satisfied. Once that screenplay's done, you do it again. And again. You need to get it to that point where at least other people will be satisfied with it, and as long as they are, then I have to be. The goal is you're writing this stuff to sell it, so you have to have the knowhow to be able to do it.

Jose: What do you consider the best-written movie you've ever seen? What would you recommend to someone who wants to learn movie writing?

Shane: One of the absolute best, and one of my all-time favorite movies for a lot of reasons, is *The Taking of Pelham One Two Three*. I always say that's one of the best dialog movies I've ever seen. I've never read the script, but based on the final movie, every single one of those characters is memorable from the main crew all the way down to just the beat cop. Everybody has a line that is instantly memorable, quotable, funny, poignant, or whatever. To me, that is the ultimate, perfect screenplay. Even if the screenplay wasn't exactly that movie, it inspired all these men and women to do it justice. That's really what your screenplay should do; inspire people to do really great work.

Carl Gottlieb, shark wrangler. Photo by Daniela Wood

Carl Gottlieb

Jaws (1975)
Jaws 2 (1978)
The Jerk (1979)
Jaws 3-D (1983)

Jose: When did you first fall in love with the movies?

Carl: I grew up in the heyday of the studio system. In my little neighborhood in Manhattan there were two big showcase theaters and four independents that showed second and third run pictures, including foreign films, so there was never a shortage of good movies. If you wanted to go down to 42nd Street, you could see three westerns, a cartoon, a Pete Smith specialty, and the news all for a quarter. So, yay movies!

Jose: Of all that abundant cinema in your formative years, can you point to one that you consider the definition of cinema?

Carl: Yes! It's a corny old studio film with a magnificent cast. It's been remade many times; even as a *Get Smart* two-part episode. It's a movie called *Prisoner of Zenda*. The version I love is the 1937 version with Ronald Colman, David Niven, Mary Astor, Madeleine Carroll, Raymond Massey, and Douglas Fairbanks Jr., who's never been more dashing. I've learned since then that that film had some of the best fencing sequences ever done in movies. It's a romantic, swashbuckling, old-fashioned, bodice-ripping, tear-jerking movie. It's just a delicious old black and white delight. I can watch it anytime.

Jose: I've seen a version of that film, but it was in color.

Carl: Probably with Farley Granger in it. They made a color remake of it in the 1950s. That was a shot for shot remake in color with a different cast who had none of the skills of the original cast.

Jose: And what spurred you to become a part of the movies as a writer?

Carl: When I was first starting, I was doing the Smothers Brothers show on CBS [*The Smothers Brothers Comedy Hour* (1967-1970)], and somebody, who was a fan of the Smothers Brothers, was doing an article for a high school paper, and they asked me, "How did you get here?" "Look around the room," I said, and there was a group of young writers, which included Steve Martin, Rob Reiner, and Mason Williams, the poet. "Everyone in this room is a result of their whole life so far. There are a series of decision points, almost like in a game, where you come to all these forks in the road and you make choices based on necessity or whim or curiosity, and each of those takes you down a different path and on each path you meet people who either want to work with you again or never want to work with you again, or vice versa." I've always been facile with words. I won composition prizes in high school, I was the editor of one humor magazine in one college, and I wrote a weekly column at the next college, the Syracuse University School of Journalism, where they published a daily paper. I was always good with words, and I was also a theater major, where I ended up drifting into stage-managing and the techie side of it. I found myself in The Committee, as a stage manager for one of the earliest and best improvisational companies; founded by some Second City people who wanted a theater of their own. We opened the show in L.A., where we were favorably reviewed by everybody. The Smothers Brothers saw me there as they were putting together a new writing staff for their summer replacement show, so I got to be in that writer's room, which led to being picked up for their Sunday night primetime show, which led to an Emmy for Best Written Musical, Comedy, Variety

Carl Gottlieb, right, working on Smothers Brothers with pre-white hair comic genius Steve Martin, left. Photo courtesy of Carl Gottlieb

show. We rotated writing assignments between us and the one that won the Emmy was the one on which my partner, Lorenzo Music, and I were head writers. He went on to create shows like *Rhoda* and *Newhart*. And then one job led to another. I made a decision, it was foolhardy, but it was a decision. I said, "I'm only going to work in show business or writing. I'm not going to be a cab driver or a bartender or any of those other jobs that people do to earn money," and I kind of stuck to that.

Jose: In your experience, what are the differences between writing for television, as opposed to film?

Carl: The great thing about writing for television is also the worst thing about writing for television. The worst thing about writing for television is writing under pressure. You've got to come up with things on time. When episode three finishes shooting, they've got to start episode four, and the script had better be ready. Time is inexorable and it's unusual and expensive to take time off to finish a script, so you just write harder and harder, and work longer and longer hours to churn out the material. That's the hard part, the constant pressure of time, especially if you want it to be good, that's even harder. The great thing about television is that once it's done, they shoot it. It's not like with a feature where you wait around for a director or a star to be attached. That's a long and torturous process. In television, you write, they shoot it and it's in the can, for better or worse. That's the thing about television. You're writing under pressure, but you're delivering product that gets made, and there's nothing more valuable to any writer of script entertainment. Seeing your work done in the collaborative process gives you new insights. Now, it's different for novelists or people who are writing personal films or art films. That's a different animal, because there you're working as an artist, and not as an ordinary screenwriter. Screenwriting, since the beginning, is a craft, which can be mastered much like journalism. If you know how to write a lead, you can write a news story. It's a level of craft that occasionally rises to the level of art because it's so good you have to say it is art.

Jose: When you moved on to features, did you miss television?

Carl: I didn't miss television because when I was writing features they were getting made, luckily. I had the pleasure of seeing the material done at a level of expense and excellence that you didn't get on television. With a feature you get care and attention; with television things are a little more haphazard.

Jose: How did you meet Steven Spielberg and start that relationship?

Carl: Steven had just come to town, and we had the same agent. Steven was a contract director at Universal, I guess I was still working in the Committee, and we became friends. I was five or six years older than him, so I was the one who introduced him to the circle of filmmakers and writers I knew. My house in those days was something of a salon. When you're an actor in the world of improv, you just know a lot of people, so actors, and musicians and writers were always over just hanging out, and Steven was there.

Jose: So, how does TV comedy writer end up writing *Jaws*?

Carl: Steven's first theatrical feature was *Sugarland Express* (1974), which was very well-reviewed by the critics, but it didn't perform at the box office the way the studio would have wanted, Steven felt he needed to do a more accessible movie, or at least one where you don't kill Goldie Hawn's boyfriend. He saw *Jaws* in the office of Zanuck and Brown, that story's famous, and he sent me a copy of it with the message "Eviscerate it" on the cover. So, I wrote a long memo, because that's what you did in those days. I had no notion of getting the job, I just wrote a memo on what I thought of the material. At the same time, Steven said, "You know what would be good? If you came on as an actor. Go through the script and find a part for yourself in the movie." So, I did, I liked Meadows, the publisher of the local paper, and in the script that I read, Meadows had a lot to do. It was a good part; he was like the second villain after Murray Hamilton's character. So, I went through the process and was cast as Meadows. Steven said, "It'll be great to have you around. You can help with the extras and the improvisation." Steven, even then, was very big on letting actors fill in the spaces. Then I guess he showed my early notes to Zanuck and Brown, and this was three and a half weeks before principal photography; the script was not in good shape. Steven called me on a Sunday morning and said, "I'm having bagels with Zanuck and Brown at the Bel Aire Hotel. I showed them your notes and they want to meet you. Can you come out?" I jumped in my car and I drove to the Bel Aire Hotel. We talked for five or six hours. They said, "Steven's going to Vineyard to start shooting. Can you go along and work on the script?" I had to quit my day job, which was being the story editor on *The Odd Couple*, but it was a feature. In those days, the dividing line between features and television was much more pronounced. In those days, doing a feature was much better than doing a half hour comedy show, so I said yes. I gave my bosses one day's notice, and then a few days later, Steven and I flew to Boston where he was going to cast extras. We had a two-bedroom suite, with a living room in the middle where he could see actors and we could talk, and I started re-writing the script.

Jose: Nowadays the shark has taken on a pop culture, tongue-in-cheek kind of disguise, and I'm as responsible as anyone having written the film *Mega-Shark vs. Mecha-Shark* and the novel *Sharcano*, but was there ever any concern back then that the topic of the film would be deemed too ridiculous or too much of a B-movie for a big studio to tackle?

Carl: No, not at all. There was a very popular documentary called *Blue Water, White Death* (1971), which sold us on the fact that Great Whites were killers. So, it was not a stretch to make the shark the killer, that was the unique element that made the novel such a best seller. The novel was doing great business, and just as a pop best-selling novel, Zanuck and Brown had reason to option it. The funny thing was when they were debating the size of the shark. In real life, a sixteen- or eighteen-footer was a monster, but the studio wanted it to be a leviathan; they wanted it to be Moby Dick. Joe Alves was the first employee on *Jaws*, once he did the research he found out that when the sharks get longer they get fatter, so thirty-foot shark, if one ever existed, would be a VW. It wouldn't look graceful and it wouldn't look terrifying. They compromised on twenty-five feet. Twenty feet is about the longest you'd find in nature.

Jose: A lot has been written about the tumultuous making of the movie, and most of it came from your book *The Jaws Log*. How does a writer find a way to work with a director when there is so much difficulty on a production?

Carl: A lot of it was that we were young and didn't know any better. We did things that were a little daring, and we took whatever steps we thought were necessary. We took the script apart and started putting it back together again, working under the limitations of what's built, what we could shoot, what we had permits for, and the days the extras were coming. Steven had learned, I guess on *Sugarland Express*, that one of the problems of being a director on location was that there was a lot of time wasted at the end of the day. You look at dailies and then you have to figure out where you're going to have dinner. Who's coming to dinner? Do we wait for them to take a shower or do we go straight from dailies? So, Steven said, "You know what, the studio has the resources, I want to rent a house on the Vineyard. It's great; you can save your per diem. I'll get a house that has like three or four bedrooms. You'll stay there and that way we're never farther than shouting distance. That way if either of us has an idea in the middle of night we're there." I recommend that, as a relationship, to live with the director. To this day, with the exception of working with actors I loved and trusted on stage with the Committee, *Jaws* was the happiest collaborative experience of my life. Everything worked. I was spared the worst part of all that because the last three months of shooting was getting the shark stuff, and when every line of dialog was finished. I was wrapped and I went home. Steven, Roy, Ricky and Robert had to stay and finish the fish stuff, which was very difficult.

Jose: It's obviously a testament that the film is a masterpiece and is considered by many, myself included, as the greatest film ever made. How does *Jaws* affect your career?

Carl: Of course, at the time nobody knew what it would do. I had already started another film with Richard Pryor, *Which Way Is Up?* (1977), and in between the time the film wrapped and came out, I still had to earn a living. I got paid SAG and WGA scale for acting and rewriting *Jaws*. So, I wrote four NBC specials for Flip Wilson, and then *Which Way Is Up?*, and then *Jaws* came out and it was a phenomenon. Then Steven became Steven Spielberg, and at that point he became less accessible. I was offered a dozen rip-offs, like *Paws*, where a Kodiak bear threatens a town in the Pacific Northwest, but my criteria for taking any writing job is: have I done this before? If I've done it before, I ask if I want to do it again. If I haven't done it before, I say, "Okay, let's do that!" I'm real sorry I never worked with Steven again, because I think we had chemistry. We could have been Billy Wilder and I.A.L. Diamond.

Jose: Let's talk about your chemistry with Richard Pryor, because of all the people you could make a movie with, how did you find yourself writing *Which Way Is Up?*

Carl: On the Flip Wilson specials I had done, Richard had been a guest on two of them, and he knew my work. Richard had a cyclical life. First *The Flip Wilson Show*, which was produced by Lorne Michaels, who even then knew how to book guests, had Richard Pryor, Lily Tomlin, and Peter Sellers as guests. Talk about a sketch-writer's dream. Richard was starting to slide at that point. Then, we did a special without him, and then, we did a third show with him when he was getting really famous, but he was deep into cocaine and cognac, and he picked a fight with an NBC page. It was a big scandal. Richard had some violent episodes in his career, but he was great and he liked what I wrote for him. I wrote a great sketch for him and Lily Tomlin. Sellers was a pain in the ass; he didn't want to rehearse, he wouldn't work with the others, and he had old sketches that he had done in England that he wanted to repeat. He didn't want to attempt any new stuff. So, anyway, Richard knew me as a writer, and somewhere in there, post-*Jaws,* I did some uncredited writing on *Car Wash* (1976), which was an urban comedy in which Richard had a hilarious cameo. The guy who wrote the script, which was an adaptation of an Italian film by Lina Wertmuller, was a socially conscious, politically active African American from Oakland, who really wasn't a screenwriter. The studio wanted a re-writer, the producer agreed, my name came up, and they hired me. I re-wrote the script, and in the Richard Pryor body of work, it's well-received and considered his best film by some critics. At one of the wrap parties, I was introduced as the writer, and everyone was looking past me, searching the room for the Black guy.

Jose: How does one write for a comedian so distinct as Richard Pryor?

Carl: For one thing, you live with him. By this time in his career, he was going through the healthy phase. He was dating Pam Grier and she was making sure that he was on a good diet and that he was exercising, because she was very fit. So, he was very clear-headed and we were living in a vacation cottage in Barbados. We spent two weeks together mapping out the whole movie and I took copious notes, and I like to think I have an ear for dialog, so after talking with Richard 24/7, you pick up his rhythms. The best thing about writing on location with actors is that you see and hear what they're doing with dialog. So, when you're writing new material you can tailor it to that voice you've just heard. I could write for Roy Scheider, or Robert Shaw. I could write for all those people because I knew what they would sound like, and the same was true for *Which Way Is Up?*, and that worked out ok.

Jose: Did you know beforehand while scripting that Pryor was going to play three very different roles, and if so, how did you script that?

Carl: I was just writing three characters, until we learned that he was going to play all three, at which point I had to adjust the dialog. The old man is basically Mudbone, the character from Richard's act, and Richard had done Black preachers before, so by that time I knew what he would be doing. It's easy to write for a uniquely talented performer *if* you have an accurate ear for his performance.

Jose: No worries about being pigeonholed into one thing, because you go from big Hollywood movie to a small, urban comedy.

Carl: Yeah, exactly.

Jose: But they knock on your door for the return of the great, white terror when *Jaws* 2 comes around. It seemed like a no brainer, but how did you become involved?

Carl: Zanuck and Brown, whatever their virtues as producers, were old school, greedy, and stingy. They offered me *Jaws* 2 at scale, and I'm the guy who made a significant contribution to the film that made a billion dollars. I found that insulting. Let me share with you an anecdote that will underline what I just said. A guy named William Gilmore was a production manager on *Jaws*. He had been a production manager for Zanuck and Brown on at least two or three of their pictures, and he basically worked for them and not the studio. Bill did heroic work getting *Jaws* in. I mean, he risked his job. He did a lot of things to keep Steven shooting, any one of which could have gotten him fired. So, the movie comes out, it does all this business, and Zanuck and Brown call him into the office. They say, "Here's a big screen television set." That was his bonus. Not a car, not a check, but a fucking $1,100 TV set. At which point, he quit. In that same vein, they offered me scale, so I told my agent, "No, that's insulting." And they wouldn't budge, they were not in the mood to negotiate. I passed, but I said to my agent, "They'll be back and it's going to cost them." Sure enough, they did it on the cheap with John Hancock and Dorothy Tristan. By the second week of shooting, they realized that Hancock was in over his head, and the script was no good, and they were thinking of replacing the director. I was still friends with Verna Fields, who won the Oscar for editing *Jaws*, which got her an executive position at Universal. I'd go to the dailies for *Jaws* 2 out of curiosity, and she would be shaking her head saying, "What's he doing? Oh my God!" I know a little bit about filmmaking and I could see that this guy was making "Moviemaking 101" errors; just terrible mistakes. It was a $25 million budget, and they weren't going to trust this guy with the franchise because they worried that he was going to fucking wreck it, so they fired him. It's very hard to fire a director once production had started; it's not often that it happens. At the same time that they were going over that decision, they said, "We also have to do something about this script, because it's not working." A one- or two-week hiatus had been built into the schedule during which they'd move from Martha's Vineyard to Florida, where they could shoot in a more controlled location. So, they said, "We've got to get a new writer to get to work right away while we find a new director."

Jose: Did you alter the script much when it finally came back to you?

Carl: They wanted kids in jeopardy and didn't know how to do that, so I came up with the gimmick that would give us kids in jeopardy. I made it up, I didn't even know if it was true or not, but I assumed there was such a thing as a cruising culture same as there was in the San Fernando Valley, only instead of cars it would be boats. They would be hot rod boats and there would be teenagers in them and that way they could all get into trouble together. Once I pitched that idea, everyone said, "Great idea, let's hire Carl," and it cost them a lot more money because they were in trouble, and they had to have somebody, and I was the perfect choice. I made a very good deal.

Jose: Were you happy with what you were able to do with *Jaws 2*?

Carl: In its time, it was the most successful sequel ever made. Artistically, it was well-received. I mean, everyone knew it wasn't an art film, but in terms of serviceable film, it's a good sequel. The shark eats a helicopter. I love that. It was well-made and it wasn't an embarrassment, and it wound up making a tremendous amount of money.

Jose: Was there ever a discussion about why a second shark would attack Amity Island, or if it was going to be related to the original?

Carl: Well, the first shark was pretty definitely dead, so we just had it be a second big shark. That's all it was, a second big shark. And the third shark is a different shark, too, in *Jaws 3-D*. That was a mama shark; she had babies. In the last film of the series, *Jaws: The Revenge*, the writers presumed the shark followed the Brody's for retribution! I never touched the script, and I have yet to see that film, to this day.

The High-Concept Massacre

Carl Gottlieb on set with Chief Brody himself, Roy Scheider.
Courtesy of Carl Gottlieb, ©Universal Studios

Jose: How do you deal with a character, like Chief Brody, that has to basically go through the same thing over again? How do you approach that similar territory in a fresh way?

Carl: One of the things about sequels, which certainly the last decade has taught us, is that it doesn't matter, as long as the same people are back doing the same things. I think it was Sid Sheinberg, who said this when we were worried about *Jaws 2*, "Listen, you have people over for dinner, and you make them a lovely fish dinner, the next time they come over you don't want to give them roast beef. They liked that fish, so you make that again." He and Wasserman were protecting the franchise. In those days, it wasn't called a franchise, but that's what it was. So, under the "If-you-served-them-fish-once-serve-it-again" theory of filmmaking, we made *Jaws 2*. The hard part, and this is where today's bad producers, bad directors, and stupid writers fail, is identifying what it was in the original that drew the audience. Sometimes it's not the hero; sometimes it was the way of approaching the material. For example: In *Iron Man* (2008), it wasn't the suit, it was Robert Downey Jr.'s performance. That character was so well-played. The hard part about sequels, or adaptations, is identifying what the essential element is; what is the thing you are trying to reproduce? When you put a two at the end of a title, the audience comes in with a certain expectation and sometimes it's hard to figure out what that is.

Jose: So, it was hugely successful when it came out?

Carl: It did hugely well, and I know for a fact it did well because, although I wasn't a profit participant, part of my deal was that I was given a bonus based on its performance at the box office, so I had the right to see the statements as they came in, and whenever it grossed a certain amount of dollars, I would get another bonus check. It was very successful.

Jose: Why didn't Steven come back for the sequel?

Carl: When *Jaws 2* came up and I had been offered it initially, he was doing post-production on *Close Encounters of the Third Kind (1977)*. I went over to see him and I told him that they had offered me the picture, and they had done the same to him. I asked him if he was going to do it, and he said, "No, I don't think so. I got something else I want to do." He wasn't keen on it, and Steven had an unerring sense of art, commerce, and studio politics. He understands all of it, and I think he understood that it was not in his best interest to make a sequel. It wouldn't do anything for his career. All he could do was fail, because when the first one had become the number one movie of all time, that wasn't going to happen twice in a row. He wisely said no, but I didn't have points in *Jaws*, and I didn't have the income from it that he had, so I still had to work for a living. I was a journeyman writer. Also at that time, Steven and George Lucas and John Milius were talking about forming a company and doing pictures together, and if I were him I would have done the same thing. It was around that time that our lives went separate ways.

Jose: Nothing can be more separate from *Jaws* 2 than your next film, *The Jerk*, which is considered by many to be one of the funniest movies ever made. How did you come to be involved with that one?

Carl: I knew Steve Martin from the Smothers Brothers show, and I had stayed friends with him. He was getting bigger and bigger as a comic, and an executive at Paramount, a great producer named David Picker, believed in Steve and gave him a three-picture deal. Steve said, "I've got a chance to write my own movie, but I've never written a script before. You've written *Jaws*, and the comedy with Richard Pryor, would you collaborate with me?" We worked and played well together, so I said, "Of course." The first few drafts that we did of the script were very different from the film that was released, it was more satirical, more serious. A subsequent writer named Michael Elias did a lot of work on it. Then, of course, Carl Reiner did a lot of uncredited work, because he was the director, but under the Writer's Guild rules he didn't do enough work to qualify for a screenwriting credit. But again, that was another very happy collaboration until a point where they needed a re-write. In those days they rarely gave points to writers. I had learned my lesson on *Jaws*, and my agent asked for just one point, or even half a point, but they said, "No." They wanted to keep it all for themselves. That's when I said, "Sadly I can't continue," so they got Michael Elias and went on without me to make the movie.

Jose: Did you have any designs on directing *The Jerk*?

Carl: Sure! While we were working on the script we made the short subject, *The Absent-Minded Waiter* (1977), which I directed in hope of directing the film we were writing together, which Paramount would have supported. But by that time, David Picker had been ousted at Paramount by Michael Eisner and Barry Diller, who scrapped his projects. It could have gone a whole different way. But when they ousted Picker, Steve Martin's team, including Picker, went across the street to Universal and sold it and I was out of it. But *The Absent-Minded Waiter* did get an Academy Award nomination in 1978 for Best Short Film, Live Action.

Jose: What's it like writing with Steve Martin?

Carl: Well, Steve is not an out-going guy. He's a rather quiet person. Writing with him is not like writing with Mel Brooks, who never stops pitching. Steve's a thoughtful guy.

Jose: Do you have a favorite moment from your time with him?

Carl: We were sitting around trying to figure out what to write about. The first page is always the hardest. Steve says, "You know, there's a line that always works in my act whenever I say it. Good or bad, if the act is dying, whenever I say it this line is a saver." So, I asked him what the line was, and he said, "I was born a poor Black child." And I said, "Wait a minute, what if you were?" So, we wrote the first scene with the Black family, and I won't say the script wrote itself, but it became an easy movie to write. When you got a solid beginning like that, it's not hard to continue, so we did and the result was *The Jerk*.

Jose: Then Jaws calls you back to the ocean, and in 3D no less. Are you sick of that damn fish by this point?

Carl: Well, I liked Joe Alves, he was a good pal, and he was going to direct it, but it was the same scenario as last time. They started with a script that didn't work. Luckily, they realized it before they started shooting, but it was very close to production. They flew me in to see the location, down at Sea World, in Florida. I saw the location, I had some ideas, and we talked it over. Because it was 3D, a lot of the elaborate effects shots could not be altered. I mean, I had to write for the set. That was the job, to work with what was there. On *Jaws 3D,* I mostly worked on developing the characters and pacing the story.

Jose: Was it always going to focus on the Brody family, or was that your idea to connect the films?

Carl: Under the "Give-em-more-fish" theory, you kind of had to have the Brodys in it, but this time we concentrated on the boys. I knew Dennis, because he was in my film, *Caveman (1981)*. The trick was to get a cast that could presumably play the Brody brothers, and that was Dennis Quaid and John Putch. We also had the formidable Louis Gossett Jr. We had to woo him. I had to ride out with the producers and the director to his house in Malibu to pitch him the story and tell him who we were. But again, having worked with Richard Pryor gave me cred with Louis, who Richard had idolized. When Richard was a kid, he had studied with Louis in an acting class. Hollywood is a small town. I had a good time making that movie.

Jose: That's great, because I really like *Jaws 3D*. I'm a sucker for shark movies, but I know that's the one that most fans take issue with, and maybe it was the 3D goofiness that gets in the way for them.

Carl: There was a cheapskate, uninformed producer on that picture. Zanuck and Brown were not uninformed; they knew how to make movies, but this guy knew less about making movies, and thought he knew more. Universal knew that *Jaws 2* had cost $28 million, and they were *not* going to spend that again, so *Jaws 3D* was jobbed out to an independent Executive Producer named Alan Landsburg, who wasn't saddled with studio overhead or contracts with the teamsters. He could do it almost like an independent film, but he was very chintzy and cut a lot of corners. The worst corner he cut, which just takes the balls out of the movie, was the last 3D shot of the shark crashing through the control room. The shark is supposed to be terrifying, and making the audience jump and cower like it did in the first one, but this time the shark is moving at the pace of the Goodyear blimp; he's slowly coming toward the camera. We only got one take, and that tight-fisted producer wouldn't go for another take, so the movie concluded with a finale that sucked. Most of the audience leaves with a bad taste in their mouths, not because the movie isn't good, but because the last thing they see is inept, and that's unfortunate. The real producer, a good guy named Rupert Hitzig, couldn't get Landsburg to spring for one more take.

Jose: Had the SeaWorld location been decided early on?

Carl: Yeah, because by now we had learned that you had to control the water, otherwise the water would control you. We didn't have to shoot an open ocean, we didn't have to justify the shark, all you had to say was, "The gate's open, something got in." That's classic horror film construction, that's what we did. You know, they all work to one degree or another, unfortunately for the sequels the first one was so good. How do you improve on that?

Jose: I know you didn't work on *Jaws: The Revenge*, but were you ever approached to be a part of it?

Carl: Nope. They never asked me. According to legend, Sid Sheinberg had an idea, wrote it on a legal pad, and hired a writer. I have no real idea how the film came to be. I say this all the time to film students, "The iron law of sequels is that only the last one loses money," which is why you have so many *Police Academy* or *Friday the 13th* movies. If they make money, they're going to make another one, one way or the other.

Jose: What are your thoughts on the possibility of a remake or reboot?

Carl: You know, Steven has so much control over that franchise now, since there's nobody left but him, and he's very protective of it. I think he's been quoted as saying, "No one will remake it in my lifetime." He has the power to make that stick and he should, it's like remaking *Casablanca* (1942). Why do that?

Jose: I'd be remiss if I didn't backtrack slightly and ask you about *Caveman* (1981), because my wife is a big Beatles fan. How did you come to write for and direct the one and only Ringo Starr?

Carl: A producer came up to me and said, "Do you remember a movie called *One Million Years B.C.* (1966)?" I said, "The Raquel Welch version or the black and white one?" He said, "Both. We want to do it again, but funny." I said, "Ok," and my deal was that I was going to write and direct it. When we were casting the leading man, who turned out to be the Ringo Starr character, we were looking for a little nebbish-y person and basically it boiled down to Ringo or Dudley Moore, because there weren't a lot of actors who could do that. Dudley passed, but Ringo agreed to do it. We had a ten or eleven week shoot in New Mexico. We used some stop-motion animation from Jim Danforth and David Allen.

Jose: How did you go about writing the script in terms of dialog for this movie, because it isn't typical human speech?

Carl: The thing about *Caveman* was that the dialog was not dialog, it was gibberish. For production reasons, it was formatted like a normal screenplay, but each dialog block of nonsense syllables came with the stage direction "As if to say....," so the actors all got the intent. We had a basic vocabulary, and we made up the words. The thing that annoyed me the most was that when I went to get more work as a director after that and they said, "Well, we don't know if you can direct dialog."

Jose: Now, I want to talk to you about one of my favorite comedies, and this will probably surprise you, but I loved *Doctor Detroit*. How did you get involved with that one?

Carl: I like that movie, too. You're one of the few, so thank you. On that one it was the same thing; they were in trouble. I had known John Belushi and Danny Aykroyd since the *Saturday Night Live* days, and when they were at Universal they had a bungalow on the lot; it was like a dorm room. They were working on *Doctor Detroit*. The script was developed from a very funny *Esquire* magazine short story by Bruce Jay Friedman, and I guess the script was in trouble. The director, Michael Pressman, hired a writer by the name of Robert Boris, who incidentally wrote *Some Kind of Hero* (1982), the only Richard Pryor movie that lost money; Michael had directed that. It hadn't come out yet at the time, but based on the fact that they had made a movie with Richard Pryor, they had been brought on to make this movie with Dan Aykroyd. They started shooting and it became obvious that Boris may not have been the best choice as a comedy writer and that Pressman may not have been the best choice as a comedy director. Again, it's very hard to replace a director, but they could re-write it, and somebody said, "How about Carl Gottlieb?" I don't know who said it, but I had a reputation at that point as a script doctor. In any case, I got the call and I said, "Ok." I remember I didn't even have time to get my clothes out of the laundry, so I flew to Chicago with a bag of dirty clothes, and went to work on the script.

Jose: How was it working with Michael Pressman, who maybe wasn't suited for comedy filmmaking?

Carl: I had some issues with Michael, because I would write a joke and Michael wouldn't get it, so he wouldn't shoot it, and I'd have to do something else. That was a problem. If he didn't see the humor in it, he wouldn't shoot the joke, but you keep on, you write other jokes. Michael went on to a wonderful career as a director, but not of feature comedies.

Jose: Was that the most difficult element of making that picture?

Carl: Yeah, he was not really a comedy director. And Danny was still grieving over John's death. But on that picture, Danny met Donna Dixon and they became man and wife. We hooked them up. I have a history of that; I hooked up Barbara Bach and Ringo Starr, they got married after *Caveman*. Also, when it came down to arbitration over the script at the end, I finally read the original short story, and I remember saying, "Shit, I wish I had adapted the short story that they bought, because that's funny. I could have had fun with that." The Robert Boris version missed the elements that would have been the comic elements in the film, and consequently it didn't connect commercially, even though it had Danny.

Jose: Did you and Aykroyd ever want to work together again?

Carl: Later on, I did a re-write for a movie that became *Spies Like Us* (1985), but it didn't work out. They couldn't do the script that I wrote, so they went back to an older draft, and did it as best they could. I had two projects going simultaneously, One was *Spies Like Us* and the other was *Volunteers* (1985) with Tom Hanks and John Candy, which I was going to direct. I was working parallel on both projects, and both studios said, "You've got to pick." Danny had a three-picture deal at Universal and that seemed like a sure thing because they couldn't say no; they owed him two more movies. It's what they called a "Put" deal. That seemed like the more logical choice, so I gave up *Volunteers* and it turned out that because of budgetary reasons they couldn't do my version of *Spies Like Us*. *Volunteers* got made, but they went back to the flawed script so they made a flawed movie. I sat grumbling because here were two movies I could have done, but I didn't have the clout or the authority to impose my vision on anybody.

Jose: There was no fuel from the *Jaws* fire?

Carl: No, *Jaws* was a Spielberg movie.

Jose: I see. No matter what we do as writers, the directors always get the credit for the films.

Carl: Always. It's a long story how that happened in Hollywood. In television the opposite is true. In television, the writer is god-king. And what's more successful these days?

Carl Gottlieb, typing champ. Photo by Andy Romanoff

Jose: Let's talk about the craft itself, because screenwriting is definitely a skill, it takes practice like anything else, and it's all about precision. What's the most important thing you've learned about screenwriting?

Carl: Less is more. Now, with the luxury of screenwriting software, you can overwrite, but then you get to the end and it's 140 pages and that's no good. You have to figure out how to say it in fewer words. It's not as difficult as haiku or sonnets, but it is an extremely disciplined form of writing, in which you have to communicate a great deal without overwriting. One of the hardest things for a screenwriter to do, especially novices, is exposition. How do you tell the audience what they need to know without being obvious that that's what you're doing? The worst expository mistake you can make is having one character tell another character what they already know. "Tom, you're my brother-in-law!" Don't say that.

Jose: What's your process like when you start a script?

Carl: The first thing you have to be responsible to is the story; a beginning, middle, and end. I don't subscribe to the three-act structure. I don't think Robert McKee is right, I think McKee is the death of cinema. But there is a need for a structure and a flow to a screenplay with crisis points along the way. In my case, I'll rough the story out on 3x5 cards. I'll write, "Intro the hero. Intro the love interest. Intro the villain."

Jose: You beat it out step by step.

Carl: Yeah. My friend Charlie Hauck, a comedy writer, once said, "Ideas abound, everybody has them. It's the damn words that cause all the problems. You've got to pick the right ones and put them in the right order." Writing is easy, but writing well is hard. Sometimes it's frustrating and it's like mining salt, and sometimes it just falls into place.

Jose: Give us an example of one that fell into place.

Carl: I did a show called *George Burns' Comedy Week* with Steve Martin. It was an anthology series, and we did thirteen half-hour comedies. I wrote the pilot based on an idea by Steve Martin. The two of us collaborated on the outline, and while we were talking it all just feel into place and I wrote the script. The guy who was at Universal television, who's an agent now, is fond of saying, "You know that's the only script in my experience that went from the writer to the Tower to the Network without notes." Well, having Steve Martin as Executive Producer helped grease the wheels, and not for the quantifiable star-fucking reason, but because Steve Martin has a reputation for being a professional. He's a pro and if he's going to produce it then it will have a certain level of quality that won't fall much below wonderful; Steve won't let it. The pilot was called "The Dynamite Girl," and it starred Catherine O'Hara and Tim Hutton. They did a lovely job.

Jose: How do you tackle characters in a script?

Carl: Invent a character from scratch. Know where he was born, where he grew up, and a ton of other information. This is all before the character even enters the frame. You've got to know who the people are, because you can't write dialog for people you don't know.

Jose: And how far do you go with your initial outline, do you have everything 100% worked out?

Carl: No, because there are always happy accidents. There's a wonderful literary device that appears in Victorian novels, and I tell this to writing students all the time, but they ignore me, though it makes tremendous sense. If you look at a lot of Victorian novels, many of them have chapters that begin with the words, "In which." The most startling and perfect example is in Dickens' David Copperfield, "Chapter One, in which I am born." If you think of the words "In which" at the beginning of every 3x5 card, you basically have the beats for your story. "In which we meet the hero." "In which he goes to sea." Then the fun, creative stuff begins with all the variables, and you have to weed out a lot of chaff. That's why it is so galling when a reader or a producer or story analyst or an actor suggests an alternative. What you want to do, if you're me, is to grab them by the collar and say, "Do you think I just typed the first thing that came to my head. Don't you think I thought of that and I rejected it for so many reasons that I can't even remember now? Give me some credit, will you?"

Jose: Has the industry gotten better, or has it worsened since the days of *Jaws* for writers?

Carl: The industry's gotten better for writers because of television. When I joined the Writer's Guild forty-five years ago, it was evenly divided between screenwriters and television writers. Television writers worked more steadily, but screenwriters made more money and there was more prestige. It stayed that way for thirty years. Today, as we sit here, there are 4,500 television writers earning more than $50,000 a year. There are 625 screenwriters, who earn more than $50,000 writing screenplays. This is because there are 350 to 400 scripted shows, and there are lots of writers writing those shows. The best dramatic writing being done now is on television, not in the movies. I don't know if it's failure of will, a failure of intelligence, a reluctance to gamble; I don't know what the reasons are, but I suspect it's all three. Movie writing is very tough now. For me, ageism sets in. Does anyone even want to look at a film written by a seventy-year old man? It's tough.

Jose: Do you see a lot of ageism despite your track record?

Carl: Oh, yeah. Because of *Jaws*, I don't have trouble getting meetings, but I do have trouble talking about my project because when I get to the meeting all anyone wants to talk about is *Jaws*, not the new film I want to pitch. So, I'm luckier than most writers, because having written some iconic films gets me in the door, but then I'm faced with young people of either gender who don't remember the films that were an influence in my life. They've seen *Casablanca*, but nothing beyond those canonical Hollywood films.

Jose: Is there one film you would recommend a screenwriter watch immediately if they haven't?

Carl: I don't think I can do one, but I've got three; *Day for Night* (1973), for how the collaborative process works, *The Magnificent Seven* (1960), for sheer story structure and character, and probably Buster Keaton's *The Gen-*

eral (1926), because of the construction of the jokes. I think Keaton was better than Chaplin.

Jose: Looking back at your career, the good and bad, was it all worth it?

Carl: Oh, certainly it was worth it. When I think back on my life, there are very few decision points that I would want to do over again. I feel I made the right choices. The lesson I learned was that movies are collaborative. They are made by a group of people. Also, the job comes first. Everything is subservient to the story, the movie, the show. I mean, "The show must go on" is not just a facile excuse for putting actors through a hard time to get the shot, it is an article of faith for those of us who make movies: we must put the thing we're doing ahead of everything else, which is why there is so much domestic strife in the lives of creative artists. It requires an almost monomaniacal obsession with the thing that you're making.

Jose: What do the movies mean to you in the end, immortality?

Carl: The most that any artist can hope for is that your work somehow becomes part of the culture.

Jose: If you had to do it all over again, would you?

Carl: I certainly would—I've had too much fun to even consider doing anything else.

Part-time fashion model, full-time screenwriter, Trent Haaga.
Photo courtesy of Trent Haaga

Trent Haaga

Citizen Toxie: The Toxic Avenger IV (2000)
Deadgirl (2008)
Cheap Thrills (2013)

Jose: So, I think it's safe to call you a movie nerd?

Trent: I've always been a movie fan. I'm of the generation that's pre-VHS. I grew up in a town that didn't even have a movie theater, you had to drive forty-five minutes to get to the nearest two-screen cinema, so movies were an event for me. I didn't have cable television or anything. Movies were super exciting and whenever I got to see one I was entranced. I just grew up being a movie fan.

Jose: Is there one film that you hold up as template of great screenwriting?

Trent: I didn't really start to notice stuff like that until later in life, but obviously the movies that affect you are the ones that brand you when you're a little kid. *Escape From New York* (1981), and *The Road Warrior* (1981), or the original *Dawn of the Dead* (1978), these are all the things that branded me. It wasn't until I worked in a video store when I was in high school that I started to watch the Scorsese films, and started to pay attention to foreign films, and started to expand my world. Low-budget horror and John Carpenter were the gateway drug to me expanding my mind. Is there a movie with particular writing that sets it apart? I don't even look at it that way. The script of *The Road*

Warrior is so sparse, Max had just a couple lines of dialog, but the script is all about the setting and the westerness of it, and it's great. It depends, of course. Some great movies come from bad scripts, and some bad movies come from great scripts, and I know this from having worked the way I have for so long. *Double Indemnity* (1944) is one of the best scripts ever, and it's because of that crackerjack dialog. I don't normally read other people's scripts, but I read that script. You know, you write a movie these days and a character has five lines of dialog and the notes will come back, "Whoa, this is way too much talking," but then you go and look at the script for *Double Indemnity* and Billy Wilder's written Fred MacMurray a three-page-long monologue! I would never give that to a modern day actor, though. The styles are completely different. I would rather listen to Fred MacMurray talk about some dame's gams for a page, than another movie where a guy is yelling, "Look out!"

Jose: Your cinema has a very in-your-face style, so I would imagine the blank page really lets you cut loose. What lead you to screenwriting from your love of movies?

Trent: You don't realize on any sort of level that there had to be some guy who sat down and wrote movies when you're little. When you read a book—and I'm a voracious reader—the author's name is right there on the front, so you know that this came from the brain of somebody. But when you watch movies as a kid, you think they somehow just magically appear. You don't think about the human beings who put it together. But the older you get and get more into movies, you begin to understand and you become aware that there's a screenwriter, but of course the director is king, right? You're interested in who the director is. So, I started writing because I said, "I want to be a filmmaker and how am I going to make one without a script, so I got to write a script." That's how I got started in screenwriting, with the intentions of making an independent film. What happened was I kept writing stuff, and showing it to people to convince them that I was the right guy to direct a movie, but they kept saying, "We love the script, but you've never directed anything. We'll give you money for the script." Well, hell I'll take money, because I'll come up with something else, and that's how I ended up on the screenwriting train.

Jose: You managed to parlay this love of films into a career. Did you decide to go to film school, or did you parents say, "You've got to go to college, so pick something?"

Trent: Yeah, that's exactly what happened. My dad worked in coal, my mom was a stay-at-home mom, but she graduated nursing school when I graduated high school, so they had a bit more income, and they said, "You get to go to college." I wasn't really interested in going to college. I figured I'd get a job working in the coal industry like my dad, or something. I grew up in a bunch of really cruddy, small towns in the Midwest. I loved movies, I was the only guy in my whole school who was into movies, but that didn't tell me that I could go and do them. No one I knew did them. I didn't know anybody who knew anyone who did them. The idea that I would be able to do it was not even feasible. However, my parents were like, "No Goddamn it, we worked hard and you're going to go to college." I laughed and said, "All right then, I'm going to go to film school," you know, thinking I'm going to waste their money. I ended up going to film school in Chicago, and I honestly thought I'd get my degree and end up going back to the mid-west, but I ended up moving to New York. I worked a ton of jobs that had nothing to do with the film industry for three years after getting out of college, and then I stumbled into Troma, and I got my first hit. I've been chasing the dragon ever since.

Jose: Let's talk about that first hit. Were you a fan of Troma films before?

Trent: Oh, yeah. I grew up on *USA Up All Night* and seeing the re-runs of *The Toxic Avenger* (1984) and all that. *Class of Nuke 'Em High* (1986) played at my local Cineplex, and I dragged my friends out to go see it. Afterwards they were like, "This was terrible, we're never going to let you pick the movie again", and I thought it was the most amazing thing I'd ever seen. So, yeah, I was a Troma fan from way back, and I was working at an internet company that did all the entertainment content for CompuServe when I stopped by Troma's fresh, new website and they said they were looking for extras. I went to my boss and I pitched him a story where I would go be an extra for a day on a Troma movie and take a whole bunch of pictures, and he said, "Yeah great, go ahead." So, I went and I auditioned to be an extra.

Jose: You had to audition to be an extra on a Troma movie?

Trent: Yeah, and I didn't have a headshot or whatever. I just went in and I said, "Look I'll write a story and spread the word if you guys hire me to be an extra, and if you kill me that would be amazing." They kept calling me back, and calling me back, and gave me one of the lead roles in *Terror Firmer* (1999). Had nothing to do with writing, but that's how I got my foot in the door. I had written some scripts and I gave them to Lloyd, because he was kind of a hero of mine. I don't know if he ever read them. He might have given them to one of his assistants and asked them to read it, but regardless when it came time to write *The Toxic Avenger IV*, which was six months after we had finished *Terror Firmer*, he called me in and offered me the job.

Jose: That must have been a dream gig, seeing as you worshipped at the temple of Troma, to take on their most famous character.

Trent: Absolutely! Listen man, you know when Indiana Jones pulls the Ark of the Covenant out of the box and the angels sing and the glow comes up, that was like Lloyd saying, "Hey Trent, you're going to make *The Toxic Avenger IV*. Money is no expense. This is going to be our biggest movie ever!" And the thing is that I had shot *Terror Firmer* and then I had gotten married, but I had put off my honeymoon to go to Cannes to promote the movie with the whole Troma team. I did that for sixteen days, and when I came back I was going on my honeymoon five days later. Two days before my honeymoon is when Lloyd calls me in to his office to offer me the job, but he says, "We need the script right now, because I'm trying to get these investors behind it, and it needs to be done immediately." I say, "Great, but you know I'm going on my honeymoon." He says, "That's no problem, you can write it on your honeymoon. All we need is a beginning, a middle, and an end." That was Lloyd's favorite thing to say. But that was the first time I got paid to write a script. I've got pictures of me on my honeymoon sitting on a beach in St. Thomas with a notepad on my lap, cranking out pages for *The Toxic Avenger IV*.

Jose: Damn, talk about stressful work environments: a deadline and wife giving you the stink eye. Were you able to finish on your honeymoon or did you not want to risk divorce?

Trent: It wasn't like he said, "You need to come back in seven days with the script," but I think he gave me a little bit less than two weeks, and one week of that was on my honeymoon. I didn't finish the entire thing on my honeymoon, but I came up with the story and everything, tons of notes, wrote some of it, and then furiously finished writing the first draft when I got back in five days.

Jose: How is Lloyd in terms of notes? Is he easy to please or is he picky?

Trent: The thing is everyone really loved the first draft, and Lloyd was really up on it, but then what happens is there are just a lot of people throwing out ideas. They all read it and say, "Wouldn't it be funny if . . . ." or "isn't it exciting if . . . ." Our job is to take in the notes from everybody. Throw out the ones that are really crappy, or try to hide them, and keep Lloyd happy. The one thing people don't understand when they give you notes is that they're only thinking about the one little piece they're looking at. It's like I built a car and in order for this car to run all the components need to fit together just right, but then someone comes along and says, "Could we make the tires really,

The High-Concept Massacre

really big?" And you say, "Yah, I could, but you got to understand that I have to change the drive train and switch the axles . . . ." Then, at the same time, there's another guy telling you about the antenna, and another guy telling you about the bumper, and another guy telling you about the fuel injector, and you have to change all these things to keep everybody happy.

Jose: That's a perfect analogy. That's exactly how it is. They don't understand that one small change affects other things.

Trent: If you've done your job right, and if it's good. Lloyd will say, "I've got this crazy idea, just throw it in there," but this was my first job and I was saying, "No, these alternate dimensions have to stay straight. What happens here has to affect what happens there. If we did this in this scene, then it can't be that in that scene, this doesn't make any sense!" It was a huge struggle, and a learning experience. You know it's interesting, Troma taught me how to just do it, but then it was later on that I learned how to do it right, but I'm glad I learned that way because with Troma the sky was the limit and you needed sheer force of will to make this movie happen no matter how crazy, no matter how anarchic, no matter how many things change, you get it done. Whereas, later on, I was given tighter budgets and restrictive shooting schedules and whatever else the realities of making a movie are. Troma doesn't make a movie in a real way, but I learned, and I learned in a way that kept me motivated and excited. Being at Troma was very exciting because it was you against the world, whereas if you're making something for Charles Band it's not you against the world and it's you trying to beat this deadline of titles that have already been sold and you have x amount of days to shoot the movie and it has to be of a z-quality caliber. Lloyd Kaufman gets to do whatever he wants, and he doesn't care who he pisses off, and he doesn't care who's happy or unhappy. It doesn't matter, he's doing it for the sake of creation, and it's insane.

Jose: Well, you can tell when you watch a Troma film that there's an anything-goes, anarchic vibe through the whole thing.

Trent: Completely! I mean the first cuts are always four hours long. It's crazy.

Jose: Sometimes it works, and sometimes it doesn't. It worked with *Citizen Toxie*, which I really enjoyed, and I consider it my favorite of the series, because I think there's a lot more to hold onto in that one.

Trent: Wow, thanks man. I tried. I tried real hard on that one, man. Lloyd told me when we first sat down, "We are going to make a $3 million Troma movie, it's going to be our biggest movie ever," and then by the time we made it he said, "Look we only have $250,000, but we're not going to change the script. We'll still have good and evil Toxie, we'll still have good and evil Kabuki Man, we're still going to keep the car chase, we're still going to blow up the school, it's just that we're going to do it for a fraction of the price."

Jose: How is the script treated on a Troma set, because there is this sense of anarchy, and I'm wondering if stuff gets thrown out by the actors, who would rather say whatever comes into their heads?

Trent: With the actors, generally, they're non-SAG and not experienced. There are exceptions, of course, but when I did my thing in *Terror Firmer*, I'd never acted before in my life, and I was playing this big role. I was just so excited to be there, and wanted to be liked and professional. I think it's later when you get actors that think they're smarter than you and they're going to change it because they're better writers than you, that's when that comes into play. But generally, the people are there because they're excited to be there and they're trying to do whatever is on the page to make everybody happy. So, I didn't have any issues with that. Except for Lloyd saying stuff like, "What if we had a clown on a unicycle? Look at this background extra! He's a clown and he's got a unicycle. We need to write something in right now for him!" For example, evil Kabuki Man sees an old lady on a walker and he runs over the old lady, crushing her head. So, we shoot the stunt man as the old lady, we do the whole gag that was in the script, and Lloyd says, "Wouldn't she defecate and urinate all over herself?" That's not in the script that she shits and pisses everywhere, but then we had to do a whole set up to make that happen. Lloyd comes up with things as a result of us doing stuff on set, but the actors, no. Generally, they did what was written.

Jose: When you look at Lloyd, he's such an interesting character. He went to Yale, so he's no dummy, and yet he makes these wacky films that no one can make except him, and that anyone not in the know would imagine were made by someone who'd never even heard of Yale. It's great that he's found this niche to really let his filmmaker freak flag fly.

Trent: He created the niche. I mean, that is the key, right? Isn't that what any of us are trying to do as artists? You can look at a thing and say, "Oh, that is undoubtedly a Lloyd Kaufman project." He succeeded at doing what we're all trying to do.

Jose: After all the shitting and pissing old ladies, what becomes of *Citizen Toxie*? From what I remember, it was fairly well-received.

Trent: Yeah, people liked it. In many ways, it was good that my first paid job was the fourth in a relatively successful cult movie franchise, where anything goes. It was interesting, because when it came out people said, "Okay, cool, another *Toxic Avenger*, we've been waiting for it forever," but in a weird way, I think it's aged well. Now it's been about fifteen years since we made it, and the Blu-ray just come out last week, so as a result you see some new reviews popping up. At the time it came out people said, "Wow, this is crazy! Okay, moving on." Whereas, after fifteen years people look at it and say, "Wow, this is really, really crazy!" I think it becomes more appreciated, as it gets older. The kids who were first exposed to it when they were thirteen are now pushing thirty and they look back on it the same way I look back on *The Road Warrior*. They appreciate the things they loved as a kid even more, so it seems to be gaining in its popularity. When you look at it compared to the other ones, it's trying a little bit harder; it's a little bit wackier. It's a weird movie, man. It's pretty bonkers.

Jose: Does *Citizen Toxie* affect your career at all in terms of forward momentum?

Trent: Nah, not at all. Not at all, and that's the world of the writer who isn't doing anything but out there selling specs. It's funny, when I talk to Troma people, my Lifetime channel movies are like my little dark, dirty secret that nobody knows about, but when I'm in the office at Lifetime, the Troma movies are my little dark, dirty secret that nobody knows about. So, the movie coming out doesn't get me a call from Michael Bay saying, "Hey, I need a new whatever . . . ." Nothing happens. I got paid $750 to write it, and I also produced it, but $750 for writing and that's it. I got a copy of the Blu-ray from Lloyd last week, so I guess I got something out of it. But you know what, it's a cumulative thing, right? The more you work, the more people that you meet become contacts, I mean you never know. I hate gambling, but my entire career is full of gambles.

Jose: You must have one, so give us a good example.

Trent: I did *Killjoy 3* (2010), and I didn't really want to. The only reason I played Killjoy in part two is because they hired me to produce and they said, "Look, we don't have enough money to hire another actor, and you're going to be there every day, so you play the clown." Okay, I'm a team player, so I did it. Years later, they call me up and say, "We need you to come back and play the clown for part three," and I'm stunned, I say, "Are you making a part three? Are you kidding me? Nah." Then they say, "We're shooting in China," and I sighed and said, "All right, I'll do it." I went to China, shot this movie, and while I was there I ended up meeting this guy who was in the textiles industry over there, and he financed my directorial debut. So, what I'm saying is take a risk. Throw it out there. You never know how one job tumbles into the next. That's the way I look at it.

Jose: A working writer is a hustling writer.

Trent: There are a lot of guys I know that are way more successful than me because they sat down and said, "You know what, I'm only going to write specs. I'm going to take a year to write this, then I'm going to take another year to take it around, and it's going to take two years to get made, and then it's going to be huge!" I'm a blue-collar dude from the Midwest. I can't sit around for three years hoping that I score half a million dollars. Sure, it would make it worth it. If somebody told me, "You're guaranteed half a million dollars if you wait three years and just work on this one project," then that's what I would do, but what do I tell my landlord?

Jose: Plus you have a family to worry about, which is a whole other added stressor for the working writer.

Trent: Yeah, I got two kids and a wife. This business is set up for people that *can* wait three years to get a project off the ground. The people that can wait three years don't really even need to get a project off the ground, because they got a trust fund, or some family money, or whatever. It sounds like the pitiful, poor kid bitching that everything is stacked in favor of the richies, but you know what I mean. In this business, you either have to do what I do and keep your nose to the grindstone and crank out projects for little money, which could ruin your reputation. I've sort of painted myself into a corner a little bit, and with something like *Deadgirl* or *Cheap Thrills*, I kind of chip away at some of the paint, but I haven't gotten any big offers. Writer's Guild won't even let me into their union. I've had thirteen movies made, and I cannot get into the union.

Trent with Courtney Cox on the set of *TalhotBlond* (2012).
Photo courtesy of Trent Haaga

Jose: That's the unfortunate drawback to working in the arena that we do, because to them they don't count as real movies.

Trent: No, no. Look, I wrote this Lifetime movie that Courtney Cox directed, and I got paid scale. That movie came out on DVD, and got sold to foreign territories, and Courtney Cox, who is awesome and deserves everything she gets, is getting residual checks from the DGA, and she was in it, so she's getting stuff from SAG. Courtney is great, God bless her, but she doesn't need any more money. I got paid, and that's it. I've never gotten a residual check because I'm not in the union. I don't qualify. I'm not a real writer, as far as they're concerned.

Jose: The ironic thing is you've probably written more than most writers currently in the WGA.

Trent: Yes, absolutely. I know this to be true.

Jose: Let's talk Full Moon. You put in your time at Troma, and then hop to Los Angeles to work at Full Moon and write *Hell Asylum* (2002).

Trent: We shot *Citizen Toxie* in 1999, and I moved out here at the end of the 2000, and we shot three movies for Full Moon in the fall of 2001. Charlie Band went and sold three movies to Blockbuster Video. It was three titles for movies he didn't even have. Then he came back and said, "Here's three titles. You guys need to write, produce, cast, shoot, edit, and have these movies ready to go." The first one we did was *Killjoy 2* (2002), and that was in August, and it was scheduled to come out in January. Next month was *Prison of the Dead 2* (2002), and then after that it was *Dead and Rotting* (2002). So, while we were working on *Killjoy 2*, the Producer, J. R. Bookwalter, came to me and said, "We need to start shooting *Prison of the Dead 2* in three weeks and we don't even have a script. Do you want to write the script?" I agreed, and they said they'd pay me $500. I was already slated to produce the thing for $1,500, so I'd make $2,000 the next month, which was great! I finished *Killjoy 2*, then hopped on a plane to the east coast because I was acting in a movie with Debbie Rochon, and there I wrote the script in my hotel room at night while I was shooting a movie. They decided after I wrote it just to call it *Hell Asylum*. Then September 11 happened, and I ended up being stuck on the east coast for an extra two days, which allowed me to write the rest of it. I finally got on a plane, flights were all screwed up, but I got back to L.A. I hopped in the car with my computer, I drove straight from LAX to the Full Moon offices, plugged in my computer, printed up the script, and handed it off to someone, and said, "Run off like seven copies of this, here's the movie we're going to start making." Nine days later, we were shooting it, and eight days later, it was in the can. You can diss on *Hell Asylum* all you want, but the fact of the matter is we went from no script to movie in the can in three and half weeks.

Jose: Do you prefer that mode of filmmaking, where you get the movie done come hell or high water, or would you prefer to tinker and be more precious with it?

Trent: Split the difference, I'd say. Personally, in my opinion, when I'm at my fourth draft, the script is about as good as it's going to get. Maybe that's my ego talking, I don't know, but what happens is you get some good ideas and some good notes for the first few drafts, and then by the fourth draft I'm thinking, "This is pretty solid." Then somebody comes by with notes for a fifth draft and they're not good ideas. I feel there's a certain point where you're pushing the envelope and you're beating a dead horse. You're actually making it worse. You're losing whatever the thing was that made you want to make it. At first you're incorporating stupid ideas, but you're trying to maintain the integrity, but after a while you're saying, "What's the easiest way for me to incorporate this stupid idea?" Once you fall over that lump, there's no real going back.

Jose: I've been in a position where I'd be six of seven drafts into a script and I've lost track of what's happening in the film. They ask me to change a line or a situation, and I'll just do it, only later to realize that it affects this and that down the road.

Trent: But then you just give it up, because if nobody else noticed, why bother? I'm enthusiastic and easy to work with up to the fourth draft, but then somewhere around the fifth I'll say, "All right look, I'm going to incorporate these notes, but I've already told you that it's not a good idea, so you're obviously not listening to me anymore, but you're the one paying, so ok. I'm going to do what you say. I'm not going to do it badly on purpose, but it's a bad idea. I'm going to do this to the best of my abilities, but I'm not going to beat myself up about this anymore." Sometimes you get to that point.

Jose: It's hard because writers who care get married to ideas and moments, and to disconnect and not be precious about certain elements feels like cheating the material, however that's the toughest lesson screenwriters must learn.

Trent: I know this happens to all writers, it must. There will be things in your writing that you'll say, "You can't cut this! I'll miss it! I'll miss it so bad!" But when the movie comes out, no one else knows that thing that was cut and that thing that you miss. They only judge a movie by a script when a movie is bad, and if the movie is good, no one ever notices it. They'll say the director's a genius!

Jose: How'd you like working for Full Moon versus Troma?

Trent: You know what, at Full Moon I think I actually learned how to make a movie, and make an actual working schedule that you have to stick to, because you have to. The thing with Troma is that there is an army of people working over there for free. Lloyd can do whatever he wants to. Charlie Band doesn't have the magnetic personality that Lloyd does, where he gets these fans of anarchy or whatever. People will show up on a Charlie Band set, but they're doing it because they need to get paid. So, now you're paying people and you can't just show up and make it up as you go along. I feel like I got a closer resemblance to making a movie from making the Full Moon movies, but I think that the Troma movies are better movies, because they've got art to them. With the Band movies, you want to make better movies, but you're given so little time, so little money, and so little resources. In many ways, it's not driven by this youthful enthusiasm that Troma has.

Jose: Well, it's more of a business for Charlie. The Troma movies are insane, but there's an artful integrity to them that doesn't exist with other film companies.

Trent: Right, and look I know there are fans of the Full Moon movies, and the directors and the writers are trying to some extent, but it's for a different reason. The only reason Lloyd makes a movie is because he wants to be punk rock, or he's got something to say. But the reason we make *Killjoy 5* is because *Killjoy 4* made enough money that it justifies making a fifth one. I mean, we start shooting *Killjoy 5* in two weeks, and I'm the lead, I'm the clown, but I haven't even seen the script, and we'll have five days to shoot the whole thing!

Jose: Let's talk about *Feeding the Masses* (2004), which I thought was a fun zombie movie. How did that one spring into existence?

Trent: I was contacted by the director, Richard Griffin, he said, "Look, you've written some stuff, it's been made, people like it, you're not in the union, you can work on your own, you don't have an agent or a manager, so I want to do something with you. You've seen *Dawn of the Dead* (1978), right? You know that news station at the beginning? I want to make a movie about those people." So, I sat down and cranked out *Feeding the Masses*, and it's just

The High-Concept Massacre

one of those ones that kills me. I just heard a review a few weeks ago and they were saying, "Wow, this script has some things to say, and is relatively intelligent," but everything is a little bit hampered by the amount of money they have and the amount of time, the actors abilities, and things like that, you know what I mean?

Jose: The reality is that the quality of the finished product doesn't always match the scripted reality.

Trent: Yeah, totally, and that was the first time I broke four digits for a screenplay. It was with my third produced screenplay. I put my foot down and became a thousandaire. It was a very exciting time.

Jose: Quick turnaround?

Trent: Yeah, I wrote the whole thing in a couple of weeks, and then I got notes based on what they could and couldn't pull off, but amazingly enough a lot of the stuff I put in there they tried to pull off, and it was a noteworthy attempt at what I had written. What I'm good at is being able to say, "Well, how much do you have, where are you shooting, and how many days?" and then I will try to tailor-make this thing to help. This is why the producers at Lifetime Channel love me, because I have a pretty good grip on what they can and can't do, if they can achieve it, and how much is too much jibber-jabber. But talk is cheap, they say, and in a Lifetime movie you want the people to talk a little bit, but not too much.

Jose: The reality of production is a great bit of knowledge for all screenwriters to keep in mind.

Trent: Absolutely. But at the same time, it kills me, because I never write big movies. I never write big movies because every time I write something I say, "Maybe I could sell this, and if they get Brad Pitt in it then it's a $30 million movie, but if they don't we could still do it for $250,000," and that's the world that I'm stuck in, because it's the world that I've worked in and have an understanding of budget and how hard it is to make a movie. Therefore, I don't write big movies because if I write it and it doesn't get made, then I just wasted my time. I can't justify taking my time to write something that if worse came to worse I couldn't figure out how to get it done.

Jose: Once you have an idea you think is workable, how long does it take you to write a spec?

Trent: It really depends. A lot of times I'll come up with a great idea, but then I'll let it sit in the back of my head and I'll write two or three jobs, but the whole time though I'm kind of turning this thing around in my head, and when I get that window I can sit down and I usually go pretty quickly because I've been ruminating on it for such a long time. Plus, I enjoy it. When I write specs I feel like I'm getting to do what I want to do, so I feel invigorated. It's not torture and it's not like a "job" job, but with a "job" job you get a paycheck, with a spec you don't. I just wrote a spec that I thought was one of the greatest things I'd ever written and I can't get anybody to pay attention to it. Whenever I sit down to write something for myself, it's impactful and there's a bit of raging at the world, so initially people say, "Fuck no, dude! No one is ever going to make this." Eight years from now, someone's going to make it and they'll be considered a genius. *Deadgirl* and *Cheap Thrills* sat around forever because they kept saying, "You cannot make these movies, why did you write this? What are you, stupid? Write me something that I can sell." I wrote *Cheap Thrills* and I bring it to my agent and he says, "What did you do?" I told him I wrote a spec because that's what he asked me to do. He says, "No, you're supposed to come to me and give me five ideas and I tell you which spec to write." I say to him, "What? You're like a sales guy. You can take ice cubes and sell them in Antarctica." He shook his head and said, "No. I'm not even going to take this out. I'm just going to stick it on a shelf and next time you think about writing something you tell me what it is, and I'll approve it." Seven years later, it got made into an audience award-winning movie at SXSW [Author's Note: SXSW is an abbreviation for the South By Southwest Film Festival held annually in Austin, Texas.] and everybody loved it. It was the same thing with *Deadgirl*. I wrote it and eight years later it got made and became a huge cult hit.

Jose: Well, let's talk about *Deadgirl*. If you were to just read the synopsis, it wouldn't really seem appealing, but beyond the gross-out concept the film is surprisingly deep and it becomes a very dramatic type of horror film. Where does that idea come from?

Trent: Those are the kinds of movies I really like and those are the kinds of movies I'd actually make if I was given my druthers. The two specs I've sold I feel are very similar. They're kind of dour and dramatic, but wrapped in the genre. That's what I do, that's what I would love to do given my own freedom. I'm the horror guy, I'm the Troma guy, because these are the people who gave me a chance, but because you do that you have to sort of fit into their sweater. *Deadgirl* is my sweater, that's what I do. I wanted to cleanse my palate and write something that I wanted to do. I loved *River's Edge* (1986) and *Heathers* (1988) when I was a kid. I loved all these juvenile delinquent movies, I didn't want to make a horror movie, but I knew that I had to keep my toes in there, otherwise nobody was going to make just a juvenile delinquent movie. To me the dead girl could have been a sack of gold or a magic ring, ultimately it was about powerless kids gaining power in a terrible way. It was harkening back to the way I grew up, and the kids I grew up with. Many of the kids I grew up with are in jail, or they're dead, or they started having kids in high school. I put all that together and *Deadgirl* came out. I gave it to Lloyd after I wrote it and I said to him, "Lloyd, if you direct this, people will be expecting one thing, and you're going to blow their minds." He said, "This is a great script, but I can't do this. I don't want to blow their

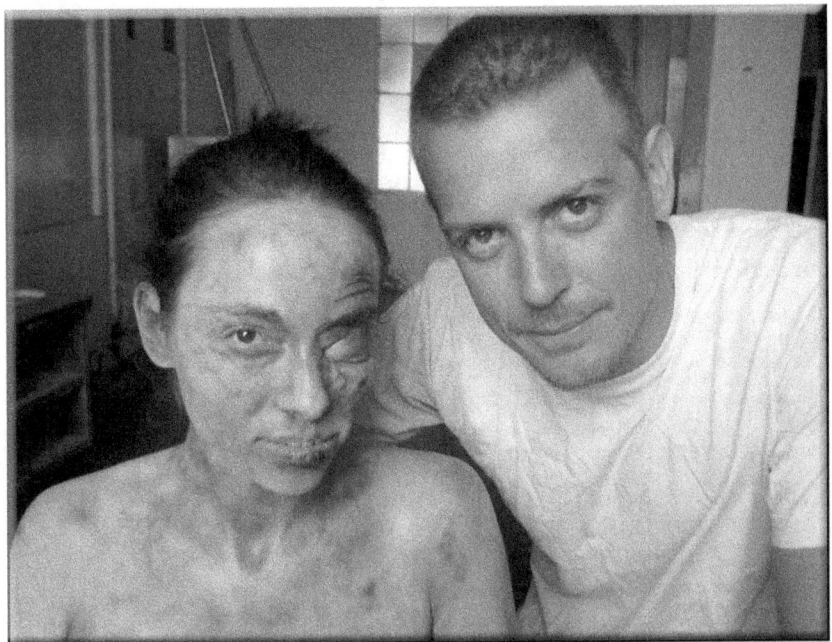

Trent with the titular *Deadgirl*, Jenny Spain. Photo courtesy of Trent Haaga

minds. This isn't my thing. It's not me." So, it sat on a shelf forever, and then I gave it to some directors as a writing sample, and they ended up coming back to me and saying, "We love this script, we want to do this movie," and I said, "You've got to be kidding me!"

Jose: What I really appreciated from a horror fan perspective was that the characters came off as real people, they weren't the typical teenaged idiots you see romping through horror movies nowadays.

Trent: Yeah, I was a social outcast, I think most writers are socially outcast, and yet we're asked to write the jock, and the slutty cheerleader or whatever, because they're standard tropes, but my specs are based in a world that is my point of view. People don't have awesome lives; they kind of have shitty lives, and are under a lot of stress and pressure. They're not popular or whatever, so I just wrote about the kids I hung out with.

Jose: What was the reception like?

Trent: We premiered at the Toronto Film Festival's Midnight Madness. Nobody knew who we were. It was a couple of first time directors, and the guy who wrote *Toxic Avenger IV*. There were only eight movies picked for Midnight Madness, so it was a pretty big deal. We sold out a 1,500-seat theater for a midnight show, and it took off. It's because it did exactly what I wanted it to do from the get-go. This movie could impact people. It could make people skeeved-out, but they're not going to be able to not watch it. It's like a car crash and that's what I wanted to replicate. It's not supposed to make you feel good, you're not supposed to escape, you're not supposed to masturbate to it, that was not the intention, but if you do then fine.

Jose: Author intent was carried through.

Trent: When I wrote this script, I had this tingly feeling, and sometimes I get that. When I wrote *Deadgirl* and *Cheap Thrills*, I had this feeling inside me. I know these are challenging movies, I know that, but when I wrote them I had so much of my essence inside them. It goes right back to this new one I wrote. One company said, "I couldn't finish reading past this one scene, it was too upsetting." That's great, except you're supposed to keep reading. I'm trying to upset you, but you're supposed to push through the upsetting and come out the other end of this experience.

Jose: *Deadgirl* was seemingly the biggest thing in your career at this point, did that help you move up a rung in the Hollywood hierarchy?

Trent: It's interesting, because *Deadgirl* started to go at the same time that Lindsay Lohan, Olympia Dukakis, Shirley MacLaine, Rosario Dawson, Giovanni Ribisi, all these big actors, had signed on to this other thing I wrote. It was a black comedy about old women getting insurance policies on homeless people and then running them over with their cars.

Jose: What happened there? I'm surprised it never got made.

Trent: Oh, people loved the script, they loved it. What happened was that the guy who was the producer made all this money selling Omaha steaks or something and he was a rich dude. He hired me to write the script, and I said, "You're crazy, because you're going to hire me to write a script about homeless people and old ladies and you'll never get it made." He said, "Whatever, I'm rich, here's $3,000." So, I wrote the script, thinking I just took this guy for three grand, but then a month later I get a call from one of the producers who said, "Go get today's *Variety*, you're not going to fucking believe this." I went to grab it and my name was on the front page, because they had attached MacLaine and Dukakis to play the old women. At that point, everybody wanted it. I was going into meetings at Miramax and Focus and all those places. The rich guy said, "Well, if everybody wants it then I'm just going to borrow money and make it myself!" He thought he had it all under control and he got eaten alive, he lost a ton of money, and the movie never got made. To top it off, no one else will come get the script because it's still got like $1.5 million in arrears attached to it, so if anyone did want to do it, they'd have to pay off everyone who had invested already, and now it's toxic. At the time that they were getting ready to shoot that, we were prepping *Deadgirl*, and I got signed because my name was in *Variety*. Nobody knew about *Deadgirl*, but all of a sudden everyone knew who I was.

Jose: Your career was catapulting before *Deadgirl's* success.

Trent: Yeah. I remember I left the set of *Deadgirl* to go meet with Paradigm and get signed by them and they said, "Oh, we're all into *Poor Things*. Love that script." I said, "Well, I just came off the set of another one of my movies," and they wanted to read the script so I gave it to them. Afterwards they said, "Oh, ok. So, what are you? Are you the writer who does movies about old ladies killing homeless people or the guy who writes about people fucking zombies?" I shook my head and said, "It's the same type of movie as far as I'm concerned." You know, the temptation is there and you're doing the wrong thing in a moment of conflict, but one's got a zombie fuck slave and the other's got a million dollars. But they didn't get it, they said, "No, one's a horror movie and the other is a black comedy."

Jose: They tried to put you in a box. Quantify you.

Trent: Yeah, yeah. They said, "Nobody makes black comedies, and even though *Poor Things* has bigger people attached, we're going to sell you as the horror guy." I don't even really think that *Deadgirl* is a horror movie, per se. Horror movies have lots of people screaming and cars that won't start at inopportune moments.

Jose: *Deadgirl* is horrifying, but more of a drama if you really look at it. I know folks were really impressed by that, I certainly was.

Trent: Yeah, *Deadgirl* was received incredibly well, which was super vindicating to me because people told me for so long that it was never going to get made, and if it did get made then certainly no one would like it.

Jose: Had you searched for representation prior to that?

Trent: No, that wasn't really my thing. Ostensibly, I have a guy who's my manager, but I don't really use agents or management or anything like that. They always say, "Write me an idea that I can sell for a million dollars with one phone call," and I say, "How about I just write what I write and you sell it because you're so awesome," but then they'll come back and say, "No, that's not the way it works. The way it works is you write what I tell you to write because I know I can sell it." They're just making their job easier and my job harder, so fuck those guys.

Jose: Honestly, I've been represented by managers twice in the past, but any of the jobs I've gotten have either been through connections or plain old hustling.

Trent: Yes, that's how it works, unless you want to get in there and play the game. A buddy of mine, a young guy, just came into town not too long ago, and he just sold a spec for more than I've ever been paid for anything, and it wasn't even an idea he wanted to do, or was excited about, but his manager sat him down and said, "Here's what we should do. Look at this movie, and this movie, and this movie. Let's do a movie like that." It took him a year and a half and he hated it, but he sold it for $100,000, and now he's getting all the meetings. I feel it's going to be painful for him, because he sold a script for something he wasn't in love with, but now any jobs he's ever going to be up for are more versions of the thing he didn't want to write in the first place.

Jose: Well, they say if you want to be a real writer then don't go into screenwriting.

Trent: I wish the people would be more upfront. That they'd say, "You're a writer and I don't give a shit, fuck you, just do what I say". But no, when you're in the room they want to suck your dick and tell you how great you are. They think your ego is so fragile that they have to blow smoke up your ass, even though you know and they know that they're blowing smoke. They just need to remove that aspect. It's funny, I look at it sometimes like I'm a Macdonald's employee and I come in and say, "This is how you fix the fucking Egg McMuffin."

Jose: Continuing with that theme of writing what you want to write, let's talk about your other spec-turned-movie *Cheap Thrills*. It's a brutal film, but it doesn't start out that way, and before we know it, we are sucked into this very believable psychological horror show. Where did this idea come from?

Trent: That whole movie came out of the fact that I was going through a bad time. Periodically with me, if things aren't going well, I'll say, "What are you doing? What are you doing with yourself, man? Once again you've painted yourself into a corner and you have no other options and you're not making money!" You know, I had a kid. Max, my first kid, was just a little baby, and one day I was sitting in my office and saying, "Man, I got to keep writing, I need to keep going," and if somebody came by right now and said, "Chop off your finger and I'll give $15,000," and I could give it to my wife and she would be happy and less scared, I would do that. That's literally how that started. There have been things like that before, but most are home invasion movies. Mine was not a home invasion movie; it was a home invitation movie. This is an opportunity for you to win some money, but you can walk out anytime you want to. The big difference was that I never empathized with the people who said, "Oh no, I have to chop your finger off or they're going to kill my baby!" This time it's you, all the onus is on you. How far are you willing to push yourself, and you can walk out whenever you want, it's your decision. That's the difference; it's man's own greed, or his own inadequacies. I see the world that way. The rich are all sitting around laughing while we all fucking fight for their table scraps. That is absolutely how I see the world, and this movie is a literal translation. Two friends, who should be uniting to kill these rich people, are killing each other. This is a common thematic thing in my work.

Jose: Yeah, the political undertones are all over *Cheap Thrills*.

Trent: Right, it's not subtle, but wrap it up in a genre thing and it's an easier pill to swallow. The class struggle thing, it's an idea that always resonates with me.

Jose: It's also not an easy-to-sell concept in Hollywood.

Trent: Yeah, my agency said, "What are you doing? This is sick and twisted and weird and not fun. It's stage play, dude. We're never going to be able to make this thing for a $150 million. We can't sell this." Once again, I only write things that I think I could make on my own if it doesn't sell, but they only want me to write things that only a studio could make and that's where the disconnect between me and representation happens all the time. I put it on a shelf, like they told me to, because I believed them.

Jose: Later to be retrieved and dusted off.

Trent: Years later. Evan Katz was a writer I knew who took me to meet some people who were trying to make seven $1 million movies. They were looking for straight-up horror specs, and I didn't have those. When I'm left to my own devices I don't write straight-up horror movies. I told them the closest thing I had was *Cheap Thrills*, and I pitched it to them, but they didn't want to make that one. But Evan said, "Hey, that sounds really cool, and I'm looking for a project to direct. Why don't you send me that script?" I sent it to him and he said he wanted to make it, and I was like, "Yeah, sure whatever, no one's going to make this movie," but just like *Deadgirl* it got made and it ended up being a big cult hit. So, you would think after two times, people would listen to me, and I got the third one right now, but nobody wants to touch it with a ten-foot-pole!

Jose: Well, according to your track record, just wait a few years.

Trent: Yeah, the problem is that as I keep getting older and older, waiting eight years becomes less of an option.

Jose: *Cheap Thrills* doesn't revitalize your career?

Trent: No. Once again, I'm vindicated because everyone told you no, and one person said yes, and you were right, but you can't call the people who said no and say, "See? I told you I was right." You can't even do that, right? So, I sit down and say, "Hmm, that worked so I'm going to write something else," but it's sitting on the shelf collecting dust because nobody wants to make it. I don't have any power. I'm not big enough. These movies were all cult hits, and people love them, so I think they'll last the test of time, but it didn't make anyone into a stinking rich millionaire, and that is what you have to do. I still haven't done that yet. It's with anything, really. In this country, it doesn't matter if you're a millionaire because you sold crack cocaine and ruined people's lives; the important part is you're a millionaire. Art versus commerce? Commerce always wins.

Jose: That's a lesson kids don't get in film school.

Trent: Yeah, exactly. Look, this is how I feel about it. At the end of the movie, the guy is standing there, his soul is charred and blackened, and he is physically destroyed, and has murdered someone for a big pile of money. What happens next? Well, it's up to the individual to interpret. The people who love money will say, "But he got all the money!" For me, he's the shell of the man he was, he lost who he was to chase the money. That's symbolic of my own career. I keep shooting myself in the foot because I keep doing the things that I want to do, and I'm not rich as a result of it.

Trent directing his first film, *Chop* (2011). Photo courtesy of Trent Haaga

Jose: Let's talk about that last shot. I saw it at a screening at the Vista theatre, and the last shot of our would-be hero brought laughter and applause, but I thought it was just profoundly sad.

Trent: It is. It's totally sad. It's supposed to be depressing and it is.

Jose: It's a powerful statement to make for those paying attention, however.

Trent: I was at that screening, and I think an even more powerful statement was that they were taping an entire podcast about the movie right before the screening and did they invite the writer? No. See how that works? No one cares. Even if you make a movie about four people in two rooms talking, they still don't care about the writer. I would never downplay the importance of a director, but I would like for people to uphold the importance of a writer every once and awhile, particularly if it's a movie that could have easily been a stage play. If it had been a play, then I would have been king, right? It's a slightly bitter pill to swallow, but you have to if you want to be a writer.

The High-Concept Massacre

Jose: It's the sad fact of our careers, but we stay because we love movies, and in your case, video games as well. Let's talk about your work on the survival horror game *The Evil Within*.

Trent: Yeah, the game had been in development in Japan for three years from the guy who created *Resident Evil*. It was well on its way and had a release date, but when they started doing test plays, the feedback was the dialog and storyline were confusing, because basically they took the Japanese script and ran it through a translator. With no context, the dialog just didn't work. So, they got a hold of me, and they flew me out there. I played the game for a couple of days, and then rewrote all the dialog for them to re-record. They paid me really well and they paid me on time, but I was thinking, "Wait a minute, you have the best game designer, the best graphics guy, the best sound guy, the best composers, you hire the best actors, but there was not a writer on this game?" They spent $300 million on this game and don't think to hire a writer. I'm not going to tell Shinji Mikami what traps to build, but maybe if I'd been around from the beginning, the game characters and the story could've had a little something more to them. This was just random, though. I knew a person, who knew a person, who knew a person that needed somebody, that's how it happened.

Jose: It's all about whom you know, ultimately, no matter what you end up writing. That's sound advice for anyone who wants to become a working writer. You have any other parting words of wisdom?

Trent: Just be completely ready to accept the consequences of what it is you've chosen to do. I think that's what it is. Dream as big as you want, but be realistic at what this is all about. I've succeeded to the level that I'm at because I didn't have ridiculous aspirations. I understood that this was equivalent to digging coal, except with a word processor and that's the truth. Some people make a movie and then spend a year hanging out by the pool deciding what they want to do next. But for me, the reality is I work with people that have to get up at five o'clock in the morning to drive to Valencia to hold up a light all day long. You have to look at your job like you're a P.A. or grip, except you happen to be a writer. If that's the head that you have on, then you'll probably be able to make it, because ninety percent of what this is all about is perseverance, and you can't persevere if you're disappointed at where you're at and you give up. I continue to put my nose to the grindstone and hopefully it will pay off, and if it doesn't I'll die and it won't matter how much money I have. But fifty years from now, because I'll for sure be dead by then, maybe some twenty-year-old kid will find one of my movies and it will change his life. Maybe that'll happen? It's counter-intuitive to what all the books say, but just shut the fucking hole in your face, get off social media as much as you can, try to make some shit, cross your fingers that it's a hit, but be prepared for it to suck. Instead of me spending three days with a sniper rifle, hoping to hit a guy between the eyes, I'm just going to kick in the door with a shotgun and start blasting shells in as many directions as I can, as fast and as hard as I can. It's not going to be as clean, or as neat, or as amazing, but it will achieve the same outcome eventually. That's the way I look at, and that's my terrible advice.

The smokin' serial killer biographer, Stephen Johnston.
Photo courtesy of Stephen Johnston

Stephen Johnston

Ed Gein (2000)

Bundy (2002)

The Hillside Strangler (2004)

Starkweather (2004)

Jose: Let's start at the beginning, Stephen, how did you fall into screenwriting as a career?

Stephen: Actually, I always wanted to do it, since I was a kid. One of my earliest memories is that my parents had left the television, which was a nineteen-inch black and white portable, in my bedroom for some unknown reason. And unbeknownst to them, I was staying up to watch movies. I was maybe eight years old, and I mean I was young enough that I didn't really know what movies were, but old enough to know that I was attracted to them. On late night, Creature Feature Theater, *Frankenstein Meets The Wolf Man* (1943) came on, and I was right in front of the television, because I had to have the volume way down so my parents wouldn't know I was watching, but I was mesmerized, and even though I didn't really know what it was, I knew I wanted to do *that*. As I grew, I became knowledgeable that movies were made by people and they weren't these mysterious things, and I said, "Oh, I want to write those." So, when I went to school, I went to Columbia College in Chicago and studied screenwriting. That was very much the path I was on. I took the directing courses because you had to, and I'm sure I will direct at some point, but I've never been that person that innately hated screenwriting, and I've never understood why it gets so disrespected. Yes, the director is certainly significant, but he or she is handed the script.

Jose: It's true it does get disrespected. Everyone is more than happy to tell you how to make your script better.

Stephen: Yeah, I was thinking about the rise of television shows and show runners. Television writers are far more respected than screenwriters. Makes you think that maybe you're on the wrong side of the desk. But my heart is still in the movies. The reality is that I like that closed structure and formula. It would be interesting to explore the same plot over the course of a season or so, that's intriguing to me, but at the same time I would think I'd get sick of it. I kind of like to tell my story in a hundred pages and be done with it.

Jose: I also think movies last longer than TV shows, because sure, a show will end and it will come out on DVD or Blu-ray, but how many people rewatch it or talk about it? People still talk about movies from the twenties and thirties and they're revered.

Stephen: That's very true. Also, there's a quality to TV shows, even though they are more respected, they are consumed and spat out and gone. There are plenty of television shows that people love, but they don't really look at it with the same critical eye that movies demand. I think movies get that a little more, because television doesn't seem to prompt that from the mass viewership.

Jose: I think because of their contained nature, movies instantly feel more special, like a novel.

Stephen: Yeah. I think that as better as narrative television has become, I think there's a tendency on people's part to say, "It's just a television show," and for whatever reason people aren't as quick to do that with movies.

Jose: Is there a movie out there that you would consider above reproach in terms of screenwriting?

Stephen: Well, obviously something like *Chinatown*, but you know, you could even look at something like *Halloween*. You would never hold that up as an example of a well-written script, but in its own way it's actually profoundly well-written, because it lends itself to the movie as well as it does. There's that old adage, you can make a bad movie from a good script, but you can't make a good movie from a bad script. A lot of that stuff from the 1970s wouldn't be made today. It would be read and they'd say, "We don't know what to do with this".

Jose: So, you graduate college, and then what, you head for Tinseltown?

Stephen: Yeah, I packed up my car, came out here with all my belongings, crashed on a buddy's couch, and within a couple of weeks I had a job as a PA, which turned into a PA job on Disney's *The Jungle Book* (1994), where my job evolved into being the point person on the lot. The production was in India, but my job for like twelve months was to go sit in an office by myself, and if anything came up that needed to be dealt with stateside, that was my gig. But it was great because I drew a nice, steady salary, and there were moments of chaos, but long stretches of me just sitting there and reading or writing and hanging out. But the point of all that is that me and this guy named Mark, the assistant to producer Raju Patel, became pretty good buddies. It's one of those things when you meet someone early on and you know they're not only serious, but they seem to have something going. You meet a lot of people who say, "I'm going to make movies," but you can kind of tell that's not really going to happen for them. It's the difference between the people who are talking about the material versus those who are talking about money and fame. Anyway, when I was in Chicago I had written a script called *In the Light of the Moon*, which was about the Wisconsin killer Ed Gein, and Mark had read that. Sometime later, Mark had started working in film distribution, and he walked into the offices of Hamish McAlpine, and Hamish has a bust of Ed Gein on his desk. Mark says to him, "Oh, my buddy Steve wrote a movie about that guy." Hamish says, "No way, no one would write a movie about that guy. I'd love to read it." Mark told me to send my script over to him right away, and two weeks later I'm having lunch with Hamish and he loves my script, and six months later we're in pre-production. It happened that quickly. That movie won Best Picture at Sitges, and a respectable amount of accolades, but most importantly it made a ton of money on video. The year it came out, if I remember this correctly, it was 25th on the list of the Top 25 Highest-Grossing Videos of that year, and it was the only one that wasn't a studio release. It made money, not necessarily for me, but I was able to keep working based on that.

Jose: It shows you that networking pays off, because you never know who you're going to meet. Your creepy little serial killer project could be someone's dream project and you'll never know unless you make connections and spread the word. But I'm curious why you chose Ed Gein out of all the others?

Stephen: It's kind of funny, because I don't really remember how I stumbled across him. Well you know *Silence of the Lambs* (1991) is based on him, *Texas Chainsaw Massacre* (1974) is based on him, and at some point I wondered why everything was based on him. If the dude is that fascinating, tell the story of that guy! There is that old movie with Roberts Blossom, *Deranged* (1974), which is about Ed Gein, but I hadn't seen that until after I had written my script. But I don't specifically remember the germination; I guess I just decided to tell the story the way it actually happened. I wrote that and it was my intention to make it myself for like $100,000 dollars. I had formed a friendship with Scott Spiegel, who I had met at a convention years previously, and was so impressed that he had co-written *Evil Dead 2* (1987), and he was impressed that I knew who he was. So, when I came out to Hollywood, I gave him my script for *In The Light of the Moon* and I told him, "This guy wants to buy my script and he wants to make it, but I don't really know because I want to make it myself." Scott said, "What are you talking about? Are you kidding me? Somebody wants to buy your script and make it a movie? What are you crazy? Sell it! Whatever happens, your toes are still tapping, you got the music in you."

Jose: I've had my brush with real-life serial killers with my forth film, *The Divine Tragedies* (2016), which was based on the Leopold and Loeb murder of 1924. These guys fascinated me and I wanted to explore their mentality and their way of sensing the world around them, so I'm curious if there was something about Ed Gein that you really wanted to explore.

Stephen: I'm fascinated by the psychology, and not by the gore. I'm fascinated by what drives people to that stuff, Ed Gein specifically. This guy lived in a small town where everybody knew everybody else, and he was able to do the most deplorable, heinous acts, and yet people would have him babysit their children. Nobody caught on that there was something wrong. He was grave robbing and had body parts at his house. That's a weird duality there, a great psychological dichotomy. I mean, we live in a world now where you kind of except that there are horrible things that happen in the world, but back then no one would have even thought of that happening in the 1950s.

Jose: Absolutely, and a big reason why *Ed Gein* works so well is because you have Steve Railsback playing him, and I've always been a huge fan of his work.

Stephen: He was great. The person we had in mind was Harry Dean Stanton. He turned it down, and I think it was a health issue. Maybe that was his excuse, but ultimately he had to bow out. Then Steve came on board and I said, "Well, that's ok!" He's a very nice guy.

Jose: I think that's what works for the character, too. Railsback comes off as a good guy, a plain-Jane guy next door, and most of these killers were regular looking folks.

Stephen: I think that's a good point. Steve had this inherent nice-guyness that comes through, and I'm not saying that Harry Dean Stanton didn't have that, but I don't know that he exudes that nice guy quality that Steve did. One of the greatest moments of my life was that I was a guest at the Texas Frightmare Weekend convention and I was at a table with Steve, and we were signing *Ed Gein* merchandise. That was pretty cool.

Jose: That's awesome. All thanks to *Ed Gein*. And because of that film, serial killers became a cottage industry for you.

Stephen: Because it was so successful, yeah.

Jose: Next on the chopping block, so-to-speak, was *Bundy*. How was he chosen as your next victim?

Stephen: That was Hamish McAlpine. *Ed Gein* made money and it was creatively successful. I don't want to be entirely mercenary, because the conversation involved more than, "Hey, let's make more money", but had *Ed Gein* not made money, we wouldn't have had the conversation. But we went in to these things saying we wanted to make a good movie. The way I remember it, I'm pretty sure it was Hamish and Mike Muscal, Mike being the other producer, who came to me and said, "Hey, we want to make another one about Ted Bundy." I don't think I was a part of the conversation about who they wanted it to be. They came to me with it. I said ok, and I went off and wrote the script in six months.

Jose: What was the research on that like? Intensive or cursory?

Stephen: I got all the books that I could and read everything. With Bundy there are quite a few, but with Ed Gein there were only like two or three. Oddly enough, there haven't been many on him, but with Bundy there were like a dozen. That process happened pretty quickly, but I guess that depends on how you define quickly. To me spending six months to research and come up with a viable screenplay was quick, but to some people that might seem like forever. But when I say six months, probably three months of that was reading and note taking, and stuff of that nature.

Jose: Was casting in place, or did you have anyone in mind while writing?

Stephen: One of the first who was potentially going to play Bundy was Danny Huston, because Hamish was buddies with him then, and I don't know why that didn't happen. Of course now Danny's a pretty successful guy. But then Michael Reilly Burke came on board, and that happened fairly quickly.

Jose: Did you help Michael prep for the role at all? Maybe shared your research with him?

Stephen: I didn't have much involvement with that film, in particular. I don't want to say that director Matthew Bright and I didn't get along, but he didn't want anything to do with me from the get-go. I mean at some point, fair enough, it's his movie and he's making it. I didn't have much involvement with that except writing.

Jose: Did he re-write you?

Stephen: He did. In fact, his name is on the script. Although, to tell a Hollywood behind the scenes story we actually had to go through litigation. He wanted first place on the script, and I said, "Absolutely not," and the Writer's Guild agreed with me. I don't know how familiar you are with the arbitration process at the WGA. They go through and read and all the drafts of the script, and I think I had done four drafts of the script at that point, so the WGA sided with me. I actually had to sign something that said I didn't mind sharing screenplay credit with him. That was one of those eye-opening Hollywood experiences. You'd like to think that everyone plays fair, but they don't necessarily.

Jose: And it always seems that the writers are the ones that get shafted. I've had that happen a couple of times, one of which a director came along and tossed out my script and wrote his own. At that point, I just asked for story credit, which was partially intact in the finished film, and the rest of my money. Also I've run into people asking for credit just for giving notes on a script.

Stephen: And that's something I also find really bizarre. I don't want credit for something I didn't do. If Robert Towne came along and said he'd give me co-writing credit on *Chinatown*, I'd say "I had nothing to do with that. I appreciate the offer, though." I just think that's a weird thing for people wanting to take credit for something they didn't do. A buddy of mine is in a similar situation, he went into a television project with somebody he thought was a good friend of his, but the moment they started to get success, this guy became the quintessential Hollywood monster. Now they're not speaking, because this guy basically wants to take credit for everything, even though it was a 50/50 creative split. My buddy's heartbroken because he found out that this guy he thought was his friend wasn't his friend. Why even do that? There's enough credit and enough money to go around. Why take someone else's credit?

Jose: I've had run-ins with people who I considered friends who turned sour on me, and it's awful when it happens, not just professionally, but personally.

Stephen: Yeah, and again I think it goes back to those people who are drawn to this business for the wrong reasons. It's a weird thing. People talk about people with ego, but to me if someone wants to take credit for something that they didn't do, that's a person with a weak ego. I don't see that as egotistical, I see that as being an emotional infant. My ego is pretty damn strong, which is why I'm capable of saying, "I didn't write that, I don't want credit. Or, I did write that, therefore I need credit." Who's got the bigger ego, the person who needs to steal someone else's thunder, or the person who's creating the thunder?

Jose: That's a great line; I'm going to use that down the road. It's very true, but I'm sorry that happened to you on *Bundy*.

Stephen: Movie turned out great, though. The movie, as it exists, is great. Eighty to eighty-five percent of it is what I wrote, so it's not like I watch it and I don't recognize it, it's still what I wrote, and Matthew Bright as a director is a talented guy, so it worked out. That's probably, to a degree, something that I could call a favorite thing of mine. That movie is very serious, but it has a slight edge of black humor to it that Matthew actually understood.

Jose: And that one was successful as well, which catapulted you into a third serial killer opus?

Stephen: Yeah, it did well enough, and then we did *Hillside Strangler*. Bundy metamorphosed into *Hillside Strangler*, and in point of fact Matthew Bright wrote the first draft of it. I never read it, but nobody was happy with the script, and so they brought me in. I remember specifically avoiding his script, especially after my experience on *Bundy*. They told me, "Don't even read it, because from a legal standpoint let's not even open that can of worms." So, much like with *Bundy*, I just submerged myself in the material and wrote the script. Chuck Parello, who had directed *Ed Gein*, came back and directed that. But that was sort of the end of the road, creatively speaking. You can make an argument for sort of the evolution of the killers. You have Ed Gein, then you have Bundy, who was the first modern serial killer, and then you have the Hillside Strangler, who was a duo. You have pre-modern, modern, and post-modern. From a creative standpoint, I felt we were done.

Jose: Did you ever feel pigeonholed as the serial killer guy?

Stephen: A little bit. I was interviewed by *Fangoria* magazine, and the first line of the interview was, "The go-to guy for serial killer movies." But at the same time, if that's your complaint, it ain't too much to complain about. It led to conversations and meetings and other things. I think a lot of people have a tendency to lament too much.

Jose: You're done creatively, but you return to serial killers a couple of years later with *Starkweather.*

Stephen: *Starkweather* was actually for my buddy, Mark Boot, who had introduced me to Hamish originally. I got paid, but I essentially wrote that as a favor for Mark, because he was trying to get up and running as a producer. I don't actually remember where it fit in chronologically, but he asked me, "Hey, can you write something about Charlie Starkweather." That was the genesis of it. He could get a movie made based upon me writing it and it being about a serial killer.

Jose: Why Starkweather? Was that out of your hands, too?

Stephen: The way I remember it is that it was Mark's idea. It's funny because people say, "So, you're fascinated with serial killers," but no it's because people hire me to write about them. I mean, yes I do find the psychology interesting. But I think it's that thing where people from the outside looking in always think that everyone makes the kind of movies they want to make, where in reality it isn't that way usually. If someone approaches you to do something, you do it.

Jose: Most writers are hired employees; it's not always up to you to decide what to write about.

Stephen: Right, absolutely. I've had pitch sessions where I've gone in and said, "This is what I want to write, and I want you to pay me to write it," but by and large if somebody comes to you and says, "Here's the amount of money we're paying, and this is the subject we want you to write about," I'm sure there are people out there that are successful enough to say no, but I'm not that guy.

Jose: That's something that people considering screenwriting nowadays should keep in mind, that not every working screenwriter makes a living wage writing a script.

Stephen: Remember when the guild was last on strike, several years ago? I remember reading something online that said that the average salary of a Writer's Guild member was something like $900,000, and talking about how greedy writers were. But that's the average, because you have people like Akiva Goldsman, who makes millions, and then there are those of us on the other side of the spectrum. I mean, do they really think that every guy in the Writer's Guild makes that kind of money?

Jose: There's a big misconception about writers and their worth. There is so much subpar stuff getting made today, but most of it is written by underpaid writers who don't necessarily care about the material, but need to pay their rent, or simply eat that day.

Stephen: Yeah. I like being in a place where everyone can make a movie, but at the same time it's really not a good idea that everybody can make a movie. The people that I encounter that want to give me their scripts, I try to be fairly judicious. I refuse to be dishonest, but I also don't want to be soul crushing. I always try to find something positive to say, but sometimes you just want to say, "You know, maybe this is not your thing. Maybe you should go find something else to do." But everybody who wants to make it in Hollywood has a script. That doesn't mean they're worth reading.

Jose: Spin that around the other way, too. There are so many scripts out there, that a masterpiece of a script might never get read just because of the sheer glut of material.

Stephen: Oh, sure, sure. I actually read a script recently that a friend of mine gave to me, and it was really impressive. It read like a giallo-style film, and I was blown away, but man I don't know who's going to make that.

The High-Concept Massacre

Jose: Well, the whole spec market is kind of dead. Say you walk into a place and pitch them your idea. They might love it, but they'll ask you to write their giant squirrel thriller instead. They aren't necessarily looking for your material. They'll take your material as a sample, but that's it.

Stephen: You know, it used to be that you could make movies for $5 million and everybody got paid pretty well, and it was professional. Those movies don't really happen anymore. You have $100 million movies, or you have the Asylum. That's unfortunate for everyone. I can enjoy those bombastic Hollywood releases, but they're rarely ever good. But the Asylum-style movies are as good as those movies, because it's the same sort of cynicism. They have no pretense that they're making a good movie, it's all about money.

Jose: Considering that *Ed Gein* was the only script that wasn't prompted by money, is that your favorite of your serial killer quadrilogy?

Stephen: I think *Bundy* is my favorite one, but it depends on how you want to define it. *Ed Gein* is my favorite, even though I had written movies before that, but that was the first one that I felt was a professional motion picture. We made that for $850,000, but that was my first professional film. So, in many ways I'd have to say that was my favorite. In terms of finished product, *Bundy* was pretty damn good. *Hillside Strangler* is too, but *Hillside* is so bleak. When my good buddy saw it he told me, "Boy, that is not a date movie." It's true, it's so unrelentingly bleak, and it's effective and I'm proud of it, but it's kind of one of those movies that you feel you want to shower right after watching it, whereas *Bundy* has enough of an edge of black humor.

Jose: Do you miss serial killers, as crazy as that sounds? Ever feel you'll return to that well?

Stephen: Hamish and I have in fact re-partnered, and we're doing another one. It's about the Moors murders that happened in the UK in the 1960s. It was a young couple, and they were child murderers and rapists. Hamish is from the UK, and he's wanted to do it for quite some time. We're gearing up for a shoot next summer, and it's going to be pretty good. One of the biggest expenses is going to be music, because we're going to get Beatles tunes and stuff. We're pulling out all the stops.

Jose: Now there's so much serial killer ephemera in pop culture so you have to find a way to stand out. When your initial serial killer films came out, the subject matter wasn't as pervasive.

Stephen: No, we created the serial killer biopic. This sounds incredibly egotistical, but if you go to Wikipedia, and I didn't write that, I don't know who did, but someone wrote that Hamish McAlpine and Stephen Johnston created the serial killer biopic. We didn't do it intentionally, it just sort of happened, but now there are tons of them out there. Even I go, "Again with serial killers? Enough, people, enough!"

Jose: And have you sort of taken that serial killer overload into account with the Moors murders script?

Stephen: That was the thing, yeah. We said, "Well, if we started this thing, we're going to end it." It's time to put this thing to bed.

Jose: So, this'll officially be your closing chapter on the whole sub-genre?

Stephen: I would have to imagine so, yeah. You know, never say never, but creatively speaking I don't know what else can be brought to it.

Jose: These movies are creative endeavors, obviously, but how does that work when you're dealing with the life story of a person from a legal standpoint?

Stephen: If it's a true-life story and it's all established and a part of the public record, it's basically fair game. We did get sued on *Bundy*, because there was one thing and I don't know what it was, because I try to take great care that it's all on record. But Bundy's girlfriend had written a book called *The Dark Prince*, I think, and after the movie came out she said that we had included something in there that we could have only known if we had read her book. I don't know what that claim was, and I don't think I did that intentionally, but the long and short of the whole thing was that she was given $10,000 bucks to go away.

Jose: A film I wrote and directed, *The Haunting of Whaley House* (2012), was based on a famously haunted historic home in San Diego. We weren't able to shoot there due to production logistics, but we still used the name, and I know they came after the production company, but I was told not to worry about it, and I never knew how it was settled.

Stephen: I think a lot of time people come out of the woodwork and they know they aren't raising a valid claim, but they know that chances are good that they are going to be given some amount of money to go away. I'm not saying that's the case with Bundy's girlfriend, she may have truly felt she had been aggrieved, I don't know. But if you truly felt you were aggrieved, you'd want more than $10,000 to go away. If you set your sights so low, it kind of says that you're not that bent out of shape.

Jose: It's one of the pitfalls of filmmaking, all the legal issues that could arise from simply wanting to tell a story and entertain.

Stephen: It's a fact that a film production has to take out insurance for the potential that you're going to get sued, kind of like malpractice. Doctors and filmmakers have to have malpractice insurance. People have a skewed view of money in the film business. Sure there are $100 million movies, but you see that movie is very different from a $1 million movie. That's a lot of money, but not when you're making a movie. It's not like anyone is getting rich on that movie.

Jose: Some people see a production crew and they think it's extortion time, because I've heard some crazy stories of what they've had to do to make sure the locals play along.

Stephen: There was a movie I wrote called *Deadly Charades* (1996) back in the day, which was the only time in cinema history that the same person was the writer and also the on-set security. We shot up in the Hollywood hills, and there are like $10 million houses up there. Honest to god, one of those people living in those houses played their stereo super loud so that we couldn't shoot, until the UPM [Unit Production Manager] went and paid them $1,000 to turn their stereo down. A person living in a house worth multiple millions of dollars basically extorted us for $1,000, just because they could, and there wasn't much we could do, because we couldn't go away.

Jose: How *did* you fall into erotic thrillers of all things?

Stephen: Initially I was hired to re-write something for Mystique films, because my buddy was working on those as a co-producer. *Playboy* was the corporate entity, and Mystique got the financing to make a slew of them, maybe half a dozen or something. However it was one of those things where they were up and running before they had the money, kind of a cart before the horse type of thing. So, they had the script for the first one they were going to do, but it was dreadful, and obviously it was going to be dreadful, but I when I say dreadful I mean it was questionable whether or not it would be a coherent film. They gave me the script on a Friday, and I re-wrote it over the weekend. When I handed it in they said, "Do you have anything like this that we can shoot?" I said, "No, but give me a couple of weeks." I think I did three other erotic thrillers in various guises after *Deadly Charades*. Basically all they wanted was for me to tell a story and make sure someone gets naked every ten minutes, but I tried to bring what I could to it.

Jose: I'm curious how that works format-wise. Do you write "sex scene happens here" or do you describe every grunt and thrust?

Stephen: Oh no, I described it, but the way I would do it would be, you know, they kiss passionately . . . as they take their clothes off . . . That way I would fill a page, because when you're reading the script you kind of want it to pace accordingly, so it plays out the way it should.

Jose: What's the writing process like for you in a typical script, let's say you're writing something just for you.

Stephen: I suppose my approach to everything is kind of the same. I don't really write chronologically, I just sit down and throw shit out there. As things come to me, I just put them down on paper. Even with *Ed Gein*, which was based on a real guy, I would just write what I thought would be scary and it slowly started to form. Obviously, you have to have some idea about where you're going, you can't be willy-nilly about the whole thing. There has to be some kind of narrative idea in your head, but I kind of let it form itself in a weird sort of way. It's like chiseling away at a big chunk of marble and slowly it starts to form what it wants to be. Different writers have different approaches, and my way might sound goofy or New Age-y, but I let the story tell itself. If you come at the material from a love of movies, on some level you should have an intuitive notion.

Jose: I think that's an important skill for a screenwriter. Learn how to be your movie's first audience member and if you can see it play out in your head, it's very easy to write down what you see happening. That's always my approach, and that's why I can write fifteen to thirty pages in a day because the movie is breathlessly taking *me* on a ride and I want to see what happens next.

Stephen: Right. When I say I let the story tell itself, what I mean is that my internal movie theater is so well versed, so as I sit there and the projector in my head kicks on, I start to see it, and if I can see it, then one assumes that other people will see it.

Jose: One should develop their movie knowledge to expand their movie language skills.

Stephen: If you're a screenwriter, watch anything. Watch everything. Whenever I start a movie, I always finish it. I've seen *Plan 9 from Outer Space* (1959) multiple times!

Jose: Let's talk character; any pet peeves about character building?

Stephen: I hate that movies are populated by just detestable people now. Why does a movie like *Halloween* work as well as it does? Because you believe that they're real teenagers, and not only that, you believe that they're people you could have been friends with, and when they start getting murdered, it matters. Whereas in half of these new movies, you want them all to die. You come to realize that a lot of writers think that someone is a character just because he's an asshole. Well, yeah that's a character, but that doesn't make them people, or people I want to watch for ninety minutes. If the point is that the guy is supposed to be an asshole, then fair enough, but if you get the group dynamic going and there is one guy who is such a detestable asshole you start to wonder why they're hanging out with this guy. When I was in high school, I didn't hang out with people I didn't like. I can deal with a lot of shit, but the cynicism I can't.

Jose: What are your thoughts on notes and rewrites? Are you combative or do you just kind of do what you can to appease the producers?

Stephen: I'm a little bit of both. I'm not one of those writers that are threatened by notes. If it's a good note, and thematically makes it better, then I have no problems with it. I mean I've gotten notes that asked, "Can we change the Chinese restaurant to an Italian restaurant." I don't care, it's a restaurant, I could have just written restaurant. A while back, a buddy and I were doing a ghost project for Twister pictures, about an old camp that was haunted by the ghost of a little girl. We had done about three drafts, and we went in for a meeting to go over notes and one of the producers says, "Maybe the movie ends with the little girl's funeral." Me and my buddy looked at each other and I said, "It ends on a funeral? The entire movie is about her haunting the place!" That was basically the end of that project, because my buddy and I were done. We were either on totally separate pages or he hadn't been paying attention to anything we had said or written. So, I'm open to notes if they're valid, but I have no qualms about telling them they're not. But if being accommodating means being one step closer to getting your dream of making a movie realized, well then you're a fool if you don't. There are plenty of times when someone has stuck to his or her guns, and nothing happened.

Jose: Speaking of meetings with producers, where do you stand on the agent/manager dilemma—worthwhile, or don't bother?

Stephen: As of now, having had both and once being at ICM [International Creative Management], I have neither one. But the reality is that if you're in a certain stage of the game, you need someone looking out for your best interests, but the key is to make sure they're really looking out for your best interests. If you have someone who represents you and they're not looking out for your best interests, if they're looking at their ten or fifteen percent, they might push you to do things you don't want to do, and maybe you shouldn't do. I've known people who've been pushed into things that they didn't want to do, and I know occasionally that has to happen, but there's a difference if the thing will be detrimental. I mean, there are plenty of meetings you can't take unless you're represented, so if you want to go into those offices and have those meetings, you have to have someone behind you. At ICM, I was on a talent roster with Wes Craven and John Carpenter, so I was a small fish in a very big pond. I've been remarkably fortunate that I could actually get away without having representation for a long period of time. Most everything I've done has all been a matter of knowing somebody who knew somebody. I once had an agent who was King Shit on Turd Island, but I don't think I ever got a job out of that guy. I had meetings, but it never lead directly to any work. I'm not an anti-representation guy, but I can't be entirely pro, either.

Jose: That's good advice; most of it is hustle and sweat. Any other nuggets of info you'd like to leave future screenwriters with?

Stephen: Write. Learn the craft. At this point I've written probably thirty-five feature-length scripts and about twelve of those have been produced. A lot of them will never see the light of day, because I had to write like five scripts before I knew what I was doing. I went to film school and learned the craft, but if you're not writing, you're not doing it. If you want to write, then do it, or do it just to find out if you even *want* to do it. I think it's not uncommon that people think they want to write and they start, but quickly realize "I don't want to do this." And if you don't want to do it, you're probably not going to be a good writer. I mean, there are times when we have to work, and it is work, but it's not like I have to force myself to do it. My advice is simply that you study the craft, but make sure it's a craft that you want to study. If it's drudgery for you to sit down and do it, then you probably shouldn't do it. It can be work when you're on your fifth round of rewrites and you're getting more notes, but that's part of it. It's like music. If you get into it because you want to be a rock star and get a lot of chicks, obviously that works out for some guys, but the only way you can guarantee it is if you learn your instrument and you play it as well as it could be played. It may take a while, and you may not get all the chicks, but eventually people will notice. There is so much bad writing out there, that if you can establish yourself as a person who at the very least is not bad at it, you'll get asked to do it again. At the end of the day, my advice is: don't suck.

Ally Sheedy was *Maid to Order,* but Amy Holden Jones was made to write. Photo courtesy of Amy Holden Jones

Amy Holden Jones

The Slumber Party Massacre (1982)
Mystic Pizza (1988)
Indecent Proposal (1993)
The Relic (1997)

Jose: When did your love affair with the movies begin, Amy?

Amy: I came in backwards, because I didn't have a love affair with movies; I had a love affair with making documentaries. I started with studying still photography and documentaries at MIT. I studied still photography with Minor White, and documentaries with Richard Leacock and Ed Pincus. I made a film there called *A Weekend Home*, which was a cinema vérité documentary about a weekend going home to visit my parents that won the AFI National Student Film Festival. It was about my parents and what it's like for a kid seeing their parents as an adult, and there were some significant problems in my family. There were no categories, whether it was fiction or whatever, there was just a first place and it won. The judges were Martin Scorsese, Fred Wiseman, and it was either Eleanor or Frank Perry, one of them, and at that time that was really the only substantial student film festival.

Jose: That must have bolstered your confidence greatly in terms of documentary filmmaking.

Amy: I tried to make a living in documentaries, and I couldn't. It was much harder then because we shot on film and it was too expensive, and frankly the problems for being a woman were enormous. I was going to quit and go back to film school, but I wrote Scorsese a letter because I saw that he was prepping a movie in Columbia. So, I wrote a very short letter, and I hoped he'd read it, saying, "Do you remember this movie, *A Weekend Home?* Do you think I have any chance of making a living in film?" He called me up and said, "Meet me in New York." It turned out that he had loved *A Weekend Home* so much that he went and made a very different documentary called *Italianamerican* (1974) after seeing mine. It had inspired him, though his is completely different, and very happy, which mine wasn't. So, I asked him, "What do I do? Do I give up?" And he said, "Come be my assistant on *Taxi Driver* (1976)." So, that's how I ended up backing into features, but I had no real experience or passion for fiction at all. I was much more interested in cinema vérité-form of photography. My teacher Richard Leacock was one of the founders of cinema vérité.

Jose: What an amazing place to cut your fiction filmmaking teeth. I can't think of a more exquisite training ground than the set of *Taxi Driver*.

Amy: It was an amazing film school. Marty was wonderful. He treated me like a fellow filmmaker, because he had really loved the documentary. You know, I never considered I'd be anything but a director. I was that arrogant because I had done well at the MIT film school and won the biggest film festival in the country, but I was a complete neophyte about it. Marty brought me in to see the dailies every day, so I could see the whole process, and I remember in dailies not understanding why there were no sound effects, in other words that it was just the live sound. But you know I picked it up as I went along and he had me helping him with the storyboards and things like that. It was a very intense shoot. People don't realize that it was a very low-budget movie, about $1.3 million, and a total of eight weeks, mostly nights. Then, I got to be involved with the cutting, and saw it go from a three-hour rough cut to the final. The editors were the most supremely talented in Hollywood.

Jose: How did you get involved with Roger Corman?

Amy: The reason I worked with Corman was because Marty believed that everyone should start with Corman, because he had. So, I was Marty's assistant through post-production, and then he sent me to Roger Corman, when he was looking for an editor. Marty said, "Prepare yourself, because it's not going to be like this," which it wasn't. Joe Dante and Allan Arkush hired me to edit their first feature for Corman, which was *Hollywood Boulevard* (1976). In features, they didn't hire women directors, and you had to have a skill in-between to make a living, and you had to make a living. I had always loved editing, so I just moved into editing. Editing, in those days, which was the late 1970s and early 1980s, was an area where they let women work. In the crew picture I have of *Taxi Driver,* there are about seventy people there, and three of them are women. They were hair and makeup, wardrobe, and me. So, I ended up in the Corman School for a while, because he hired tons of women. First of all, because he liked strong women, and second of all, they work cheap, which is all he really cared about.

Jose: *Hollywood Boulevard* **is an interesting editing challenge, because wasn't it made from bits and pieces of other movies?**

Amy: Yes, it is. Joe was an editor for Roger, of trailers mainly, and he and Allan got the idea that they could get Roger to let them direct if they wrote a script that used the expensive action scenes from a bunch of his existing movies, and just linked them with some new footage. It had a ten-day shooting schedule, if that. It was a lot of editing, but on the other hand Joe is one of the great editors of all time, so I don't think he would have hired me if he didn't think I knew what I was doing, and he hired me off of the same documentary, *A Weekend Home*, which tended to win people over. It was a blast, it just didn't last very long. Then I cut trailers for them for a little while, but it was not really regular work.

Jose: Did you ever work with Scorsese again? Was it ever something you guys discussed?

Amy: What happened was that videotape had come in and they had to let a whole bunch of people into the editor's union. The rule was, at that time, to be a union editor you had to have worked eight years as an assistant editor before you could be a union editor. But to let all these videotape editors in they had a one-time thing, which was if you had worked ninety days non-union in a certain category you got in on that category. I had worked as the grade one editor for Corman, and I got in at the age of twenty-six as a union film editor, when no else was that age because of the eight-year requirement. So, I worked a couple years as an editor, and I cut a documentary for Scorsese called *American Boy* (1978), while he was on the lot doing *New York, New York* (1977). I also cut one of the worst Hal Ashby movies; it was called *Second-Hand Hearts* (1981). I was then even supposed to cut *E.T.* (1982), because I was cutting *Corvette Summer* (1978), and I got that because I was cutting on the lot with Marty. It was cut at Lucasfilm, so all the cuts were seen by Lucas, and by Spielberg actually. In the interim was the Ashby picture, but then Spielberg offered me *E.T.*, which was kind of amazing for the age that I was. The script was wonderful, but I knew if that happened then I would be a big editor, and I'd always wanted to be a filmmaker. I went back to Roger and he said, "You would've had to have directed something like what I do in order to get a job with me. The documentary is great, but that's not what I do."

Jose: This is where *Slumber Party Massacre* comes in?

Amy: I took a script off his shelf called *Don't Open The Door*, which was a horror movie written by Rita Mae Brown, a famous feminist. I re-wrote some of it, but I basically shot the first ten pages of it, because it had action, suspense, and a dialog scene. We had a crew of four people. My husband, who had shot *Taxi Driver*, was the cinematographer, and my next-door neighbor was the soundman. I cut it nights on Joe Dante's KEM [Author's Note: A KEM is a type of flatbed editor used for cutting film] when he was doing *The Howling* (1981). When he would finish at the end of the day, I would go in and cut. Then when I showed him the reel of film I had, he called up Roger and said, "You should look at this." I said $1,000," because it was all shot on short-ends and with deals. He said, "You have a future in the business. How much would it take to finish the movie?" I had never read the rest of the script, I had only read the first ten pages, and I had no idea what happened after that so I just threw out, "$200,000." He said, "Okay, you're in pre-production." Then I had to decide whether I was going to edit *E.T.* or direct what became *Slumber Party Massacre*.

Jose: You're sitting on a green light for two great projects, the decision is really up to which would benefit you creatively, because financially I'm sure *E.T.* would have been the right move.

Amy: I decided to roll the dice, and Spielberg was very gracious and released me, and hired Carol Littleton, who did a great job. Then I read the rest of the Rita Mae Brown script and it was not a good experience. Suddenly, I was in pre-production and I had four weeks to re-write and prep my first movie, which I did, and that was the first time I had written a screenplay.

Jose: How much did you change?

Amy: I completely re-wrote it, except for the basic premise, which is a feminist one, about a driller killer. It was a metaphor, but it was maybe a bit too obvious. Rita's script wasn't a comedy, and I turned it into a comedy. I gave it to Roger and he said, "You can do this. You can write." So, we shot the damn thing in four weeks for $200,000 dollars with a crew of twenty people. It became *Slumber Party Massacre*.

Jose: That's a really fun film that still holds up very well, but it's a complete turnaround from your documentary, cinema vérité days.

Amy: I didn't set out to do a *Slumber Party Massacre,* I was more on the arty farty side, but all of a sudden I was doing these movies for Roger Corman. A certain number of people told me I was a fool, but it was the training ground for everyone in those days, and in fact the movie made a fortune for Roger and he remade it over and over again. He thought it was great, but most of the reviews were, "How could a woman do this?"

Jose: So, you did get some flak for being a woman director doing a half-naked chicks getting slaughtered movie?

Amy: I guess they missed the comedy. I guess they missed the fact that more boys die than women, and much more violently than the women do. And they missed the fact that it had this feminist theme, which came from Rita Mae Brown, and was all about the fear of getting laid for the first time. I think it's hilariously funny. I looked at it again recently, for the first time in thirty years because it played at a revival house and the place was packed. The damn thing plays and it's very funny. That underpinning, which came from Rita Mae Brown, is clear when you watch it now. But anyway, it didn't get me anything in terms of directing. Nobody hired me for anything.

Jose: Even though most of the Corman alumni got bigger gigs, it didn't pan out equally for you?

Amy: All of the men who did that, including Marty himself and Jonathan Demme and many more, immediately moved into mainstream movies, but women did not direct, except for comedies. I wasn't offered anything at all. I didn't have a single meeting.

Jose: How does your next film, *Love Letters* (1983), come about then?

Amy: I went back to Roger. He also distributed art films at the time. He distributed all the Truffaut films and all the Fellini films and so on. He had two networks of distribution; the theater and drive-in near you for the exploitation films and the art film circuit for the Truffaut and Goddard films and all that sort of stuff. I asked him if I could do something for his art film circuit and he said it had to have some exploitation element to it. It had to have some salable item. So, I sat down and wrote the script for *Love Letters*, where the salable item there was sex and nudity, and he loved the script. He was great to me. He just green lit it, and off we went.

Jose: What inspired *Love Letters*?

Amy: What inspired it was that I had fallen in love with the cinematographer on *Taxi Driver*, Michael Chapman, and I had moved out to California. He lived in New York, and we wrote each other letters. I had all these letters from when we were apart and I thought, wouldn't it be interesting if someone's daughter found all the letters and got interested in all that stuff. It was also inspired by the art films of the time, like *Shoot the Moon* (1982) with Albert Finney.

Jose: What had you learned on *Slumber* that you put to use on *Love Letters*?

Amy: For *Love Letters* we had $400,000, but the trick was to make a film cheaply, and you had to have a very limited number of locations, because the moves ate up all your time. If you only had a certain number of days, you couldn't spend a half a day moving your crew. You had to be in one place, then once you were lit you could go over and around stuff. There were other ways that money was saved, too. Sometimes Roger would take away our generators on *Slumber Party Massacre*, so we would have no way to power the lights, and he would say, "Just point the car headlights into the house," and of course that didn't really work.

The High-Concept Massacre

Jose: How did *Love Letters* do?

Amy: That one went a different route; it went on the entire festival circuit, across Europe too, and it got great reviews. It got a great review from Siskel and Ebert.

Jose: I had no idea that Corman did festival runs, that's interesting.

Amy: He sent his art films to those, but he never made many prints of them. He didn't want to send it out, he really just wanted to sell them on video, which is what he did and they did very well on video, but you had open in big cities to get a video release.

Jose: I'm curious if you ever considered coming back and helming the sequels to *Slumber Party Massacre*?

Amy: He asked me to, but I was trying to not do exploitation films. I was busy writing stuff for myself to direct, and I wrote *Mystic Pizza* after *Love Letters*, and Roger would have made it, but he wasn't going to give me any kind of a budget. So, I set it up with Samuel Goldwyn Films, which was a terrible mistake.

Jose: Well, that's what we're here for, the terrible mistakes. Please kindly spill the beans.

Amy: It turned out that it was Samuel Goldwyn Jr., the son, and he didn't actually make movies, he just distributed them, so he kept movies in an endless state of development. He had this fear of starting a shoot. So, he optioned the script with a verbal agreement that I would do one pass for him and then he had four weeks, I think, in which to green light it or return it to me. I did my part, which was a third-act re-write, and he then began to hire other writers to work on it. I never had any deals on paper with Corman at all, I didn't know much about contracts, and my agent, I was with Gersh then, had not finalized the contract so this guy made up what he thought was the deal and then he sued me to sign it, which would have given him *Mystic Pizza* for $5,000 for the rest of my life. The Writer's Guild arbitrated it and it took about a year and a half while that was going on, and I made *Maid to Order* (1987) in the interim, which was a re-write of someone else's script.

Jose: Let's talk about *Maid to Order,* because I remember that movie very fondly. How did you come to be involved with that one?

Amy: It's one of my favorites actually. So, the machinations were going on to try to extract *Mystic Pizza*, and this script came along that a friend of mine, Holly Goldberg Sloan, had written the first draft of, but she was kind of in the weeds about getting through her second draft and she asked for help. We sat down together and re-wrote it. She gave me shared credit, and I brought her on as an associate producer on it. We set it up and were given $4 million to go make it. First we went to Demi Moore, and she passed. I sent it to Ally Sheedy and she took it immediately. Then Demi Moore, who it turns out had never read it, tried to get back on it, but it was too late. We shot that one in thirty-two days, which was an improvement over the twenty we had on *Slumber Party*. I love that movie.

Jose: Was there any studio tampering with the script?

Amy: I never had any problems with that with Roger, or with anybody, really. I got plenty of that from Samuel Goldwyn, though. I mean, he was horrible; only the Writer's Guild stood between me and him. Ultimately, he lost because what he was trying to do was illegal. There's no such thing as an endless option on someone's material.

Jose: This is your first big studio film, so does this finally put you in another bracket career-wise?

Amy: We had a blast making that film, and it got decent reviews, and it did really well. Now, there were several films of that size that came out around that time, but the others were all directed by men, and all of those men got offers and went on to big careers, and I got nothing. Not one offer.

Jose: What happened with *Mystic Pizza*?

Amy: I lost it. Once you've optioned your script to somebody, if they are willing to pay you your directing and your writing fee, which is called pay or playing you out, they can then own the screenplay. Goldwyn Jr. had lost, but pay or played me the full amount, which was still pretty little, and owned *Mystic Pizza*. He then went on to hire a very nice man, who had never directed anything, and by then I had directed three features, and he completely re-wrote it into the ground. Then he hired Randy and Perry Howze, because they had written a draft of *Maid to Order*, and I had re-written it, so we split credit on it. I guess he thought it was some sort of payback by hiring them to re-write me, but we were friends. So, they actually took the script and returned it to the original script. They did eliminate one of the girls, who was a rich girl, and was the equivalent of Mickey Rourke in *Diner* (1982), which was the inspiration for *Mystic Pizza*. Pretty much what they did was multiply existing scenes, so it was long enough, because they had lost a quarter of the script with her gone. Nobody would have gotten shared credit, but I didn't arbitrate it because I was grateful to Randy and Perry for returning it to the original script, and I didn't want their names gone because they had done me a great service. The script was widely read over Hollywood so everyone knows it's my script.

Jose: The movie went on to be well-regarded, but are you happy with the finished film?

Amy: I'm pretty happy with it. I think the casting was brilliant, I really do. It was cast by Jane Jenkins and Janet Hirshenson and they were just young casting people then, but they became two of the biggest casting people in Hollywood.

Jose: Now, the big question: how does the writer of *Slumber Party Massacre* and *Mystic Pizza* add the family-friendly *Beethoven* (1992) to her filmography?

Amy: I love *Beethoven*, too. In a funny way, when I look back, I love the comedies most. After *Maid to Order*, after I had seen the other male directors move on and I had nothing, I decided that I needed to do a big movie and then I'll get a chance to direct a little movie. This was in the era of *Big*, the changing-body movies, so I had this idea about a dog that turns into a man, and I went to Ivan Reitman's to pitch it, but they didn't want to do it. As I was leaving, I saw this script called *Beethoven*, and I asked them, "Is Ivan doing a movie about Beethoven?" They said, "Oh, wait a minute that's a dog movie, and you just pitched a dog movie. Why don't you take a look at it and see what you think." So, I took a look at it and I came back and said, "I think we should do this, this, and this." They didn't know if they should hire me or not, but they hired me on a weekly basis. They were already in pre-production, too. I rewrote the opening sixteen pages, and Ivan read them, and he said, "Ok, just keep going, this is great." He would give me notes every sixteen pages or so, but basically it was a dream experience as a writer, and I rewrote the whole thing cover to cover during pre-production, and that's how *Beethoven* came about.

Jose: Was there ever a discussion on whether Beethoven should talk? I've always wondered about that, because it seemed like most animal movies employed that gimmick, but *Beethoven* didn't.

Amy: No, they didn't discuss that, because the original writer, who took a pseudonym because he didn't want his name on the movie, was more interested in the story of the father, which is kind of what's so strong about the original.

Jose: Did anything happen with your dog-man movie?

Amy: Ultimately, I did write it as a spec and sold it for a tremendous amount of money. It was bid on by three different people, one of them was Amblin, and I went with Turner Pictures. It was a very big spec sale. And Spielberg, when I did not sell it to them, sued Turner saying that I had stolen their idea. It turned out that they had a movie about a bunch of pets that turned into people, so they didn't want to see another one made, or something. Turner was scared, but they had to pay me, and they paid me a very big fee. I had to make the choice: do I give back the fee and get the script back? My agency said, "Don't do it, because you will never get this made if Spielberg opposes it." So, I kept the money and it never got made.

Jose: And this wasn't because of some hidden animosity between you guys that went back to *E.T.*?

Amy: I hope not. I never spoke to him personally. I suppose I should have picked up the phone and tried to call him. That probably would have been the smart thing to do. But they were angry that I hadn't sold it to them. There was an aspect of that in those days. If you're the most powerful guy in Hollywood, you throw your weight around.

Jose: There are currently eight *Beethoven* movies. Did they ever approach you for a sequel?

Amy: Yes, they asked me to do *Beethoven 2*, and I did a treatment for it, which they paid me very well for. I can't remember why I didn't do it; I think I got involved in something else. I think I wasn't actually available. The treatment was fun, I called it *Beethoven & Sparky*, and it was going to be about him and the little dog that plays big in the finale. They had a buddy adventure.

Jose: Switching gears cinematically, *Indecent Proposal* comes into your life at this point.

Amy: Producers Tom Schulman and Alex Gartner had a book, *Indecent Proposal*, and they told me, "Don't read the book, because we don't want the book. We want the title, and it's about a rich man who offers a poor man a million dollars for a night with his wife." I actually did read the book, but I threw it out. It's about Arabs and Jews; it's very strange. I wrote the first draft of that and then everybody at Paramount got fired. That version had her go to have sex with the rich guy, and she can't do it, but he gives her the million dollars anyway to destroy the faith between the husband and wife. So, when the entire administration at Paramount changed, and it actually changed twice, the new people came in and said, "We want her to really do it." So, it was a completely different script, and I thought about whether I could do it, so I looked at the films of Billy Wilder, which almost all of them are about selling yourself. I wrote a new outline and I got excited about it again. That draft went in and the producers really liked it. I was at ICM then and someone there slipped it to Adrian Lyne and then he was the director and that was that. I was actually dubious about it because *Flashdance* (1983) was not exactly the way I wanted to go with *Indecent Proposal*, which was changed in the third act. I have sole credit on it, but a number of people worked on individual scenes for Robert Redford, but the film was cast off of my draft.

Jose: The movie has a very solid cast, especially Redford who, in my opinion, manages to define his later years in acting with that role.

Amy: Woody Harrelson was not who Tom Schulman or Alex Gartner or I wanted. We didn't think he could stand up to Redford and it was necessary for her to go back to her husband in the end. There was a meeting in which I said, "I don't know how to make it work that she would leave Redford for Woody." Adrian replaced me and brought in a series of people who worked on the third act. I think that Adrian identified with Redford; he did not identify with the young husband. He threw the movie to Redford in the third act, and I don't think it works, actually.

Jose: You finally get a chance to write and direct another big theatrical film with *The Rich Man's Wife* (1996). What was your experience on that one like?

Amy: I think it wasn't as much fun as I hoped it would be. *The Rich Man's Wife* is not my favorite, and I think what happened to me was that I had started to become a writer, and not a director. I had set out to be a director, and there had been so many years between *Maid to Order* and this one that I had become a writer, and a writer gets to work alone in a room and do what they want to do. In directing, one misstep in casting and the whole thing falls apart. Halle was the name that got the movie made, but she's done a lot of thrillers and they all have a similar failing like *The Rich Man's Wife*. I don't know what it is, she does a very good job, but I don't think she should do thrillers. I don't know, I'm not crazy about the movie. I found I really didn't like directing, but I still really loved post-production. I didn't really love the 'dealing with the actors' part of it. *Maid to Order* was much more fun to do.

Jose: Was that a hard thing to realize, or do you think it was maybe just the genre you were playing in?

Amy: I think that the thriller was maybe not my thing. Horror I could do. But when you think about when I did horror it was really comedy-horror. I don't watch *The Rich Man's Wife*, it was really a rough shoot. One of the actresses, not Halle, was mainlining heroin and every day was a struggle. I ended up preferring writing. In fact, I could have directed an episode of the television show I did two years ago, *Black Box*, and I didn't want to. I had no interest in it at all.

Jose: What would you do different if you had a chance to go back and do *Rich Man's Wife* again?

Amy: I wouldn't have cast Halle, but I don't think that's the only thing. When I look at the picture, any scene that she's not in I think basically works, and the stuff that she's in doesn't work. I don't really know why that is. The funny thing is every director has a movie that doesn't really work. I mean, no one is watching *1941* (1979), and I would watch *The Rich Man's Wife* five times before I'd see *1941*. When a woman directs a movie like that, it would basically stop her career, where with a man it would just be forgotten. I mean, it wasn't like it was a huge failure or anything; it did fine; personally I wouldn't watch it again. I didn't want to direct ever again after that. The real reason was that I was impatient with actors. I just wanted them to go in there and do their job. I didn't want to have to do all the political stuff. It's been my experience that the really good ones just go in there and do it, but it's the ones that make you talk to them a lot are jerks, usually.

Jose: Let's talk about *The Getaway* (1994). The original is my favorite Peckinpah film, and I thought the remake was pretty good, too. Was that daunting to take on the reimagining of a classic film?

Amy: It was Fox, I believe, that came to me. The original writer was Walter Hill, and he was going to direct it, but he bowed out and wasn't going to do the rewrite for some reason. I was brought in to work on the Kim Basinger character, because he didn't do women very much. I didn't think I'd get shared credit on it, even though I did a lot of work on it, but he wanted me to have it. Mostly what I worked on was the relationship and her character; she was pretty much nothing. Walter Hill is not about writing women. I actually did action stuff too, like the big action scene at the end I completely rewrote.

The High-Concept Massacre

Jose: Your next real genre credit after *Slumber Party Massacre* is the monster-in-a-museum romp *The Relic*. What was your experience on that picture like?

Amy: I was totally rewritten on that one. When I handed in my draft, the producer called me and said, "You've launched this like a cruise missile. We've immediately gotten it green lit by Paramount. This is fantastic." She went off to do some movie with Spielberg, but she handed it off to her second-in-command, who had been the partner of Peter Hyams, who ended up directing it. They never went to A-list directors, they went right to him, and he was someone who always rewrote original writers and he went through several different writers. I never even met him. After writing the script that got the movie green lit, I never met the guy. They used a team to complete the final draft, which was a complete mystery to me because I had just written Paramount's biggest movie, *Indecent Proposal*, and they gave the script to a team, who still work today, who had just written Paramount's biggest flop. That director was well known for cycling through writers. He was not a good director.

Jose: It seems like you had a good luck with your writing assignments, in terms of them getting made.

Amy: Everything I did up to that point got made, and then I wrote two animated film for Dreamworks that didn't get made. I did *Casper 2,* and that was a script I really loved. They didn't do it because Christina Ricci wouldn't commit to it, but I loved that script. That was the first one that I had worked on that didn't happen. I had done a big pass on the live-action *Jetsons* movie, and there were a million people who had done a pass on that. I realized that I had written every genre; I'd done horror, action, comedy, drama, and science fiction. I hadn't done a Western; that was about it. Anyway, I was sort of bored with it, and decided I'd try to do television. I went to Brillstein-Grey, who were doing a lot of television then. I told them I wanted to do television, and they were indulgent, but not terribly interested. They explained to me that at that time, which I believe was 2004 or something like that, they were mainly doing procedurals, so you had to do a detective show, a medical show, or a legal show.

Jose: Those can be very dry, I'm personally not a fan of those, but I assume that information really struck a chord with you.

Amy: My father had been a doctor, and he had a floor for impossible-to-diagnose diseases, so I came up with a cross between a detective show and a medical show. This was the year before *House M.D.* Mine was called *The Seventeenth Floor,* and all three networks tried to buy it. Brillstein-Grey chose CBS, but CBS decided to do something called *Doctor Vegas* instead, which was a really terrible script, but it kind of hooked me, and I've written and sold one or two pilots a year ever since.

Jose: Wow, that's almost unheard of.

Amy: It's frustrating because so few of them get made. I had one pilot shot at the CW, which I loved and tested through the roof, but they picked up another one, which hadn't tested through the roof. That was about Harvard medical school, and I had done different ones through the years, but since very few people do the medical ones, I kept getting asked to do those. Since then I've become the medical shows person.

Jose: This led to *Black Box,* I assume.

Amy: It led to *Black Box,* which was this television show I had on ABC a couple of summers ago. That one was originally written for FX with Ryan Murphy producing, and it was partly inspired by my father, who was a wonderful cancer researcher, but was bi-polar. I'm actually very proud of it, I think it's great, but I don't think ABC was the right home for it. I think it would still be on the air if it were somewhere else. I think it was a little too intellectual for ABC. It didn't do badly, but it wasn't a big, huge hit.

The High-Concept Massacre

Jose: A lot has been said in this book about pitching a movie, but how do you go about pitching a pilot?

Amy: You pitch the show, you pitch the concept, the main characters, what the genre is, and what the on-going conflicts are. You don't necessarily have to pitch the pilot, they buy the concept for the show, or they don't. So far, I never had any that I didn't sell. Unfortunately, the downside is that it's very hard to get on the air. A network will buy sixty drama pilots. If you sell to them, you will be one of those sixty. Then, they will shoot anywhere from four to ten of the sixty, so already your chances are one in six that you will get shot. Of the ones they shoot, if they shoot ten, four will probably be on the air. It's almost impossible to get on the air with those odds, because the four slots tend to be taken by big creators who already have shows on the air. For example, at ABC it's all Shonda Rhimes and Shonda Rhimes spin-offs.

Jose: It's funny, despite those odds, most of the feature writers I know have switched over to working in television.

Amy: Well, features have become either tiny films about esoteric subjects that make very little money, or remakes, or huge movies. I have no interest in writing a comic book movie. That's for young people, I'm too old.

Jose: Have you seen the industry change since you started in terms of respect for female writers?

Amy: No, not very much. In television only a quarter of the writers are women, and they are kept out of an enormous number of areas. *The Daily Show* has seventeen writers, and two of them are women. *Seinfeld* never had a woman in the writer's room at all. It's very strange, but it's a club-like atmosphere in a writer's room, so if the main writer is a guy, he fills it up with guys. It's one out of four television writers that are women. I don't know what the reasoning behind it is, and I've had projects fall apart because of it.

Jose: In your opinion, which is a more feasible writing career: features or television?

Amy: I think it's almost impossible now; there are no jobs in screenwriting; the jobs are in television. Nobody buys specs. And the way into television is much more logical than it ever was in features. There is a ladder system where you start at the bottom as a staff writer and only get to do occasional scenes and research for the other writers, but you work your way up to becoming one of the running writers.

Jose: Well, what advice would you give a writer who wants to start writing for the new Golden Age of TV?

Amy: Quit looking at television and go read great television scripts. Go to the Writer's Guild library, which is open to anyone, and read pilot scripts. There are diversity programs from the guild if you're either a diversity writer or a woman. Also, most of the television studios have programs to bring people in, which most people are not aware of. You can go and work in the program for a year and then they staff you on a show. There're millions of staffing jobs in television. It's tricky, but it's not impossible.

The happy-go-lucky maniac screenwriter, C. Courtney Joyner. Photo courtesy of C. Courtney Joyner

C. Courtney Joyner

From A Whisper to a Scream (1987)
Prison (1987)
Class of 1999 (1989)
Puppet Master III: Toulon's Revenge (1991)
Doctor Mordrid (1992)
Trancers III (1992)
Lurking Fear (1994)

Jose: You've been a film fan your whole life, so what kicked off your obsession?

Court: I can remember the first movie I ever saw in theaters was *Hey There, It's Yogi Bear* (1964), probably when I was four, I believe. Hanna-Barbera on the big screen, and not the entre into horror you'd expect, I guess. But, I was just lucky enough to grow up in that "monster" period. I was born in 1959, so by the mid-1960s, when I was seven or eight years old, you were completely surrounded by *Famous Monsters* and *Castle of Frankenstein* magazines, Aurora models, Castle Films, TV horror hosts, AIP, and Hammer movies in the theater. The monster boom was just insanity; everything a kid could love was around you, and with all that, I was just smitten. I became one of those kids, complete with lazy eye disease, running around reciting the credits to *The Ghost of Frankenstein* (1942) when I was six.

Jose: Can you point to one film, or a handful of films, whose writing really impressed you?

Court: The movies that blew me out of the back of the theater as far as the writing goes, that were tremendous, were *Godfather: Part II* (1974) or *Chinatown* (1974) certainly, which is of course the high watermark for so many people. I remember the first time I saw *Fail Safe* (1964) on TV when I was about twelve, and I was just fascinated by it. Of course, I love Kubrick, but for a long time I actually preferred *Fail Safe* to *Dr. Strangelove* (1964); I guess I was more comfortable with the dour dramatic stuff than I was with the satire. I love the formality of certain dramas, which is kind of a lost art, but I watched everything I could on TV, growing up in Philadelphia and Pittsburgh. When you talk about horror literature for the screen, and what really hits your ear, I think that's one of the reasons I was drawn, from a horror standpoint, to the Hammer Films; maybe just because it was British actors delivering great Jimmy Sangster dialog, or even bad Jimmy Sangster, it didn't really matter. Everything sounded so sophisticated and classical, rather than American horror movies of the era, the cool AIP flicks, that were featuring mostly teenagers. I loved those, really loved everything if it was horror, or had monsters either man-made or atomic, but the Matheson-scripted Poe films, like the Hammers, were in their own class, and certainly had a different feel, look, and sound, than other AIP movies, and I was drawn to them. Also, the Universals were a mania with me—and still are—so I was devouring the genre! But, I wanted to read the scripts, was really curious, but never was able to read any horror screenplays because they weren't readily available. I was grabbing the paperback movie tie-ins to everything, but you couldn't find published scripts. Not horror, anyway. When I was finally able to finally get my hands on some scripts through mail order, I got Dean Riesner's script for *Play Misty for Me* (1971). It's not strictly horror, but that script is just astonishingly good! Of course, he was a wonderful screenwriter, but I don't know what it was that he did, because it was a re-write, that just brought it into this whole other level, as a thriller. I love Eastwood's movie, but that screenplay, and its language, and layout on the page, it just really hit me between the eyes: what a screenwriter can do on the page. It's still one of the best scripts I've ever read in my life.

Jose: So, what kicked you in the ass and made you want to be a part of the movie business?

Court: I don't think there was ever any choice. I was pre-wired for it!

Jose: Did you go to film school?

Court: No, I never did. When I went to USC, the film program at that time was pretty much focused on graduate students. There were a few undergrads. Jeff Burr got in as an undergrad, but that was a rare thing, and they hadn't adjusted the class requirements to undergrads, and all that, but I was able to take a ton of film classes as a non-major.

Jose: How does that transition into your first film *From A Whisper To A Scream*, which you made with the aforementioned Jeff Burr?

Court: Well, I knew Jeff very well. I was always hanging around the department and helping to arrange film festivals and things like that. I actually brought Warren Oates and Sam Peckinpah down for a screening of *The Wild Bunch* (1969), because I had done a documentary on Sam Peckinpah for a Western Film class and Peckinpah and Warren were very kind to me. I actually sat between them during the movie and that was my commentary track! That was pretty wild. We were all going out for drinks after, and I saw Jeff and asked him to join us, and that really started our friendship. He knew I was crazy, but he also knew I was totally enamored with movies. He, and I, and our friend Darin Scott were all absolutely focused on the same thing. We tried to get a feature going called *The Nightcrawlers*, but it didn't happen. At that time, thanks to *Halloween* (1978), and the fact that the first *Friday the 13th* (1980) had just exploded, indie horror was huge, and everyone wanted product for the VHS market, which was just raining gold on producers. So, Jeff, Darin, and Jeff's brother Bill, formed a production company and they raised independent money in Jeff's hometown of Dalton, Georgia, and that's how *From A Whisper To A Scream* came about.

Jose: Why an anthology film?

Court: People always ask why we did an anthology, and the reason is first of all because we loved *Tales From The Crypt* (1972) and *Asylum* (1972), and not only did we love that format, but it was also practical. If at any point we ran out of money, we would have large sections of the movie shot and completed, so you didn't get stuck and have to hire a certain actor three years later. Not having your movie finished is a terrible trap to fall into and a lot of people, some we knew, who were starting out, had it happen. This was our way of sidestepping that and it worked.

Jose: Let's talk casting, because there are a whole bunch of notable faces in a movie made by three kids in Georgia, working on their first movie.

Court: Jeff was bound and determined to have Vincent Price, and we got him. Not without a few bumps in the road, but we did get him. I knew Clu Gulager well, because I had worked on a small documentary about Don Siegel when I was at USC, and I had sought him out. The Gulagers were so great to me, and I introduced Jeff, so it was natural to write something for Clu, because we knew it would be fantastic, if he played it. And he was. I met Terry Kiser through my friend Steve Carver. Jeff and I approached Harry Caesar at Robert Aldrich's memorial at the DGA, and he said (in Caesar's voice), "You got a movie? All right, when do we start shootin'?" Then Jeff and I went down to Palm Springs to get Cameron Mitchell, and he was great, a real hoot. We pieced it together through people we knew, and then people they knew, and ended up with this wonderful cast.

Jose: You were working with Vincent Price in the latter half of his career, so I wonder what an old pro like him thought of you young upstarts.

Court: Well, he took us to school a little bit. I wrote all the Vincent Price stuff. Jeff got his address, and we just went up to his house, and he ushered us into his living room. He had been baking bread and he was in an apron. He was very kind to these strangers! We told him what we were doing, and he really wasn't that interested because he had done that PBS series *Mystery* with Diana Rigg, and he had done a movie called *The Monster Club* (1981), which was one of the last Amicus films, and he didn't think that had turned out that well. Basically, he didn't want to do it in the first place, but was being nice about it. We got him to hold off on his decision until we had shot the stories and then see what he thought. Finally, he came down and looked at the film, agreed to it, and then we made a huge blunder, because we really were just inexperienced. Once he agreed to do it, we decided to initiate a whole bunch of script changes, but we didn't consult with him. We really tried to alter it to make it more elaborate, but it just wasn't going to fly, and he got a little upset with us, which is understandable. But he came down to the set, met some of the other actors, including Clu, and we talked, and he agreed to do the original script, and it was fine. But again, there's a learning curve with all of this. What we didn't know, we *really* didn't know. He was a true movie star—an icon—and should have been involved in all the changes, simple as that. It's all he wanted. He was very good to us, and I know his patience was strained, but he saw the enthusiasm we had for him, and our eagerness to do something a little wild and different. I don't think it was always to his taste, but he saw that we were sincere about what we were trying to do. Interestingly, his being stabbed in the throat by Susan Tyrell was his idea. I had written that she poisons him, because I thought it would be easier for him physically, and Vincent Price said, "Oh no, I think she should cut my throat, it's much nastier," so he gave us that one, but it was a delicate situation, since we made some silly mistakes, but he took them as our inexperience, and was nice about it.

The High-Concept Massacre

Jose: I think a lot of people starting out have a problem with that disconnect that exists between being a film fan and being a professional filmmaker.

Court: Yes, and I think there's a big disconnect. When you make that leap you never stop being a fan, but once you're a professional you're in that camp and your knowledge is different, then your experience is different, and you view things a certain way. You don't lose your enthusiasm, but it's true.

Jose: How did *From a Whisper to a Scream (aka The Offspring)* fair when it met the world?

Court: We opened at the Egyptian, before it was the American Cinematheque, and at this point I was already working with Renny Harlin on *Prison* (1987), so he came with his girlfriend. It was a rainy Friday night. A couple of people trickled in off the street, but we were feeling pretty good. I mean, we had had this long, long journey and we ended up at a theater on Hollywood Blvd., and it played across country, so that was a real triumph. So, we're standing there, and in my brain, I'm going, *Okay, I'm going to ask Nastassja Kinski out on dates now,* and all this stuff, *because I'm a big movie writer!* Then, the doors to the auditorium open and this guy comes walking out and says, "Man, this is bullshit!" That brought us back to earth, so we went over to Boardner's and got hammered! We played movie theaters across the country, and it didn't make any big box office noise, but we got some nice reviews, including the *L.A. Times*. It did just fine, and, we had a Drew Struzan poster! I'm thrilled that people even pay attention to it anymore, as a lot of horror flicks made at the same time are sort of forgotten. I'm proud of the movie, and it just had a great Blu-ray release. But *The Offspring* really is Jeff Burr's film, top-to-bottom. For my part as a writer, I'm pleased with it because I got to write dialog for Vincent Price, as silly as I did it. That was a long time ago and I look at it now and I say, "Oh boy, would I do it differently now? Yeah, I think so." I don't know if I'm better or worse now than I was in those days, but since you asked, it's fun to contemplate.

Jose: Well, a lot of things were better back then, particularly getting horror movies like this made.

Court: Independent horror movies used to be possible at that time! Tax laws were different and the studios were different. In those days, if you had an independent horror movie you wanted to do, it would take you two weeks to go to every single office of all those mid-range production companies, but now you can do it in an afternoon. The opportunity was different because you had all this different eyes looking for product. Even though now the need for product seems to be greater, and you've got all these multi-media platforms, all the money seems to only be coming from three of four sources because everything is so corporatized. If you can't get into that stream you're going to have a hard time, and that's not the way it was.

Jose: You mentioned you were working on *Prison* at the time that *From A Whisper To A Scream* hit theaters, so how did that project develop?

Court: *Prison* actually happened before *Whisper* was finished. I had a friend at USC named Mike Farkas, he was a filmmaker and he had asked me to write a treatment for him for a futuristic prison movie. I wrote the treatment, he showed it around, nothing happened. Well, he had been working with Producers Irwin Yablans and Bruce Cohn Curtis, and Yablans had developed a script he described as "Halloween in a Penitentiary." Mike told them he knew the perfect guy to work on it. So, I met with Irwin and Bruce, they were really great, and they asked me to do it. I sat down and read their script, and then I had another meeting with them and said, "Here's the problem, this has got to be supernatural. What you have is a realistic story of a convict walking around murdering other inmates. That happens constantly, it's a true story. It's horrible, but it's not horror. It has to be '*Poltergeist* Goes to Jail,'" and that's what sold them. Renny had been hired because he had made a film called *Born American* (1986), which was making a lot of noise at the American Film Market, so we met, and then went to work. Irwin kind of became my champion, because after *Prison* he introduced me to Mark Lester and that's how I got *Class of 1999* (1989), then he brought me over to TWE and that's where I did *Vietnam, Texas* (1990). I became kind of his Go-to Guy. We still talk all the time, and he's my great friend.

Jose: What was the process like turning *Prison* into a fully formed movie?

Court: Oh, it was great. I worked very closely with Irwin and Bruce. Bruce was an excellent story editor, and Irwin and I constantly bounced ideas. It took time, but the script got finished, and Irwin and Bruce then decided to dissolve their company. Irwin ended up with half the properties, and Bruce ended up with the other half, and so Irwin got *Prison*. Originally we were going to make it with Dino De Laurentiis' company, and that was interesting. We had a meeting, but the exec on it, Gary DeVore, ended up being killed. He was one of the writers on the Schwarzenegger movie, *Raw Deal* (1986). He disappeared driving back from Las Vegas, and they found his car a year later, in a culvert. That's who was going to be running *Prison* for us. Then we were going to do it at Cannon, and that didn't happen. Then, Irwin went in to meet with Charles Band at Empire. Of course, Irwin had a long association with Charlie, because back when he owned Compass, they had released *Parasite* (1982). So, we ended up being an Irwin Yablans Production that was released by Empire. Irwin brought other money into the financing, so everything didn't originate with Charlie, and we didn't develop the script at Empire. We kind of did our own thing and then came back for Empire to release it, and they did a good job, with one of my favorite posters.

Jose: I think *Prison* is a lot of fun, but were you happy with the finished film?

Court: You know, I really am. Renny and I were both mega Don Siegel fans, so we wanted a *Riot in Cell Block 11/Escape from Alcatraz* vibe, not just horror, and that was really the thing. Despite all the supernatural trappings, I still wanted it to feel like a prison movie. Of course, we had Mac Ahlberg shooting it, and Renny did such a beautiful job. We had Viggo Mortensen; a great guy, very dedicated. And Lane Smith, and Lincoln Kilpatrick, and all the others. Tiny Lister. Great cast. It was just tremendous.

Jose: And this springs you forward into *Class of 1999*?

Court: Yes, Mark L. Lester, the director, was a friend of Irwin's. We had a wonderful screening of *Prison* at MGM. Mark was there, and he asked me to work on *Class of 1999*. The wonderful thing there was that the story had been written by Stanley Mann, and Stanley is one of the Big Boys of screenwriting. He had written the screenplay to *Damien: Omen II* (1978), *Conan the Destroyer* (1984), and *Firestarter* (1984), that's how he and Mark knew each other. My God, Stanley had written the script for *Eye of the Needle* (1981), and produced *Theater of Blood* (1973)! He was a hero to me. *Class* was a non-WGA thing, so he couldn't write the screenplay, and that's why they hired me. So, I got to work with Stanley Mann, and boy I was a nervous guy showing him my pages, but he couldn't have been more helpful, or gracious. Anyway, the film went to Vestron and they hired other writers. They had different people working on the script at different times, because my commitment was done, but they always kept coming back to me, thankfully. When I was doing the final drafts, the script was close to the very first ones that Stanley, Mark and I had worked on. That sometimes happens. Scripts can go way off in the re-writing, because stories can be told a million different ways. It's experimenting. I've done it. And then, sometimes, you come back to that original thing, that first approach. Full circle. It's a long process, but that's what happened here, and Mark and I ended up doing six more movies together.

Jose: Is there anything you wrote that didn't make it into the film that bugged you?

Court: My biggest disappointment is with my original ending. My idea for the end was that the kids kill all the robot teachers, but the robots come together into this spider-like thing. But it was just not in our budget, and that movie wasn't all that cheap. It just wasn't practical, but I sure liked the full-sized android they used.

Jose: Like most of the folks I've interviewed for this book, you found your way into Full Moon movies, but end up writing *Puppet Master III*, which is a film that I'm sure everyone considers the best entry in that franchise.

Court: I had a relationship with Charlie after *Prison*, and I had worked on other projects at Empire, but none of them had gotten made. A friend of mine was going down to Full Moon for an audition, and I went with him. I'm walking up the steps and the first person I see is Charlie. So, we sat down and played catch-up, and Charlie asked me to come down and visit him on the set of *Trancers 2* (1991), which they were filming at the time. Tim Thomerson and I were already great friends, because he had been in this movie I had written called *Vietnam, Texas*. I'm down there on the set and Charlie brings up *Puppet Master*. I was a little hesitant about that because everything I had done up to that point had been theatrically released, and now, that sounds ridiculous and snobby. But Charlie wanted to do a prequel to the first film, set during World War Two, and the more I thought about it, the more intrigued I got—actually, totally amped for it. I love period pieces—so, I said yes, enthusiastically, and they gave me a three-picture commitment.

Jose: Fairly painless writing process?

Court: I submitted an outline that was approved right away and I just went for it. The writing went well and fast. I just sat there, and put on my "low-budget Alistair MacLean" hat. I remember talking with Dave DeCoteau, the director and a great buddy, and saying, "I want this to be like a Pinewood Studios Nazi movie," and he immediately got what I was going for. I loaded David down with tapes, including *Night of the Generals* (1967) and *Where Eagles Dare* (1968); he got so enamored, and inspired, with the look and attitude of those adventure pictures. That's what we pursued. I think he really liked that approach, because it wasn't one he'd done before.

Jose: *Puppet Master III* really has that authentic look, too.

Court: We were originally going to be one of the very first of the Full Moon pictures to be shot in Romania. Ted was over there doing *Subspecies* (1991), something happened and he got pushed back, so *Puppet Master* couldn't go. David and producer John Schouweiler were the ones who said, "Let's try Universal." So, that was great! There we were, on the back lot, shooting in Frankenstein village, and every time I turned around I recognized something from *Son of Frankenstein* (1939), or *Night Monster* (1942), or *Sherlock Holmes and the Secret Weapon* (1942), and on and on. I'm a total Universalite, so it was a ball. I just loved it. And, practically everyone we knew wanted to visit the set.

Jose: Let's talk about Richard Lynch. I got to direct him in my second film, *Corpses Are Forever* (2004), and he was a great, dedicated actor. Was he always attached to this project, because he looked like Blade?

Court: Richard looked exactly like the Blade puppet, and that was great. That was the whole point, that the puppet would be a re-incarnation of him. We had a very interesting experience on that movie. Since we were patterning ourselves on those big Elliot Kastner-type Nazi movies from the 1960s, we wanted an all-European cast. For the main Gestapo agent who tortures Andre Toulon, we wanted Ralph Bates. We made the offer to Ralph, and we didn't hear back for a while. Finally, we get this phone call from Virginia Wetherell, an actress from *Curse of the Crimson Altar* (1968). She was Ralph Bates' wife, and now his widow, because he had just died. He was dying of cancer in the hospital, but she had told him that there was a movie offer, and that made us feel so great. Dave and I both got really choked up about this; it was so sweet of her. Christopher Neame, who was the young vampire in *Dracula A.D. 1972* (1972), he came in and sat down with us. He was Ralph's best friend and he said, "I want you to know that if you hire me for this, I'm going to give Virginia my salary." That was quite a thing. That was very impressive. Charlie wouldn't let us do it though, and I understand his thinking. He said, "Look, we have to have an American actor in here some place, because if we don't, distributors will think the whole thing was shot overseas and I will get less money for it." From a business standpoint that makes total sense, and we moaned, but that's how we ended up with Richard Lynch, because Richard had been in *Trancers 2* and Charlie loved him, and Richard was great. So, it worked out well, but it was an emotional thing with Ralph Bates and Christopher Neame.

Jose: After tackling puppets, you tackle masters of the unknown with *Doctor Mordrid*, does that happen after *Puppet Master III* is released, or before?

Court: You know, Full Moon was set up like an assembly line, and I believe that *Puppet Master III* was in post when I started working on *Doctor Mordrid*. The whole thing with *Mordrid* was that the origin came from Jack Kirby. He had done his concept drawings and stuff, but unfortunately I didn't get to meet him. I'm a true comic book-geek, and Kirby's work was like Mount Rushmore to me, so one of my goals was to capture the feeling in his artwork. Charlie always trusted me so I was left alone to work on scenes, and bring in as many comic book elements as I could. I came up with the idea of the dinosaur skeleton battle at the end, because I've always wanted to do a giant Ray Harryhausen-type sequence. I told Charlie what I wanted to do and he said, "Go for it." So, I went ahead and wrote it. Then later we were in a script meeting, and David Allen, our visual effects guy brought up something, he said, "You know, you've included a Pterodactyl in here. How's it going to fly?" I shrug and say, "Well, what do you mean?" He looks at me and says, "It's a fossil. Fossils don't have skin. Wings have skin." It had completely zoned out on me that it wouldn't have wings, but that was a great way to eliminate one of the animated monsters. That movie was the first time I really worked closely with Albert Band, because he really directed the movie. Charlie was there, of course, but he was running the company, so he would come in and do some scenes and then Albert would take over. It ended up being Albert who primarily directed the film, just because Charlie was doing a million things at once. Albert was my guy. For me, he wasn't the director of *Ghoulies 2* (1988), that wasn't the Albert Band I thought of. I thought of the guy who wrote the screenplay of *Red Badge of Courage* (1951) for John Huston. I thought of the producer of *Asphalt Jungle* (1950), and *A Minute to Pray, A Second to Die* (1968). He really was my mentor at Full Moon. He was a great man.

Jose: They knew you wanted to direct, why didn't they offer it to you?

Court: They had already decided that I would direct *Trancers III*, so what they did was really fantastic. I would basically be inheriting the *Mordrid* crew, so I was around for a lot of the shooting, getting to know how they worked best. Some were already friends, but I hadn't directed before, so that's not how they saw me. Albert and Charlie would ask me about setups. "What do you think? Where should we go next?" Testing me the whole time, you know. It was wonderful; they were incredibly generous about easing me into that position.

Jose: *Doctor Mordrid* **is a blast. I think, despite some signs of age, it's still a great picture.**

Court: I really like *Mordrid*. I think possibly we went a little too far with having the naked girl, because it seems a little out of tone with the rest of the movie. I think Full Moon used to do that a bit; we'd be going along on one thing and then there would be an R-rated, exploitation element thrown in there. Of course, she looked fantastic, but I do think we went too far, and maybe it didn't belong in this film. They spent a little more money on *Mordrid*; it's a bigger movie, and feels a little more polished. But again, this was a great example of what you could do at Full Moon, those fun opportunities, and I was pretty thrilled that we got close to a comic book feeling.

Jose: *Doctor Mordrid* **wraps and you find yourself on the set of** *Trancers III***. Was it daunting to take on another part three, and keep it within the continuity of the previous film?**

Court: It was. The biggest issue for me for part three, really, was part two, because there were so many still unanswered questions that related to the first movie; so how do you make this work? I didn't really understand a lot of part two, and it's chronology, so when I wrote the script, it came to pairing the "Trancers" ideas from that film down, and being able to address things from both movies. I wanted to clean up the relationship with Helen Hunt's character, and we didn't even know if that would be possible because she was a big star by then, and we didn't know if she would agree to come back and do this. I really wanted to have something for Andrew Robinson, which was my big ace in the hole. His wife was my agent, and he's just a great guy, and he was such a dear friend that thank God he agreed to do it to help me, because his presence added so much. But, I'll tell you what Jose, it all boils down to this: I had discussed directing with Charlie and Albert and they were very supportive of me, but it really all came down to one person ultimately, and that was Tim Thomerson. Tim went in and had a big sit down

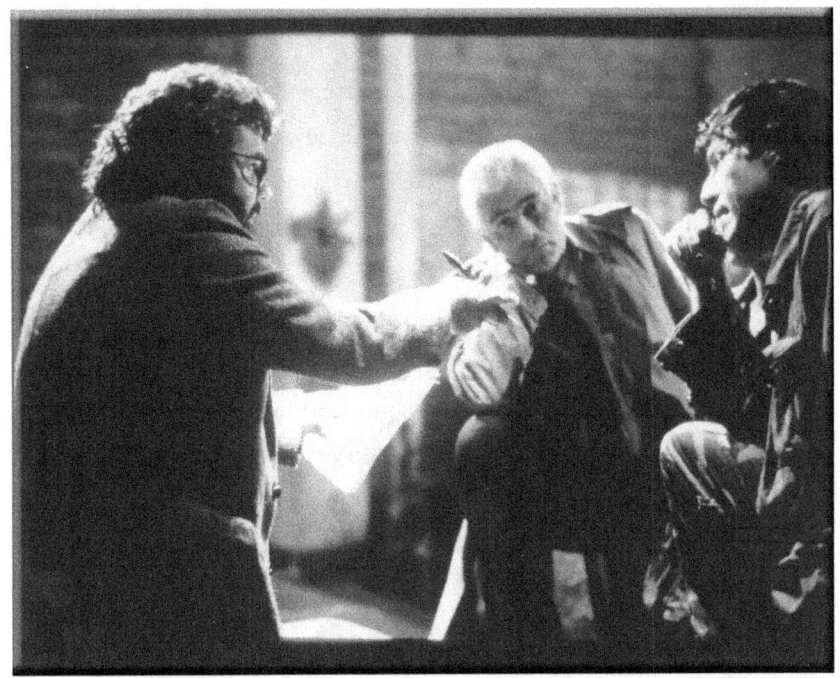

Court directing Tim Thomerson and Stephen Macht on the set of *Trancers III*. Photo courtesy of C. Courtney Joyner

and told them, "I really want to do this with Courtney, I really do," and that's what kicked the goal: the total support of the star. *Trancers* was an important franchise to Full Moon, and Charlie, Albert and Tim trusted me with it, since Charlie had been the only other director. That's a real endorsement, and I'm still grateful. When we were shooting, Tim wanted to make sure I was respected as a director on set and he really went a million miles out of his way to make it a lovely, protected environment. And Albert was always there, always guiding, always helpful, but he also stepped back if he thought I was doing okay. That was his vote of confidence. Greg Nicotero I've known since he was seven, so I asked KNB to do all the special effects makeup. That was a huge favor, as they were pretty big boys by then, working on huge projects, and they did it out of kindness, no other reason.

Jose: What inspired the script for *Trancers III*?

Court: I just watched the first one a bunch of times. Also, I knew Tim Thomerson's sensibility really well, because we were always sitting around talking about *The Big Heat* (1953) and guys like John Payne and Steve Cochran, and these types of hard-boiled flicks, so I wanted to go in that direction with Jack Deth. I wanted it to feel film noir driven.

Jose: I have a weird connection to that series. I credit *Trancers II* as the film that officially pushed me into wanting to make movies, and while it doesn't hold up, it has a special place in my heart. When *Trancers III* comes out, I'm all excited, but I get disappointed, only because the Helen Hunt and Megan Ward characters get sidelined. Was this a logistics issue, in terms of production realities?

Court: Well look, *Trancers II* made me want to blow my head off. I truly didn't understand what was going on. I don't want to sound too harsh, maybe I'll re-examine it. But the thing was that by changing the time period, it also changed the position of the characters. Megan was off, I think, shooting *Encino Man* (1992). Helen had *Mad About You*, and she was already so established as a star, that it was a question whether she would be in it at all. The thing with *Trancers III* was that it was going to be a bookend and really wrap up all this Jack Deth material up to this point. Also with the Helen Hunt storyline, it made sense that they were divorced. It felt organic and appropriate due to Jack's antics. And whom he sees in the future is Alice, as a different person, as a grown woman, who has completely changed. I thought that was a good transition for her from the young girl in *Trancers II*. To me, they were the natural directions the characters would go.

Jose: Speaking of characters, tell me where Shark comes from, because the series up to this point never had any type of alien-like creatures.

Court: I wanted to give Thomerson a different kind of sidekick and I said, "You know, he's never been teamed up with a character that is completely straight-faced and it drives him crazy." I know how good Tim is at improv, he's a major stand-up comedian, and his reactions are priceless, so putting him with another goofball, he wouldn't have anything to play off of, but if it's this slab, this giant straight-man, then that could be funny!

Jose: When I worked for Asylum they always wanted their movies to be bone-dry serious. What was Full Moon's stance on humor?

Court: I think Charlie was always angling for that. That's why he would hire people like Tim, and Sonny Carl Davis, and folks to give the movies that extra bit of personality, which I think works very well. I believe he liked the contrast with the horror and sci-fi. I mean, can you imagine *Re-Animator* (1985) without the humor? But Charlie always wanted that, at least the casting choices seemed to reflect a humorous approach.

Jose: You get another chance to direct with *Lurking Fear* (1994), which is another memorable Full Moon picture, so how did that one develop?

Court: Charlie was very pleased with *Trancers III*. So, I was a little bit of a hot tamale within the company, as limited as that honor is! Stuart Gordon was now at Disney, and Full Moon had *Lurking Fear*, so the idea of me taking over a Stuart Gordon project was scary, challenging, and also super appealing. As a genre fan, this was big stuff for me; not the budget, just to add my own spin to a Lovecraft tale. Sadly, I don't think it worked out too well, for a lot of reasons. The H.P. Lovecraft story is very internalized, so I kept running into problems adapting it. I couldn't find a way to appropriately expand it so I went way in the other direction and went with a crime-thriller structure, which I was comfortable with, and the combining of genres was something I had done before so that's what I went for. But it was a rough go, and I think I started almost wrong-footed. The thing is, even though this movie trips over itself as this kind of tangled-up mess, I think Jeffery Combs is flat-out terrific in it. But the biggest thing is that I took the easy way out with the script, which was a mistake. And when we were making it in Rumania, I just wasn't experienced enough as a director to bring a good vision to the project, and the ball just kind of rolled out of my hands. I take complete and total responsibility for the movie. From time to time, I do get some really nice comments on that movie from folks, but it's always surprising to me; they're very kind, and feel I caught a little something of Lovecraft in my weird mix. I beat myself up about that one, but not about the performances, which I think are very strong, even when the writing failed the actors, they came through. And there never was a nicer man than Paul Mantee.

Jose: Let's talk about your other brush with the *Trancers* series. You wrote *Trancers 6* (2002), but I'm curious why you used a pseudonym.

Court: Well, the only reason was that I used a pseudonym on all the films that were non-SAG. *Trancers 6* was kind of a derivation of a TV pilot script that we were trying to get going, and it was going to be with Tim, but that didn't happen. I left the project and was doing things with Mark Lester again, but I was thrilled that they got Jay Woelfel to do it. He's a good friend, and really knows his stuff. It was made under very tough circumstances, because Charlie was spending very little money at that time. It was kind of a crisis situation, and I think that Jay did a good job with what he had to work with. I respect Jay for getting anything done, because he really was fighting an uphill battle, and that's very difficult, very tough, for a filmmaker, but Jay surely did it. I was pretty much gone from the company by that point, but I did a few little favors for Charlie here and there when he asked. The Paramount days had passed, but I owe the Band family a lot, as far as opportunities, and will always feel that way.

Storyboard from *The Lurking Fear*. Photo courtesy of C. Courtney Joyner

Jose: What about your script for *Puppet Master vs. Demonic Toys* (2004)?

Court: Well, the thing is that wasn't really Full Moon. Charlie had made a deal with the Sci-Fi channel, so that movie was all them. The idea was that this was going to be a pilot for a *Puppet Master* television series. We wrote it kind of lighter in tone, like *Gremlins* (1984), and Andre Toulon was basically written for someone like Martin Mull or Fred Willard, and we ended up with Corey

Feldman. The problem with Corey Feldman wasn't the casting, it was that I was not allowed to go back and rewrite the thing so it would be appropriate. Okay, forget it, it's not an old man; it's Andre Toulon's idiot nephew. Let's do it that way and make it age-appropriate, instead of this bizarre thing they attempted. I had a lovely talk with Corey a couple of years ago. I told him who I was, and he gave me a hug and he goes, "I'm sorry, dude! I'm sorry." But again, I had no problem with him, if I had been able to alter the script properly.

Jose: And consistently, it's the B-movies with the strange choices that always seem to get made. Would you say it's easier to get into the film business through the B-movie side as opposed to hitting up the big boys?

Court: No, absolutely not. The reason I say that is because with the B-movie guys it's like a closed shop. How many people have come up to you asking to set something up at Asylum?

Jose: Many, and it never pans out for them.

Court: Forget it. They're not going to do it. They're not going to read it. Now, once you get through the wall, there you go. But trying to get through to Corman or Asylum, it's very, very difficult. Someone has to open the door, and how that happens, nobody knows. It's the "stock company" mentality, because they don't have the money, or frankly the inclination, to hire new people for each production, so they return to the writers, directors that they know, they have a history with. It's just easier, business-wise. I think once they have the machine in place, that's all they want to do, make the movies one after another, as Full Moon did, as a lot of companies did, with people they knew. It was the same thing with the scripts. These were assignments, to fill a need. So, no, I think in many ways the B-movie guys are more closed off than the big studios are. Certainly, that's the way it used to be, and I think it still holds true. But, there's also much more need for budget product now, because the streaming channels, etc., have to be fed, so that means more opportunity. The trick is to get the chance, and that's always the toughest thing, at any budget level; the eternal show biz question: "How do I break in?" As frustrating as the situation is, no matter what, it always boils down to writing being the key, to get noticed, through a reader, or an agency, or script contests, or whatever. You can make a YouTube short, and put it up, but if it's not well written, with a good joke, or message, it won't have impact. Even at five minutes, you have to have your script.

Jose: What has your experience been on the big studio side?

Court: Well, it's been a mixed bag, actually mostly good, but frustrating. I've done quite a few things at Warner Bros. I worked with I was over there to be involved with the Hammer things when Richard Donner owned the library, and wrote a thriller for Paul Maslansky's company that made the rounds, got very nice coverage, but wasn't made. I sold a spec script to John Watson and Pen Densham called *Black Gloves*, another thriller, when they had their deal at MGM, and we got to the final rounds, but the company changed hands, and all the projects from the previous regime were shelved. That's kind of "Hollywood typical," unfortunately. I really liked those guys, and that project, and they really tried to get it made, but management shifts and all that stuff, very tough to fight. At Fox, I was brought into a werewolf movie called *Silver Strike*, and that didn't go beyond development, but I really like the producers, and they recommended me to a number of other studios, and I was hired at Universal and Sony; so made some money, which was nice, but wasn't making the movies. Sheldon Lettich and I are old friends, and we've co-written a few scripts together, that have been optioned by studios, but not yet made. At the mid-range studios, when they existed, I had a streak of working for Cannon, New Line, Atlantic, TWE, and the whole gang. Some of the flicks got made, and I also did lots of re-writes, and ghostwriting, so it all evens out. But the majors are very tough to crack, and unless you have a hit or something, it's even more difficult to stay in business. There were writers who became millionaires, having only written scripts on development deals for huge movies that never see camera, but that was also during a time, years ago, when studios were spending lots of development cash, which they don't anymore. And writers, who were repped by the biggest agencies, get packaged into huge deals, and on the studio "A Writer's" lists—which I certainly never was of course—have a fantastic advantage, because they're already in the studio game. But with all that, you can still break through, but you have to accept certain realities about the business, and the business-side is one of those realities. Lots of factors are involved at the studio level, so it's complicated. And, to have anything go the distance, or stay at that table for project after project, especially when they don't get made, that's a rare thing. But it does happen. I've worked with some great people, who've made huge movies, but they're developing a hundred projects for a studio that plans on making eight films in a year, so that's tough odds to beat, on top of everything else. Every time you have a crack at the studio thing, you know you can make some money, but when it's over, and there's no movie or whatever, you can be back to square one.

Jose: Do you have a favorite pitch meeting from those days?

Court: I've sold a few things on pitches, but those stories aren't too interesting, because it was just a case of me talking, and them buying. But I have a disaster that I think makes a point about the process, unfortunately! I went to Warners to pitch on *House of Wax* (2005) for Dark Castle. I met with the guys, because they'd read a screenplay of mine that they liked a lot. They said, "What do you think about *House of Wax?*" Knowing Joel Silver's the executive producer I said, "You don't want to do *House of Wax*. You want to do *Mystery of the Wax Museum* (1933), because that's the gangster version of it." They hadn't seen it, so Joel Silver watches *Mystery of the Wax Museum* and he goes nuts, and loves my suggestion. So, suddenly, I have to come in and pitch my "gangster version" of *House of Wax* to Silver, all the execs at Dark Castle, and everybody at Village Roadshow, who were going to co-produce. But I couldn't find my "zinger," those ten words that say everything about the concept and gets everybody excited. I couldn't find my own story, and I was going nuts. Talking to friends, struggling like hell, and the clock's ticking. I kind of had something, so I go in there, and I was so nervous that I crashed and burned about forty seconds into the pitch and I had about eight minutes to go. It just got worse, and worse, and worse, and I kept thinking, "Please, let me get the fuck out of here. I'm blowing it! I know I'm blowing it!" I didn't get the job, and it was so awful that I lost complete and total confidence for a while. That is something that people don't take into consideration. You get these opportunities, and when it goes, it goes great, but when you fail, the failure is crushing. It has so many reverberations and it washes into your other work. You really have to have a tough hide to get through that stuff, and I certainly have one, but that screw-up hit me hard, because I would have loved to have done my version of a classic. If I had gotten the *House of Wax* job, it would have certainly changed my year, and put me in with Dark Castle, which I really wanted, but boy, I just couldn't get my mind around an appropriate pitch that would have worked for those guys. It happens. The writers that got the gig came up with "the house is actually made of wax" killer story, and Paris Hilton starred, so, there are good and bad failures, I guess, but their concept was very clever. As an ironic footnote, a few years later I found out I was on the list of writers for a sequel to *Jonah Hex* (2010), if they were going to make one. The film bombed, of course, but it was for the same people, so that made me feel better about my *House of Wax* fiasco.

Jose: You've recently found solace in Western novels. Was that something you've always wanted to tackle?

Court: What ultimately happened was that the bottom dropped out of the B-movie market, and the A stuff wasn't really coming my way anymore. I was reaching that point too where I was not going to be the guy that Platinum

Dunes was going to call for the remake of *Texas Chainsaw* (1974). I wasn't on that list. I was too old, I was too out of sync with everything, and all that perceived bullshit. The Western is something I've always loved and wanted to pursue. It wasn't that the opportunity presented itself; it was that there were no other opportunities. I said, "The hell with it, I'll just do it."

Jose: Was there a big difference for you, becoming a novelist as opposed to a lowly screenwriter?

Court: As far as image goes, and writing identity, when I started writing the novels it was amazing how much it changed. I've been at Paramount for a year, working on a TV concept, with projects in the U.K., and something new for Hallmark. They know about my background, with Charlie Band and all that stuff, but what they cared about were the books. It's almost like cocktail party patter now, "Oh, how amusing you did a *Puppet Master* movie." One of my execs at Paramount loves that I did a *Trancers*, because that's what she and her sister rented at the video store! Makes me feel a little ancient, but what they care about is that I'm a published author, with screenwriting experience. The books have completely changed the level of the people that wanted to see me again. I'm the same guy, in the same town, and I still love the same crazy, monster stuff, and comics, and everything, but because of the books, it's like I'm a different person. The books actually brought me back to the studios, which is pretty amazing. It's the dumbest preconception in the world, but it still exists.

Jose: To them you become a real writer.

Court: That's it! Exactly correct.

C. Courtney Joyner, the novelist, displays his literary wares.
Photo courtesy of C. Courtney Joyner

Jose: I fear most people reading all this will become discouraged, but they shouldn't. These are things that every writer faces in one way, shape, or form. It should serve more as a heads up to what the screenwriter life is like.

Court: It's not a matter of discouraging anybody from doing his, but it is a matter of making sure that anybody who wants to do this is ready for the long haul, and that they really, really, really love it. There are so many disappointments, but it's just business, it's just part of the commitment to any sort of life in the arts. There aren't any sorts of guarantees. Our function in the world, when you get right down to it, is the most disposable you can think of. We're not doing water reclamation; we're trying to think up a new adventure for Michael Myers. It's all about devotion. The devotion to movies, the devotion to this process, has to really be complete, because sometimes that's all you have that gets you over the rough spots, like taking jobs you hate, or living on zero cash. We've all done it. And for those who think there aren't going to be any rough spots, they're nuts.

Jose: Any tips to help smooth out the roughness?

Court: One of the biggest things is that if you're lucky enough to get a meeting, then really do your research. I'm always stunned when I hear from development executives, because I've been on the other side of the desk, that people come in and they sit down and they talk about their own stuff with an absolute zero awareness of who they're speaking to. I worked for a producer whose dad produced the Gordon Douglas remake of *Stagecoach* (1966), and I thought that was pretty damn cool, and we talked about that, and he gave me the gig. Now, he hired me because he liked my writing, but he enjoyed that I was such a movie nut, was excited about it, which I can't help anyway! It's not like you need to know someone's biography, but you have to be aware, at least from a business standpoint, who you're speaking to and why you're speaking to them. That's a big factor. It's a reality of the heel-to-toe life of a writer.

Jose: Do you think there's a formula for success?

Court: It's what we were saying, if there is one truism in Hollywood it's that there is *no* formula. How do you get your script noticed? How do you get to the top of the pile? How do you get an agent? How does any of this stuff happen? You know what, nobody knows. People don't even know it after they've done it. Everyone has an entirely different experience, and if someone is not prepared for that, then this really isn't something they should attempt. But it does happen. Movies get made every day. TV shows get green lit every day. It's just about finding your own personal way, because the way you do it is going to be different from the way the next guy does it.

Jose: What compels you to keep going?

Court: I guess it's because I love it so much. And after the ups and downs of the movie side, I was glad I took a break from it to pursue fiction, and now I've come back to it from the other side, and it feels better, it feels more settled. I don't think there's anything you can throw at me that hasn't been thrown at me before. Good or bad, writing is just built into me, it's just who I am, and no matter what level, or form, or what have you, I can't imagine doing anything else.

The film buff turned filmmaker, Rolfe Kanefsky.
Photo courtesy of Rolfe Kanefsky

Rolfe Kanefsky

There's Nothing Out There (1991)
The Hazing (2004)
Nightmare Man (2006)

Jose: How did you get bit by the movie bug?

Rolfe: My father introduced me to Abbott and Costello movies when I was four years old. Fell in love with films through them, and watched them religiously almost every Sunday morning. Even before I knew how to write, I would tell stories to my babysitters, and started with Abbott and Costello, doing my own tales with them. I moved on to creating my own characters, Nick and Neel, who were based on Abbott and Costello and the Hardy Boys, and wrote stories with them. Then, I started going to conventions where they sold screenplays, so I started buying and reading those, and pretty much learned the format by reading other screenplays. I realized most of the stories I was writing were very script-oriented in the first place; I just didn't have the proper format, so then I started writing in screenplay form. I took a screenplay course when I was fifteen years old in New York. A friend and I were the youngest ones in the class, most were in their twenties or older, and we were the only ones who did the assignments, because a lot of people talk about wanting to be a writer, but don't actually write. So, that's how it started for me, watching movies and then wanting to write scripts.

Jose: Is there one film from your formative years that you look back on as your greatest inspiration, or would consider a template for great movie writing?

Rolfe: *Used Cars* (1980). I just saw this again recently on the big screen, and every time I see it, I'm reminded how much I love the screenplay. That is a wonderfully structured screenplay that Robert Zemeckis and Bob Gale wrote. I was very impressed with the dialog and writing in *The Color of Money* (1986). I've also always loved *The Stunt Man* (1980), which is a wonderful, very layered script that has a little bit of everything in there, but it just really works. I'm a big fan of *Psycho II* (1983), I thought Tom Holland did such an amazing job on that script, because everyone felt there couldn't be a sequel to *Psycho* (1960). It is such a wonderfully-tailored script, and I've talked with him about it and he's said he'd never worked so hard on a screenplay as he did on that one, because he wanted to make sure that everything fit within the context of the first one, so you could watch *Psycho* one and two back to back, and they're companion pieces to each other.

Jose: Let's talk about your own scripts, specifically your first feature *There's Nothing Out There*. How do you transition from film fan to filmmaker?

Rolfe: *There's Nothing Out There* started as an exercise for myself. I was in high school at the time and I had seen an episode of Siskel and Ebert, where they were talking about how horrible slasher movies are. I've always been attracted to these types of films, so I wondered how long it would take to write a teenage exploitation film. I had no real structure at all, I just wanted to see how long it would take me to write one of these things. As I was writing, I realized I couldn't do it seriously, because I had seen too many of these things. When I turned fourteen I started watching every horror film on video, because I had decided I wanted to be a director, and I realized that most first-time directors, like Oliver Stone, Spielberg, or Coppola, had started with horror films. If I was going to do a horror film as my first film, I wanted to learn the genre, and learn the rules. So, as I wrote this thing I asked myself, "Why hasn't anyone in a horror film watched a horror film?" That's something that jumped out at me. So, I created a character that was basically myself, who had seen every horror film on video and knew all the warnings and rules on how to survive a horror film. This was 1987 when I wrote this, by the way. My character, Mike would be the audience and we could do the clichés, and make fun of them at the same time. My goal underneath the goal of writing a generic horror movie was to send up all the lazy conventions of low-budget horror movies. If I do the cat scare, I'm going to make fun of the cat scare. It was very freeing. I wrote the script in five days, I've always been a fast writer, and it came together pretty well.

Jose: You beat *Scream* (1996) to the punch in the self-referential horror genre.

Rolfe: Yes! Kevin Williamson and I obviously share similar sensibilities. But at that point, nobody had done it; it was six years before *Scream*. I thought the movie turned out pretty well. I was able to direct it, and we produced it independently. My parents and few private investors put in the money. We decided to sell it as a horror film, and the comedy would spread through word of mouth, because I had done my research with *American Werewolf in London* (1981), *Fright Night* (1985) and others that were sold straight, whereas if you sold it like a goofy comedy, the horror fans wouldn't go see it.

Jose: There's a great gag in the film involving the boom microphone and an Indiana Jones riff, which is probably the only time it gets goofy, but it works.

Rolfe: It was originally supposed to be a chandelier that the guy swings on to escape the creature, but the house we were shooting at didn't have a chandelier. I went to see a movie around that time, and it was projected wrong, so you could see the top of the screen and the microphone was there. It was hysterical. So, I said, "You know what would be really fun, if the boom dips into the shot and the audience thinks it's a mistake, but the character sees it and swings out to safety on it." The audience went crazy for that. *Variety's* review said, "Someone's finally figured out what to do with the boom mic." A studio would never let us do that, unless it was a Mel Brooks movie. The most important lesson I learned is that when people think you're crazy, or people are saying, "You can't do this" about a specific scene, that's the scene that people are going to remember. That's the scene you hold on to with a passion.

Jose: Right! 100% agree. What was the overall reaction to the film?

Rolfe: The audience reaction was amazing. Every place we showed it, they were loving the film. The cat scare got ovations. It was awesome because that was my goal and they got the movie. What I was surprised about was that critics also liked the film because of the humor. There's an old rule that if you have a horror film that isn't really scary, the critics will like it because they don't really like horror films, so if you get great reviews, it's probably not a very good horror film. But we got good reviews in *The New York Times*, the *Hollywood Reporter,* and *Variety*, because they liked the humor and it wasn't a mean-spirited movie. It still delivered some of the gore and nastiness, but it was tongue-in-cheek. The only people who didn't get the film were studios and agents. It's too funny to be scary, and it's too scary to be funny, is what they told me.

Jose: Let's talk about your initial brushes with the Hollywood machine. Does *There's Nothing Out There* open any doors for you?

Rolfe: We premiered at the IFP (the Independent Feature Project) in New York. There were only two horror films there at the market, and one was our film. They accepted us because, at that time, they accepted most movies, but they didn't like horror films, so they threw us in at the end. Anyway, it was a two-week market, and I went there to pitch like crazy. I was this twenty-one year old kid telling everyone to come see my movie. There were parties every night and I was working them. A lot of people came just to see what this kid was doing, and the theater was packed, people were standing up in the back of the theater. Articles started to come out saying we were the hit of the festival. We were getting calls from studios asking to see the movie. The head of acquisitions at Universal called and told me, "We're looking for a director of *Child's Play 3* (1991), so we need to see this film right now." It was amazing. I came out for an L.A. screening, and that's when we started to hear the "It's too scary to be funny, it's too funny to be scary" thing, but I got signed with an agent; my first real agent was with William Morris. He had seen the film at the Director's Guild, when we had a screening. He loved it and signed me, but I learned later that unless you got a three-picture deal with someone, when you sign with one of the majors, they don't really push you. It's better to sign with a boutique agency that might get you work, although most of the work I've gotten through the years has been through self-promoting or just doing it by myself, because you can't sit back and wait for your agents and managers to get you work. That's an important rule.

Jose: So, it didn't necessarily kick-start your career having a rep.

Rolfe: I had a few meetings, but nothing really happened. Actually, when the film finally opened up in L.A. and got rave reviews, my agent didn't even return my phone calls at that point, which was weird because I was getting calls from studios and he wouldn't even take the calls. I was brought on to a family film called *My Family Treasure* (1993), which was a film that was unfinished and I helped put it together, and with two films done I decided to move to California. I soon found out that my two finished films, because they weren't huge hits like *Clerks* (1994) or something, didn't count. So, I had to start again. Thanks to a cousin of mine I was able to screen the film for Robert Zemeckis, which I was hoping would lead to directing a *Tales from The Crypt* episode, which he was producing at the time, but that didn't happen. He liked the movie, but he didn't love the movie. He said to me, "Look, you obviously know how to make a movie, so write a script that everybody wants and then attach yourself as director, and that's how you'll get in the door." So, I kept writing scripts, and it took about three years until I finally got my foot in the door, which happened to be with a French producer named Alain Siritzky at the American Film Market.

Jose: Would you recommend attending AFM as a screenwriter?

Rolfe: It's been very good and important to me. I go every year, and I have been going for the past twenty years. It's very hard to get meetings with people, but at AFM they're all there. If you can work your way around and get up to the rooms, you can meet people, get cards, and I've been able to get work from AFM more often than not. I didn't have a pass the year I met Alain Siritzky, who was famous for the *Emmanuelle* series. He was about to do a series based on these erotic comic books *Click* and *Butterscotch*, and I was familiar with those, so when I went in the room with Alain he was impressed that I knew the comic books. I gave him a copy of *There's Nothing Out There* and a script I had written, and he said, "Let's meet the last day of the AFM." We had lunch then and he said, "I'd like you to write and direct three or four of these movies that I'm starting this summer." He was doing these with Roger Corman, and there was already a writing team on board that were all Roger Corman people, but he wanted me on, and they were very suspicious of me because I wasn't part of the Corman world. I realized that I should prove myself, because they didn't know whom I was, so I wrote a half hour spec script of one of the *Click* movies, which is basically about a remote control that can turn women on. They read it, were very impressed with the writing, and I earned their respect with the script. I wound up turning that little script into the first episode of the series. It was a Roger Corman type of crash course. We were shooting fourteen features, back to back, for fourteen weeks in the summer of 1996. I wrote five of the fourteen, and directed four. They were movies shot on 16mm. That was a great training ground, but it didn't mean anything for getting attention in Hollywood.

Jose: During this time, while working in the erotic films market, were you ever hankering to make another horror picture?

Rolfe: I spent seven years trying to get *The Hazing* off the ground. When I first came out to California, one of the first people I met was Joe Wolf, who produced *Halloween* (1978), *A Nightmare on Elm Street* (1984), and *Hell Night* (1981). Well, they had done sequels to the first two, but they hadn't done a sequel to *Hell Night*, so I said to him, "What about *Hell Night 2: The Hazing.*" People liked the script, but nothing happened. My idea was *Breakfast Club* (1985) meets a horror film. *There's Nothing Out There* was making fun of the clichés, but with this one I wanted to make fun of the characters and whom you think would live or die by playing with the stereotypes. No one had ever had the blond bimbo turn into the Sigourney Weaver-type and that's why I really wanted to make it, which to me was worth doing the movie.

Jose: Would you consider *The Hazing* a companion piece to *There's Nothing Out There*, in terms of them existing in the same meta-world?

Rolfe: Originally, Mike Frey appeared in *The Hazing*, as a cameo. When the kids first show up at the house, he was supposed to be there warning them. He's the old guy warning them very quickly as he goes through the laundry list of things they shouldn't do this evening. It was very funny, but the producer said no because they didn't think anyone would get the connection. I said, "People will still get it if they haven't see the other movie, it's still fun," but he still said no. At the end Mike was supposed to show up again and destroy the staff, saying "No sequel." That never got shot, either. Some of my favorite gags got cut, however *The Hazing* finally got made and I'm very happy with the final result, but there were compromises along the way.

Rolfe in front of the Fitzgerald house, the main location for *The Hazing*. Photo courtesy of Rolfe Kanefsky

Jose: Let's talk compromises in terms of this film.

Rolfe: Well, it went through many, many rewrites, and I was able to hold on to it, but there were producers. First it was Siritzky, who couldn't put it together. Then we talked with the producers of *Dog Soldiers* (2002), which I thought was amazing. We were going to do it with them, but it led to one of the worst days of my life. We sat down with them and the story development guy, who worked for those producers. He had put together a questionnaire with questions like "Who is the protagonist?" and "What is this movie?" We all had to fill this out separately what our thoughts on this script were and how we see it. I'd never been in a situation like this for a finished script. Everyone had different answers, so I knew we were in trouble. They asked, "Why does it have to take place on Halloween?" I replied, "Because it's the fall and it's good timing for pledging fraternities." They said, "Why can't it be New Year's Eve?" I shot back, "Well, no one is in school at that time of year and it wouldn't make sense." They also didn't want to do the tongue scene, which was controversial. They said, "Instead of the tongue scene, what if there's a full-sized clown doll that they have to steal, and while the couple are having sex, the clown doll comes to life and starts to butt fuck the guy? That'd be scary, wouldn't it?" I said, "Yeah, could be, but where is this coming from? What movie are we making?" Writers will have this happen. Story development will suddenly have a different movie in their head, or have a script they wrote years ago that they want to try to incorporate into yours. I was in hell. So, we didn't end up working with the *Dog Soldiers* producers, but Tom Seidman, a TV producer, wound up raising the money from his own father and a few investor friends that he had. So, luckily the script stayed closer to what I had wanted it to be.

Jose: Any homosexual clown notes with Tom Seidman?

Rolfe: There were arguments with Tom along the way, as happens with the producer. I was constantly fighting this reality thing. I kept saying, "Look, it's a horror movie and there are certain things you do that are effective for the audience that you can get away with." He wanted to take out the line, when they're talking about the book, "This is Evil Dead territory." He said, "Well, we shouldn't say that." I jumped in and said, "No, we need to say that, because everyone's thinking that. That's what we're ripping off, or homaging, or whatever you want to call it. We need to be in on the joke." There's a very thin line, but people need to know that we know what we're doing. I had to fight like crazy. I've always said that the most brilliant thing about selling *Die Hard 2* (1990) was that in the teaser trailer Bruce Willis says, "How can the same thing happen to the same guy twice?" As the audience, we can now accept this movie because we know that you know that we know this is ridiculous that it is happening again.

Jose: How was production?

Rolfe: Casting took a long time, and shooting the film was not easy, because Seidman hadn't produced before and he felt we didn't have enough money to do it properly. He said, "Rolfe, you're never going to be able to make this movie. I'm telling you that you're never going to get your vision on this film, because it's way too ambitious." I said, "Well, let's try." I wasn't afraid because I had done the low-budget Roger Corman stuff, and we had almost a million dollars and an eighteen-day shoot. I've worked with much less, so I knew I could pull off this thing. He was always walking around the set like a zombie, worried about the money, and it was his father's and friends' money so I can see why, but he wasn't enjoying himself. Mostly I got what I wanted, and the movie sold and we received great reviews. I kept sending Seidman the reviews and he responded, "Wow, I guess the other horror films out there must be pretty terrible films." He just couldn't see it; it wasn't his kind of thing. He went on to direct his own family film.

Jose: Speaking of not his thing, I'm backtracking a bit, but since I've spoken to a lot of Full Moon alumni, I'm curious how you found yourself there with *The Killer Eye* (1999)?

Rolfe: Okay, well that's not one of my favorite credits, but I had a lot of friends who worked at Full Moon: C. Courtney Joyner, Jay Woelfel, and Dave Parker. Pretty much everyone I knew had worked at Full Moon at one point. I had asked if it was worth pursuing writing over there and most of the time I heard "No." In the heyday yes, but it had changed a lot and it wasn't that great in the late 1990's. David DeCoteau, who I'd been friends with for a while, had been hired to direct a movie called *The Killer Eye*, which had been written by Benjamin Carr, and David did not want to direct the movie. He hated the script and he asked me if I would do a re-write. His hope was to convince Charlie Band to let me direct it. I thought the script was fun. I said, "If I were to do this movie, it should be *Tremors* (1990) meets *Re-Animator* (1985); just this over-the-top crazy thing, and if you really want to go for it then make it a musical like *Little Shop of Horrors* (1986)." They would never do that, but I wrote this really fun script with some great gags in it. I did two or three passes on the script, however David couldn't convince Charlie to let me direct it. So, David brought in Matthew Jason Walsh to make it shootable for him, because he was doing one of his four-day wonders. That's why there's three writers credited, and David said he was really happy with the movie, so I left my name on it, but personally, I wasn't that pleased with the final result, although David did a fantastic job considering the time restraints and budget.

Jose: What are your thoughts on pen names, which a lot of writers use? After you do all the work, do you consider using a pen name as if you're throwing all that away? How do you interpret that aspect of the writing field?

Rolfe: Well, that's an interesting thing. When I worked with Siritzky, I started using pseudonyms. On our first collaboration, I kept my name on as the writer, but I took my name off as director, because I was not happy with what they did in post. The post guys did stuff to spite me and I think it hurt the film. But look, if you're doing stuff that you don't want to do and you're doing it for the money or the experience, it's fine, but you should try to be proud of everything you do. So far, and this is the big thing, 99 percent of everything I've written I've been proud of. I try to do the best job I can. Some of that stuff I never thought in a million years I'd write, but I got hired and I'm a professional so I did it. When I started, I said I'll use my real name because I'm not ashamed of what I'm doing. The problem is when you're dealing with stuff that is so low budget, or in the erotic genre, people tend to pigeonhole you and if you get too many credits like that, then that's who they consider you are. In reviews of my later films, if people wanted to knock me, they would use my late night cable credits, and not stuff like *The Hazing*. If you do too many of these things, it could hurt you. So, I've used pseudonyms sometimes because I haven't been happy with the finished results of a film, and other times it's just because I have too many credits in one genre and I don't want my name attached to stuff like that. Two years ago, I wrote twenty scripts in one year. I write fast, but that's a lot for me. Eighteen out of the twenty were commissioned, and they've all mostly been made. If they see me writing as much stuff as I do, diverse as it is, people tend to think of you as a hack. Based on that, you have to be careful with credits. Stephen King used pseudonyms because at one point in his career, he was writing too much.

Jose: An up-and-coming writer hears that someone has written twenty scripts in a year, and the first thought that comes to mind is, "Wow, this guy must be a millionaire." That is almost never the case in the B-movie world.

Rolfe: There is a big falsity between the working writers versus the Hollywood writers. They do articles when a script sells for $3 million. They don't do articles when a script sells for $1,000. The money is always an issue. You're always trying to pay the bills. Yes, twenty scripts in a year sounds like an amazing year, but with all these movies you don't get back-ends or percentages. In the old days, writers were well-paid, but given little acclaim. They didn't want them on the set and were given zero respectability, but at least they paid them well. Now, they don't pay the writer well, and they still don't get any respect. They want it cheap, fast, and good; they want all three. You try to give them all three, but there are limitations. The usual rule is you can get two out of the three.

Jose: What was a typical paycheck when you started out?

Rolfe: When I first started working for Siritzky in 1996, he was paying $6,000 a script for the late-night erotic stuff, which was not great, but okay money. I was writing most of these things in a week, so it was decent money if I wrote four or five of these things in a year. You'd make a living. Couple years later, he went down to $3,000, and the industry as a whole started to change to where you weren't getting paid what you should be getting paid.

Jose: And if you ask for more money, tell them you have a set rate, they'll just hire someone else and you're out of a potential gig.

Rolfe: Right, they'll just get someone else, because there are plenty of film kids coming out of school who would love to do something for free or whatever to get their foot in the door. The first time I got paid for writing something, I was given $250 for research, but the script was never produced. The most I've gotten paid was on *Blonde and Blonder* (2007), a comedy that I originally wrote for Siritzky. It was supposed to be $10,000, but I got paid half of that because he never had me do the rewrites. I got $5,000, and nothing ever happened with it, so I wound up optioning it to another producer, who got it to Pamela Anderson, who got it set up in Canada, and suddenly they're making the movie without telling me, and I had to fight for the payment money. It was a sliding scale deal based on production budget, and I got paid $40,000 dollars, which should have been $80,000 dollars since the budget did get up to the next payment tier, but for me that was a pretty good payday. The problem was that it was one of the most nightmarish experiences of my life and they destroyed the movie. The original producer found me and said I was supposed to reimburse him $5,000 to buy back the script, which I never did because I was supposed to get $10,000, so in my mind I owed him, but he owed me the same amount so we break even. But that's not how it worked and he got an Executive Producer credit on the film. Everyone came after me, because I had sold a script that I didn't officially own, by accident, and it was a disaster. Everyone was trying to sue me, and I had no money. I mean, here is a multi-millionaire, here's a billionaire company, and you're going after the writer? It was a horrible, miserable experience. But to this day it's still the most money I've made on a screenplay.

Jose: Well, let's talk about *Nightmare Man*. You return to your homegrown horror movie roots and make something that is completely yours.

Rolfe: After fourteen years, my parents finally broke even on *There's Nothing Out There* and we decided to try it again. I wrote a spec script years ago called *In The Web*; it's like *Sunset Boulevard* (1950) meets *Demon Seed* (1977). The movie begins with a mature actress watching one of her old movies, so it's a movie within a movie, and it's a cool little four-minute sequence. My composer, who I've worked with a lot, read the script and he loved that scene. He goes, "I'd love to see that movie!" That little scene was basically the kernel of *Nightmare Man*. I took that idea and I sat down and wrote *Nightmare Man* in about seven days. It worked and people who read it really liked it. It was a doable movie that was really smart and in my opinion it was kind of another love letter to the genre that takes you purposefully through the 1970s, 1980s, and 1990s of horror films, because it changes as it goes. We found a Brazilian producer, who put up some money, and my parents put up some money. Not a lot, it was about a $100,000. Found some good actors, and shot the film in fifteen days.

Jose: It became one of the 8 Films To Die For. What was the selection process like?

Rolfe: We finished the film and I was very happy with it, but we couldn't sell the movie. We had a producer's rep who couldn't sell it. Nobody was buying the movie. So, what happened was I went to the San Diego Comic Con, and I was walking around and saw a booth for After Dark's 8 Films To Die For, which they had just started doing the year before. My friend, Mike Mendez, had had his film, *Gravedancers* (2006), with them that past year, so I went up to them and asked them how they pick films for their festival. They said, "We have a deal with Lionsgate and we go to Toronto and all the other big fests, but are you a filmmaker? Do you have a film?" I gave them a DVD and a press kit of *Nightmare Man*. Everyone thought I was crazy, because they were looking for much bigger films than my little one, but if you don't try you'll

Rolfe with his favorite leading lady, Tiffany Shepis, from *The Hazing* and *Nightmare Man*. Photo courtesy of Rolfe Kanefsky

never get anywhere. A couple of weeks later, I get a call from them telling me they had found the press kit, but had no idea what it was for because they had lost the DVD. I sent it again, then emailed them a few days later to make sure they got the package. They responded, "We got it, we watched it, and we're showing it to the other people in the company." Two hours later, I get a phone call from them telling me they want it. It got a 500-screen theatrical release and was picked up by Lionsgate, who had originally turned it down, and it made a lot of money on video. However, we never saw a dime.

Jose: Despite it being another financial sinkhole, were you happy with the finished product compared to what you wrote?

Rolfe: The script is pretty much the movie. I think it works fairly well. I like it. It's got a good sense of humor to it, and maybe folks who were looking for a terrifying film were a little put off by it because they found something funny. This is the thing with all my films. A sense of humor is usually in all my material. I get e-mails from people about *There's Nothing Out There* saying, "The first two times I saw this movie, I hated it. Then I realized it was a comedy, and now it's one of my favorite films of all time." Sometimes you have to change your perspective to adapt to the movie.

Jose: Do you have a favorite genre you like to write in?

Rolfe: I do. I've always loved thrillers, because they combine a little bit of everything. You have action, thrills, suspense, scares; it can all be in there. Usually when I'm writing spec scripts for myself it's either a thriller, or a horror piece. I do love horror. I'm a huge horror fan, and I watch them all.

Jose: I lean more toward action specs myself, not so much horror, although most of the scripts that I've had produced are horror films. But there's something about the genre that eludes me; certainly the fandom has changed.

Rolfe: There is no other genre, I mean sci-fi, fantasy, and horror, which has the audience and the fan base and the websites as those. The horror community, I feel, has changed a little bit. They used to really want to like your film. There was a real support system in genre. Horror was always considered one step above porn in the Hollywood system. I mean Paramount was never proud of the *Friday the 13th* movies, but they made too much money to say no. It's always been the evil stepchild, the horror genre, but you can do things in horror that you can't do in other genres. You don't have to play by the rules, so you get more freedom as a writer, which is enjoyable, but you don't get the respectability. But over the years, because everyone with a camcorder or a cell phone can make a movie now, everyone thinks they can do a better job. The Internet is now filled with trolls who just seem to want to hate everything out there and knock it all. Some of them say, "This was the worst movie I've ever seen, and I turned it off after the first five minutes." Well, if you turned it off after the first five minutes, you didn't really see the movie, now did you? What are you talking about? Watch the first five minutes of *Psycho*. There's no Norman Bates, nobody gets killed in the shower. It's about a woman who steals from her boss. I mean, if you watch the first twenty minutes of a movie, especially a horror film, what has happened? Most likely almost nothing has happened! You have to build. You have to develop the characters, or there's no connection to the movie. You set up the characters so you can care about them before you kill them off.

Jose: I think that's something that's been lost, and I can blame the development process for this. A movie isn't shitty special effects; it's about the characters. You remember a movie because you remember the characters. You quote the lines, because you remember the characters saying them. That is the most important element which helps the audience buy into whatever it is, but it always seems that those pieces are what get cut first, because it's not as important to tell a good story with real human beings.

Rolfe: Yes. For any writer, I'm sure they will all agree the most brilliant show on television was *The Twilight Zone*. What Rod Serling, who everyone should study, compacted into twenty-five minutes per episode, was amazing. There was more character, more development, and more story in a half hour than in most features. Those stories have arcs and twists and all that. Everyone should study *The Twilight Zone*, it's a crash course in excellence in writing.

Jose: TV is where real character work lies nowadays.

Rolfe: Television has taken over because the writers have been given the freedom now, without being censored. By far the writing is better in television than in most movies today. There's still the independent cinema, but good luck getting any money from it, because they don't give you any advances and they don't give you any backend anymore either.

Jose: It always starts with the love of movies, but money becomes the reality, and therein lies the struggle everyone wanting to make movies, or be involved in movies in any way, shape, or form, finds themselves.

Rolfe: If everyone knew how hard it was to make a movie, no one would ever make a movie. Nobody would, it's crazy! But you do it because you're blindly optimistic and you just make it happen. You just do it. You don't think logically about the thing. That why any film that gets finished should win an award, and if it turns out to be good, it's a miracle.

Jose: How should screenwriters deal with such hard truths?

Rolfe: The thing with the writer is that when you're writing a book or a screenplay it's one person's point of view, of course. This is your vision, it's very freeing, and you don't have to answer to anyone. But when you move to the movie stage, it becomes something else. The writer is king in plays. You can't change a word in a play; it's a writer's medium; but film is a director's medium. If you can recognize three scenes from your original screenplay in a finished movie, you should be very happy. I've had that. I've sometimes had less than three scenes. Being a writer/director, which I've been able to do for most of my career, I was able to keep it more or less my vision. I've written twice as many scripts for other people that have been produced, and you always have to distance yourself if you're not the director, because it's never going to be your vision. So, either you don't even watch it, or you sit back and hope to find the kernel of the idea that you originally came up with. Most of the time, you're disappointed. But sometimes, a few things slip by. With my love of Abbott and Costello, sometimes I slip in these little Abbott and Costello routines like Easter eggs for those in the know and myself.

Jose: I do that, too. Not necessarily with Abbott and Costello, but there are a few phrases that I consider personal mantras that I used in every script, and I always reference a few things that only exist in the universe of my books. What's your favorite Easter egg that made it into a movie?

Rolfe: There's a movie I wrote called *Shattered Lies* (2002), which was a thriller with Martin Kove, James Russo, and Frank Zagarino, who also produced it. The funniest Easter egg in there is a scene where the characters are supposed to be sitting there watching Jeopardy or something on TV, and since it's in the background they needed like two pages of dialog for the game show. So, in the background I did this whole horror movie trivia thing, and one of the questions was, "What film inspired *Scream?*" Then, the contestants were giving the wrong answers, and you couldn't hear any of this, except for this one moment when it gets quiet and you hear one of them say "*There's Nothing Out There.*" At one of the screenings of the film, one of my friends heard that and shouted, "Jesus Christ, Rolfe!" I thought they'd never be able to hear it, but there it was. But yeah, you have to throw yourself a little Easter egg here and there. Tarantino and Kevin Smith have made a career out of it.

Jose: Do you think it's ever going to get better for writers again, or since it's so easy to make a movie nowadays, as we spoke about, that the respect and the money will lessen and lessen?

Rolfe: Well, I think you have to create something, whether it's a web series, or a comic book, because everything is becoming based on other medias. Something based on another medium seems to be what the studios want because they desire that built-in audience. I know a lot of people who have been trying to do that, either developing a comic book, or developing something, that their screenplay could be adapted from. There's a great story about Peter Stone. He was a great writer. He wrote *The Taking of Pelham One Two Three* (1974) and *Charade* (1963). He initially wrote the screenplay to *Charade*, but no studio bought it, they wouldn't touch it. So, he wrote a

Rolfe on set, bringing a script to life. Photo courtesy of Rolfe Kanefsky

novel based on his screenplay, and he sold his novel to the studio, which they then hired him to write the screenplay. They gave him a lot of money. He sat in his apartment for a month, twiddling his fingers, and then gave them his original script. As a writer, there are all these different games you can play, and it does work, it does happen.

Jose: But the rules to the game are always up in the air.

Rolfe: "Nobody knows anything." There is no golden rule. Everything is an exception to the rule. Whenever you're writing to try to predict what the next popular thing is, you're probably going to fail, because by the time it's written and out there, they would have moved on to something else. Look, you have to write what you want to write, what you want to see, and what appeals to you because you have to live with it, and you need to be proud of it. If you're writing stuff for just a paycheck, you're going to be pretty miserable. It's always a process, it's a journey; if you're not enjoying the journey, then you're doing it wrong. You can't always afford to enjoy the journey, but you try.

Jose: Looking back, how do you see your career up to this point?

Rolfe: I've been happy that I haven't been pigeonholed as a writer. Some people know me because of the horror things I've done, other people know me because of the talking-animal family scripts I've written, and other people know me from the late night cable Siritzky stuff, and I got the thrillers, too. It's all different groups, so it's pretty cool. I like that, because once you get successful in one thing, that's all you get asked to write over and over again. There's a famous story of the writer who wrote *A Shot in the Dark* (1964). It's one of the most famous comedies of all time. Everyone kept telling him that he was a comedy writer and all he can write are comedies. So, he say, "Oh yeah, let me try and write something horror". So, he wrote a book that did really well and it got made into a big movie, and then he became the horror writer who could only write horror. The writer was William Peter Blatty and the movie was *The Exorcist* (1973). So, what is he? He's a writer, guys; an excellent writer who can write anything.

Jose: That's a great story. It really exemplifies that writers shouldn't be boxed in and should be free to explore. You've written a ton of stuff, and explored most of the angles, so now I'm curious what your writing process is like on any given script?

Rolfe: I come up with the concept or idea, sometimes I have the ending, but I don't have it all worked out, and I write from beginning to end, I don't jump around. I don't use cue cards, which a lot of people do, and I have recommended people to do that because a lot of them get stuck on page twenty or thirty and the cue cards allow them to jump around, to see the big picture. If I'm writing a spec, I come up with the idea and I write it from beginning to end. Now, many times this has happened, which is an awesome experience; the script starts to write itself. The characters come to life and they take you in directions you didn't expect to go. It's very dangerous and you might run into holes or might not even finish it, but I tend to love that process. When I'm doing an assignment, most of the time they insist on a treatment so you have to write out this two to five page treatment that pretty much maps out the story that you have to stick to. There are a lot of writers that go off on tangents, but producers do not appreciate that. But for myself, I don't outline, I just start and go tunnel vision. Also, I never start a script unless I know I'm going to finish it. So far, I've written a 150 screenplays and I've been paid, in one form or another, for more than half of them. If I'd been paid well, I'd be doing great.

Jose: That's amazing. There are some people who can't say they've sold one script! With that in mind, you must have some advice for a fellow screen trader?

Rolfe: Listen, a writer has to write. If there's anything else you enjoy doing other than being in the film business, do it, because you'll be a lot more satisfied. But if you have to write and you have to create, whether you get paid or not, then that's what you have to do. You always want to have at least three scripts ready to go, so when you go to a meeting and pitch something you have ammo. It's also good to read screenplays and watch movies, both good and bad. The biggest advice really is to finish what you start. You have to be responsible, especially in this business. If people are going to pay you money, they have to be confident that you are going to deliver on the job. When you're writing a script, at some point you're going to hate it. You always do. You hit that one spot where you think it doesn't work at all. But force yourself to barrel through, don't go back and start rewriting the whole thing. Get to the end because once you get there, you'll probably realize it's not as bad as you thought it was and you'll have that feeling of accomplishment. The number one key thing for a writer is just to force yourself to finish it. Just know that your first draft isn't your final draft. The more you write, the more you develop your craft. That's the difference between a hobby and a career.

Sean Keller tossing blue steel at you. Photo courtesy of Sean Keller

Sean Keller

Mammoth (2006)
Giallo (2009)
Rage (2014)

Jose: How did you discover the joys of screenwriting?

Sean: I came to it very late. I didn't write my first script until I was twenty-nine. I was a musician. I started off as a singer/songwriter, and I had a publishing contract when I was nineteen. I was putting songs in movies when I was a teenager. I thought I was going to be a rock star, and then that fizzled and disappeared, and I became an actor. I did Broadway. I played Roger in *Rent* in the first national tour, and stuff like that. I was really into acting and singing, and I came out to L.A. when I was fired from *Rent* to be an actor, and I kept on reading bad scripts. As a real literature lover, and someone who had written songs and had a background in writing, I said to myself, "People are making this? Fuck, I know I could do better than this." So, I wrote a pilot on a manual typewriter; I didn't buy a computer until I was thirty. I didn't have any need for it; I was an actor. I really liked writing it, but it wasn't good, although I really liked writing it. So, over the course of a year I wrote three more scripts. When I turned thirty-one, I was really focusing on it because my acting career was fizzling.

Jose: Was it tricky to switch careers and balance a family life?

Sean: My wife was pregnant with our second kid, but she was off working, and I was staying home babysitting. Putting them in daycare was just too expensive, so I knew I had to stay home, but what can I do if I stay home? I basically stopped auditioning, and I told my wife, "I'm going to be a writer." She's says, "Ha ha, I'm going to divorce you." I said, "No, no, no, I'll make it work. I'll teach myself how to do it." So, I didn't go to film school. I perused lightly *The Screenwriter's Bible* just to get format down, but that was it. I just watched a shit ton of movies and done enough on sets, everything from a driver to boom operator, that I know how movies are made, so I figured I could put them together. Now, of course, that's quite the leap, because me figuring I could put them together doesn't mean I know what the fuck I'm doing.

Jose: So, you plunge into this new career. How long before Hollywood comes calling for material?

Sean: It was the fourth feature I wrote. It got optioned by a director, I got a $1,000 for the script, and I said, "Fuck yeah! I'm a fucking writer!" That's how I got into it. I wrote for a good two years on my own, while tending bar at night at the Beauty Bar in Hollywood, and I met a guy named Jim Agnew, who was DJing there. We would sit after last call and bitch about how Hollywood was doing it wrong and we could do it better. Then he came to me with an idea for a script, and we wrote something called *L.A. Gothic*. It was almost like an *Entourage* horror movie. John Carpenter read it, loved it, and we were attached to him for years. That's how I knew I could really do this, because John Carpenter said it was great.

Jose: I know you're a big horror buff, so it must have been pretty mindblowing working with Carpenter on a project.

Sean: He's the coolest man in the world. We would be led into a room, where he'd be there sitting behind his desk, smoking cigarettes, and there's always a cheese plate out with grapes and coffee, and he'd say "You're writers, eat. You're poor. I know. Eat, eat." He would take care of us and was really cool. But working with him consisted of him reading our script out loud to us, and every so often he'd stop and look up at us and say, "Fellahs . . . . " So, we'd be ready to scratch something out. He was really merciless in pointing out something that had been done before, or a joke that he didn't like, or somehow violated his sense of machismo. We got a real crash course in screenwriting from John Carpenter. We wrote that script for him through many iterations, even tried to make it a TV show, but timing and other things stepped in the way, but he's great, I love him. And after that we did re-writes on *The Ward* (2010) for him. The Rasmussen brothers did a great job on that, but we just came in to do some tinkering to basically make the lead active and beef up the scares. We wrote in stuff to make it feel like John's kind of movie.

Jose: Yet, you remained un-credited on it, so let's talk about *Mammoth*, which is your first official on-screen screenplay credit.

Sean: That one *came out* first, but I had written two other Sci-Fi Channel films before that one: *Kraken* (2006) and *Attack of the Gryphon* (2007), which was actually the first one. *Gryphon* came about because my friend Tim Cox, who had optioned my fourth feature, called me and said, "I'm stumped. I got a deadline. I have to turn in the script on Monday." This was a Thursday and he hadn't written a word. I went over to his place and over the course of three days, we wrote the whole feature. It was just bonkers. I asked him, "Are you going to get fired if you stray from the outline?" He said no, so I said, "Fuck the outline, let's go," and we just started writing. It was super fun, and I got paid a little pittance. But Tim looked out for me on the next one and actually got me hired to work on *Kraken*. *Mammoth* was his idea. He came to me and said, "I want to make this thing, it's going to be Looney Tunes." Sci-Fi Channel didn't do comedy; they didn't want to do anything that wasn't serious. So, he tells me, "I want to make a comedy, but we can't let them know it's a comedy," and so he sold them this idea of an alien-possessed wooly mammoth that comes back to life and sucks out people's souls with his trunk. I said, "Tim, that is the dumbest fucking thing I've ever heard." But he assured me it would work, and it started out being a send up of 1950s sci-fi movies, but it was really a send up of Sci-Fi Channel movies, which was the intention.

Jose: I have to say that I loved *Mammoth,* and it's partly because it was funny and I caught that you guys were trying to make something different.

Sean: It's a super-weirdo film, and it's not really my type of film, but Tim kept asking me to help him write it, and I kept saying no. Then I finally decided to do it and he asked, "Why? Why are you doing it?" I replied, "Because I'm terrified of this. I think I'm no good at this, and if I can pull this off at all, then I'm a writer. So, let's just try." And for better or worse, it's *Mammoth*. I actually know a couple of other people who really like it and that's super weird to me.

Jose: It's hard to have the separation from your work. You'll never be able to view it from an outsider's perspective.

Sean: I don't appreciate any of the stuff I've made yet. My career is the people I work with, not the product I make. There's nothing I like better than walking on a set and because I had an idea there's seventy people going to work today. Everyone's getting a paycheck. These people are going to make their rent this month because I had a dumb idea. That's satisfying on the deepest level, and that's what I love the most. I love writing, and I actually really love pitching, because of my background and it being performance-based, but I'm not goal-oriented, I'm process-oriented. I really love the doing, and staying active.

Jose: Let's talk about pitching, because that can be a hurdle for a lot of writers, myself included, and it such a crucial element in a screenwriting career. Since you love it, I'm guessing you have some pointers to share.

Sean: The thing is you're going to pitch to a CE (creative executive), you're going to go in and give this elaborate great pitch, and then that person is going to walk down the hall and do a perfectly inadequate job of telling his boss about it. Unless you give them the hooky, buzzy shit that they will remember, you're doomed, there's just no chance, and pitching a feature is almost impossible. I've moved into TV now and I've been doing a lot of work there. Jim Agnew and I are both performers, so both of us can walk into a room and command the room just fine. You've got ninety seconds, that's it, and if your pitch goes over eight minutes, you're fucked. I've heard people say that a fifteen to twenty minute pitch is great, but no, no one has that kind of endurance. After three minutes, their eyes are glazing over, unless you've brought in some sort of visual aid for them to look at, which I always do now, because when you walk into a room, there's this contract you enter in with the other person and they've got to look at you, but that gets exhausting, so letting them off the hook with something to look at is a mercy to them. People say it's hokey, and I feel like a schmuck bringing that stuff in, but the effectiveness is undeniable. Anything you can do to make their day more comfortable is going to make your pitch go better. Their mood is going to dictate how well your pitch goes.

Jose: Is a TV pitch similar to a feature pitch in terms of delivering content?

Sean: When we go and pitch TV, it's so character-based, because it's all about who the character is going to be in your living room every week. So, we'll put actors up as these characters. We know we're never going to get them, but we put them up during the pitch so they see the face and the name and know who's who. It's all these simple little tricks that make a huge difference, and they are all tricks. It's got nothing to do with writing, and everything to do with being a good communicator. Also the tone of your voice is going to sell the tone of your show. It's not only knowing what you've written, but knowing what you're selling. A lot of writers have trouble with that, understandably, because we live in our heads and we do a lot of worrying about things that are completely out of our control, but the way Jim and I approach everything now is one step at a time. The pitch has to please those people in the room, and that's it. If you get hired, then the outline has to please them, we're not looking at the audience yet. If we get to write the pilot, then it has to please x-number of producers, and if they like it, it'll go up the chain to the next. It's one step at a time; I'm not going to worry about how it's going to be received, or the casting, until the producers have signed off on it. As long as you chunk it out in little steps it doesn't get overwhelming, it really helps you focus on the task. It's about the work for me; it's not about the art. It's about doing the Goddamn work and doing it well enough that people say, "Ok, I want to see some more." At any time it can change, and I've been fired plenty.

Jose: It's interesting that despite our crucial positions in the film business, writers get shafted a lot of the time. We're above the line, but not.

Sean: No one would be doing anything without us, but you're treated like you're the one who pooped in the car. They want you as far away as possible. I think the people who can't do it are so intimidated by it, and so weirded out by people who can write. The executives can't, and they know they can't, because they come up with ideas and they don't realize how they don't dovetail together. They don't see the big picture properly. They can be awesome at giving you tools and notes to tweak things, but they couldn't sit down and write, because if they could, they would. These execs that you meet with, they're not dumb, they may not be creative like we are, but they're smart people. Being so smart and not knowing how to do something bothers them, so I think they consider writing this mystical process and they want to distance themselves. I see that quite often in the way people behave, and quite often working in this business you kind of wind up being a shrink. You have to manage so many egos, so many personalities, and when I see that I can tell they fear us, so you have to calm them down. This isn't rocket surgery, there are only so many words, and at some point we'll get it right.

Jose: Touching on the executives and their notes, I've heard horror stories about the now newly renamed Syfy Channel and their notes. I've had films on the channel, but they weren't ever directly made for them, so I'm curious how tailoring a script for them specifically works?

Sean: I was contracted out through a sub-company, and so they were the ones with the notes, and they were the worst. In *Kraken,* I wrote this one scene where the lead guy and girl are trapped on the sinking ship and the Kraken's babies have all been born and the thousand baby Krakens are attacking them, which I knew we couldn't afford, and the girl says, "I'm scared", to which the guy goes, "I am, too." I recall this one guy sending me the note, "Heroes are never scared, take that out." I said, "No, heroism is when you're afraid and you act anyway. When you go through with the thing that frightens you." But he said, "No, that's not how this is. Heroes don't show fear." You know, I was shooting for at least a hint of nuance, but fuck that, I guess there's not going to be any. Those kind of notes were the worst. It just makes you not want to try. But I was never the last writer on any of my Syfy Channel movies. I always walked before the last draft, because it would get to a point where the notes were untenable, and I was young and dumb and I would throw my hands up and go, "Fuck it, I'm out. Go find someone else." That's how you learn though, that's where you cut your teeth. Syfy is almost akin to this generation's version of the Corman school, or working for Charlie Band on a certain level. It's where people have to go to do a little work to make their way to the next level.

The High-Concept Massacre

Jose: The trick is not to stay there.

Sean: Oh, yeah. You've got to get out. I don't have bridges left there. I firebombed the fuck out of that shit. I made certain I wouldn't go back, and I was a young fool, I didn't know what I was doing. I've always been a little too arrogant for my own good. Working in TV slaps that out of you pretty hard, but in TV they respect the writer, it's just that the workload is relentless and you have to go fast.

Jose: When you're working on a pilot, do you develop a bible for the series as backup ammunition for pitches?

Sean: We usually just go pitch. We didn't even know how to write a pilot. I asked my manager to send me a whole bunch of samples of pilots so we could figure out how to write one of these things. Jim and I decided to write something crazy. We knew it wouldn't get made. Suddenly, instant budding war. We got an agent right off the bat, sold it to ABC. Just crazy for our first

Readying for a take on *Giallo*. Photo courtesy of Sean Keller

thing right out of the gate, and we never had a bible, we had a pitch, we had a world and a lot of background documents, but we never had to put together a bible yet, because we haven't had a show yet that's gone. I'm sure at some point we will have to, but we're not show runners yet, even though Jim and I are producers. We have a long history of giving our reps scripts and them saying, "We don't know what to do with this." Fuck you then, we'll go make it ourselves and you're not getting a percentage because you didn't do anything. That's how we made *Giallo,* and that's how we made *Rage.*

Jose: Let's talk about *Giallo*, which finds you working with Dario Argento, another big horror movie director, in a genre that he essentially defined. What compelled you to play in the giallo genre?

Sean: With *Giallo* we were just trying so hard to predict what was next. Everything was little Asian girls with wet hair or torture porn, that's what was going down, and we said, "What people really need is Euro sleaze. Why is no one making that?" We didn't set out to write a giallo; we set out to write Euro sleaze. We called it *Yellow* because the villain was jaundiced. Originally we had a different director attached, some Italian TV director, who loved it, but his schedule got too busy. Someone we knew, knew Asia Argento, so he got the script to her and she just passed it on to her dad. They translated it into Italian, and he says, "I love it, I even love the title *Giallo*". I said, "Oh shit, now they're going to call this *Giallo* and everyone is going to expect this to be straight up giallo." Dario didn't want to do anything that we had written in that were tonal references to his work, he said, "I don't want to copy myself." And we got it, he's Dario Argento, he could do whatever he wants with this movie. I'm not going to tell him how to make a movie.

The High-Concept Massacre

Jose: When he translated it into Italian, was there a considerable change just contextually from your American version to his?

Sean: Oh yeah, there's all kinds of dialog stuff that got missed; tonal things slipped, certain jokes we had written in didn't play. That's what happens, but that's also what makes it a piece of Euro sleaze. That's what makes it more like a giallo than any other thing, and that's kind of one of the things I love about it, because it has its clunks. If they had dubbed the whole thing, it would have been even better! But we were on the phone a lot and he would give us notes. The actors would give us notes. Our rule has always been if we get the same note from three people it must be a valid note. I was a little bit out of the loop on set because there were a lot of on-set rewrites going down. I wasn't there and it was just happening too fast for me to have any part of. When you're dealing with multiple nationalities and multiple languages, shit gets lost sometimes.

Jose: Are you happy with what he eventually made of your script?

Sean: We had a few casting issues and a few shooting issues, and some serious money issues. A lot of things went south on it. It was originally Vincent Gallo as the killer, Ray Liotta as the cop, and Asia as the lead chick. Asia got pregnant, Vincent Gallo didn't want to work with Asia, and Ray's agent convinced him that he should ask for more money. So, we had to go out to a whole new cast. I mean, they were all in, and then they were all out, at once, a month before shooting. But we got Adrien Brody, an Academy Award winner, and Emmanuelle Seigner.

Jose: I'm curious if it was your decision or Brody's to have him play both the cop and the villain under the heavy, jaundiced makeup.

Sean: We had cast Elsa Pataky first. They were dating and he had read the script. He got what we were doing and he said, "I'd like to work with Argento. I'll do it *if* I can play both." Come on, we get an Academy Award winner? We said yeah, and he's great. He did a good job.

Jose: You've worked with Carpenter and Argento, is there anyone else in the horror pantheon you'd love to work with?

Sean: Of course! All the rest of them. But I'm really more interested in working with people younger than me. I'm forty-six, and I'm hitting that point where I want youth and vitality around me to keep me sharp. I need to hear a different perspective. I grew up in a different generation from the people going to horror movies right now and I need to stay in touch. So, in order to stay current and fresh, I need to surround myself with younger people. I can give them little bits of advice, and they can give me vitality. It's a good exchange. Which is funny, because as a kid all I wanted to be was a curmudgeonly old man, but as I'm speeding toward that I'm realizing that was a bad idea.

Jose: The horror genre has changed now, it seems more mass-marketed than it used to be, and maybe that's just my perspective, but for you is horror your main playground or do you feel any burn out?

Sean: I still write horror here and there. I mostly write horror short stories. But with features and TV, I'm more into sci-fi and action right now because I can sell those things. Plus, you work ten years making horror movies, you kind of say all you can say in horror. I've written every kind of horror movie, I've done vampires to religious lunatics to giallo. Once you've done one or two of each of those, what else are you going to say? It gets to be a real challenge as a writer, because I say to myself, *Does this mean anything?* I try to make it a real point that everything I write means something. I mean *Rage* has got a very specific anti-gun message, and it's a gun-filled, explosive, violent film because you catch more flies with honey, than vinegar. You give people an action film that at the end has a very strong anti-gun message and a lot of people picked up on it.

The High-Concept Massacre

Jose: Well, let's talk about the development of *Rage*, formerly titled *Tokarev*. What inspired you to write an action movie?

Sean: Jim and I wanted to do something non-horror, and that was our first non-horror script together. We love tough guy films and crime films. We wanted to do one of those. There's this story about John Gotti's neighbor. Gotti's neighbor accidentally hit and killed Gotti's kid with his car. Now apparently, Gotti knew about this and was ok with it because it was an accident, but his wife went all Lady Macbeth and told Gotti to make this guy disappear, and boy did he disappear. No one knows where he went. We wanted to do a story about what happens when you fuck with the kid of a gangster. We had written it six months before *Taken* (2008) had come out, and no one wanted it then, even though it had made the Blacklist and it was sort of a big, hot script. Then *Taken* came out and a whole bunch of people wanted it. We were taking meetings all over the place, and it got over-saturated. Everyone read it and everyone passed. It took a couple more years, but we ended up making it ourselves.

Jose: Featuring the incomparable Nic Cage as your gangster.

Sean: Another Academy Award winner. We got two of them now. He's a guy who's always on time, always knows his lines, always ready to go, and the second they say cut, he's cool and relaxed. He's a great dude and he comes with a lot of baggage. There's a lot of people who hate him, but when you have an action movie with Nic Cage, it also sells in every territory on the globe. There were kids tweeting from Doha that they were going to watch it. People in Jakarta were writing, "I'm heading to the mall to watch Nic Cage in *Rage*." Everywhere on this planet you can find this movie, so that's fucking great. Did the movie come out perfect? No. But it came out pretty close to what we had written. There's certain tonal things I'd love to see done differently, but that's with every movie. My partner and I haven't lost money on a movie yet, so we get to keep making them.

Nicolas Cage kicking ass in a scene from *Rage*. **Photo courtesy of Sean Keller**

Jose: Do you have a lot of projects in the works?

Sean: Absolutely. Always have twenty irons in the fire, because if you don't you're never going to hit anything. We're always working on a lot of different projects; Jim and I are constantly hammering out new stuff. You never know what's going to happen as a writer. Pick all your battles and consign yourself to the fact that it's never going to be the thing that was in your head if a movie gets made.

Jose: How do you pick your battles? What's your line demarcation in terms of a script's untouchable elements?

Sean: I've really gotten better at being a producer about this, where I try to really think about what's best for the film. What's going to make the film work? I'm not precious with anything anymore, because I can't be. The second you get precious with something, that's the first thing they're going to cut. Every once and while, there is a line that I really love, and sometimes you get to keep it and sometimes you don't. But where I will fight my battles is specifically on subtext. I'll say, "This is what has to be said without being said, and if we don't keep a through line with that, then the weight of the storytelling is just going to collapse the story." You need to have subtext, it's like the foundation of a house. If you don't have the proper subtext, it's all surface. That's where my literary love comes in. And a lot of people who read the script won't understand the subtext. Most people will just see what's happening. That's where I pick my battles, which I didn't earlier on, but I just want to make sure I sit down with everyone involved and I tell them, "This is what we're going for." It's tricky as the writer, because the director's job is to lay those lines down. I will tell the director and the producer, but I don't tell the actors, that's the director's job, but I've often wished I had.

Jose: I write alone, in a dark room, but you and Jim have been writing together for a while now, so how does that tag-team writing process work?

Sean: Our process is very social. He comes over to my place at 10 a.m., and we write from 10 a.m. to 1 or 2 p.m., five days a week. It's really regimented. We never work too long, so we're burnt out, and we can keep on going back to the well every day. If we work all the way to 2 p.m. and we want to keep going, we'll stop anyway. We'll jot down a few notes and bullet point a few things, we'll think about it overnight, and if we're still feeling that way in the morning, we'll write that. We start at the beginning and plow. We write sequentially always. I'll be at the keyboard typing and Jim will be pacing around behind me, and we back and forth it. Our first drafts usually come out pretty smooth because we've already talked through it and edited ourselves. We think through the big dumb things. I know a lot of writing partners write separately and they'll write drafts and send them to each other, but writing is lonely and boring, and I'm too social for that. Knowing that my partner is going to show up every day is a good discipline, too. We count on each other to keep the schedule. We can usually bang out the first draft of a feature within ten to fifteen days. We'll be happy with five pages, but we like to do ten a day. It's a nice round number. Ten pages in ten days, you're done.

Jose: That's the first big hurdle, writing the script, and you're right that having a schedule really helps keep a writer focused. The second biggest hurdle is that once the script is ready, how do you get anyone to read it?

Sean: I entered competitions; that's how I got my start. I would submit two scripts a year to Screamfest for four years. I had four semi-finalists in consecutive years, and after the third year I got a manager from that. He contacted the people at Screamfest, asked them who he should be looking at, and they said, "This guy hasn't won, but he's made it to semi-finalist every year." So, she repped me and she didn't do a whole lot for my career, but she introduced me to my lawyer, who I still have, and he introduced me to another manager, who got me an agent.

Jose: The agents and the managers have become the Keymasters to Hollywood's Gatekeepers.

Sean: And we've fired a couple of people, and been dumped ourselves, it's kind of a clown car in Hollywood, rolling in and out. It's really important to have representation, but your reps are never going to do anything for you. They'll get you meetings, but they don't get you work. You get yourself the work. Unless you've written a spec that an agent sees as an overt big-dollar sale, they don't care, and they shouldn't. Their business is making money off of scripts that make money. Make peace with that, because you can't change it, and bitching about things you can't change will make you crazy. This business will drive you insane if you let it. A manager on the other hand, might take a real interest in your craft and might really help you shape your stuff. Reps are also very good at knowing the marketplace, and that's what writers typically avoid. They are valuable at telling you what people are looking for now, or what has been sold recently, but hasn't been made, and will conflict with something you're trying to sell. Having all that information is just as important as reading every day or watching a movie every day.

Jose: A lot of screenwriters I've spoken with have learned writing movies from reading screenplays. Do you read movies as often as you watch them?

Sean: I don't read a lot of scripts. I read friend's scripts. When something is really, really hot and my agent says I should read it, sometimes I'll read it. I've learned lots of tricks from it, but I think it's a trap to read too many screenplays. Especially people who say, "You've got to read *Chinatown*." No one is making that movie anymore. If you write *Chinatown* today, you're fucked. You can't sell that. If Paddy Chayefsky wrote his shit today, he would not sell it. It's a different marketplace and that is a trap that people fall into. Everyone goes, "Oh, I want to make films like this or that", everyone wants to make the kinds of movies they love, but it's a trap. If you don't contemporize it, then you're going to make something that doesn't sell, that won't find an audience, and will be an exercise in frustration because you think you're doing something great and no one is enforcing that. I've read a lot of great scripts that I've said to the writer, "No one is going to make this. I would give you notes on how to re-write this, but don't. Move on." It's tough love, and it's hard to say. It's really mean, and I hate saying it, but sometimes people need to hear that. I don't like to hear it, and I've heard it a bunch.

Jose: Writing is so internalized, but one big skill a screenwriter has to learn is accepting other people's opinions on their work.

Sean: And you've got to have some emotional armor. The notes are going to come, and getting mad at notes is like getting mad at the wind blowing. It is a waste of your energy. I've gotten to a point where I get to mentor people. I'm hanging around with young screenwriters and helping them out. The creatives need to stick together, because there are enough people telling you you can't make it. It's nice to have someone hold your hand and say, "No, no, you're good at this. Keep working." I tell them all the time not think of any note as stupid, because the people giving you notes are not stupid people, especially if it's the money people. People with money have money because they don't lose money, and if they're telling you what will or won't sell, it's because they know what the fucking market will bear. No amount of literary greatness or arrogance is going to push through that. Write it, enjoy it, then put it in a drawer, and who knows? In five years, the market might come back around to it because it changes all the time. The people in these positions have gotten there because they are good at what they do and you need to respect them for that. That adversarial nature that writers want to take is destructive. We are all in this together; you have to think of it as collaborative, because the second you do that it becomes easier to take a note.

Jose: You mentioned that if you get the same note three times, you consider it valid. So, how do you dissect a note if it rings true, but only comes from one or two readers and no one else picked up on it?

Sean: You've got to be a doctor. You've got to be able to diagnose the note. It's like saying, "My knee hurts," and there are a million little things that could be the cause of that. When someone says, "This beat isn't working," well why isn't it working? Is it because the first act didn't set up the third act properly? Or the second act turn paid it off weird? You've got to go in and diagnose it. That doesn't mean do everything they say, but figure out what's bothering them about the note. Ask them about it because sometimes you get people to come around on their own note. Also, you get to understand them and they know that you've considered their note, because people who are reading your script are considering it. Oftentimes writers don't spend as much time considering the notes that they get because it's easy to say, "Oh, this is a dumb note. They're not the writer. They're not creative like me." You can take in every note to please the Producer and turn in something that's flat; I've done it. I've done it plenty. Or you can take the time to engage them and figure out together how to make a movie that is going to make everyone happy.

Jose: As an actor, do you treat dialog in a more organic way? Do you think it helps you in constructing conversation to have that background?

Sean: I always treat it like improv. We'll know what the scene is about, what the goals are, where the relationships should turn. So, I just start writing out improv, playing the different characters in my head, and that'll usually be overwritten. I do it again right away. I don't wait. I delete and start over, and whatever was good you'll remember if you do it right away. It's become more pointed now, since we've been doing it for long enough. I don't necessarily talk like a real person, I talk like a movie person, and there's a difference. One of things I've learned is that everyone wants complexity, but a complex character is almost bad for your film in a weird way. A character should express a single point of view, and a different character, not within the same person, should express a contradictory point of view. When it's being performed, it's a lot easier to understand, but on the page, even though humans are filled with contradictions, it confuses the character's POV.

Jose: What's the biggest misconception you've run into in regards to notes?

Sean: My least favorite critique of anything is "Oh, that feels so contrived." It is! We made it! It's been conjured up, from beginning to end, with an intention. Every single thing about film is contrived and every single thing is gratuitous. What is being shown is shown for a reason. Or characters arcs; in real life, people don't have arcs in their lives. People are pretty much the same all through their lives. Every so often they have big, life-changing moments, and we've all had those, but the core stays the same. But in a movie they want your character to grow and learn things. Unless someone wants to do a piece that takes place within twenty-four or forty-eight hours, I'll say, "No, I'm not going to worry about that." I'm going to make sure that everyone has goals they're working toward, and different people's goals are in conflict with each other. Sometimes you have to make something satisfying. Jim and I for the longest time wanted to be clever. We wanted to take a cliché and subvert it and be very clever. Yes, I delight in usurping an audience's expectations, but we realized that clever is almost always the opposite of satisfying. So, I'm focusing real hard now on being satisfying, and how to do it without being cliché, or lame. I don't have to kill the dog in every script, and it's ok for the good guy to live. Sometimes people want that joy. Conversely, TV is the one place where you can be dark.

Jose: One of the big distinctions in creative expression between the short form film and the long form series.

Sean: What I love most about TV, and what's so different from writing features, is that features are all about the resolution. They are all about the third act and how it's resolved. In TV, if it's resolved, it's dead and it's over. You're writing first acts over and over again, weaving threads going in every direction at the end of each episode. It's a long game, and you don't need to worry about resolution. In *Twin Peaks*, when you found out who killed Laura Palmer, it's over. Even though it kept going, it's over! In TV you don't have to resolve it, you just have to spin it out. Also, the joy of it is that it's fast, whereas you can spend ten years on a feature.

Jose: Let's talk about those potential ten years with a feature. More and more writers are looking for financing now to get their careers off the ground themselves. As someone who's done that successfully, what advice would you give someone wanting to branch out into producing?

Sean: Looking for financing sucks every time. I have a hard time asking for money. It feels very beggarly every time, and you've got to present it like it isn't, like it's a great business opportunity. Jim and I have always tried to avoid making things for too cheap, just because it's hard to make any money on it, especially if you're not going to own the copyright on it. But we've recently decided to get together a similar amount of money for a production slate and make like four smaller films. The whole idea is to do low-budget sci-fi like *Primer* (2004) and *Pi* (1998) and stuff like that. A heady concept that can be examined on a small budget is kind of a smart path to go on. If you're not doing the things to generate revenue, if you're not being entrepreneurial, then you're going to stay broke. That is unless you're Shane Black and wrote a brilliant action script.

Jose: Everyone worries about his or her idea being poached. How do you protect yourself?

Sean: No one steals material. They don't, because you can't get away with it. If there's pre-existing stuff, then everything is fucked. Chain of title goes out the window. No one steals, but there is creative synchronicity. There *is* a cultural zeitgeist where there are multiple people in multiple places having the same idea, which happens constantly. That's why there are two volcano movies in one year, or two asteroid movies in one year. That happens because of creative synchronicity. Now, I did have one producer on one project that I was developing insist that we should have a scene like this one scene from *The Natural*. So, we wrote a scene that was similar, but she wasn't happy. We went back and forth a couple of times, but then she just took the scene from *The Natural* and plopped it in our script and changed the names. I said, "That's plagiarism, don't ever do that again, and I'm officially not listening to your notes anymore," which is a big thing to say to a major league producer who used to run a studio. There are a couple of people out there with zero scruples, but for the most part I'd say no one steals, because you can't get away with it. Everyone's out there trying to sue.

Jose: That's one of the sad elements of this business; that folks get so litigious. It can sour a person who's just trying to make a living making movies. I've met so many lifers who are bitter and burnt out.

Sean: Yeah, but that's just a prison of your own making. You don't have to be. Another key to surviving this town is to not ascribe intent to others. People's actions are their actions, don't try to think about what they were thinking when they did them. You can deal with the actions, but their intent? You're never going to know. Don't worry about what their intent is, only worry about yours. It will help eliminate all the bitterness. If you can somehow do that, you can tap dance through this town.

Jose: Would you consider that the best advice for a screenwriter trying to break in?

Sean: Well, the best advice for a screenwriter trying to break in is: don't! But, other than that, just work. Do the work. People are going to say no. Some people are going to hate the things you wrote, and some people are going to love the things you wrote. It's a crapshoot. If you don't mind living your life on a fucking roulette wheel, then go ahead and jump in. I'm all about it; I think it's thrilling that I have no clue how my life is going to shake out. My wife, not so thrilled, but I find it exciting. There's a white-knuckle terror to it. This town is terrifying; it's a tough, tough gig. If someone shits all over your baby, make a new baby. It's all about saying, "What's next?" Every time you're going out with another script it's another chance. And there is no such thing as "making it," you're either in a state of working or not working. If you have some illusion that you're going to write something, sell it, and be on easy street, then you are living in a fucking fantasyland. Be prepared for a lot of heartache. Good luck.

Screenwriter William C. Martell basking in the glory of the Raindance film festival. Photo courtesy of William C. Martell

William C. Martell

Ninja Busters (1984)
Night Hunter (1996)
Invisible Mom (1996)

Jose: Let's start at the beginning, how did you pick screenwriting as a career?

William: It picked me. I'm from a blue-collar family in the East Bay Area. My grandfather's business was water wells and farm irrigation, so I'd be digging ditches if I weren't writing scripts. My father ran away from it, and it's not like he ran to become a great artist, he ran away from it to paint and install signs. When you come from a broke family, your children are your employees, so I spent most of my youth climbing up rickety ladders up the sides of buildings holding up fucking heavy signs while my dad is drilling holes and installing them. I can't fucking stand heights, so I said, "I can't do this."

Jose: You decided to switch to mental labor as opposed to manual.

William: As a kid, I read a shit load of books. I watched a lot of movies. I was a fat, uncoordinated kid who got picked on at school all the time, so movies and books were my escape. My parents had an 8mm camera for home movies, and when I was twelve or thirteen, I used my lawn mowing allowance money to buy some rolls of film, and shot a movie with my little brother in our backyard with cardboard alligators attacking him. That was the beginning. I said, "Hey man, I can make movies!"

Jose: You discover this passion, but how does it lead to a career?

William: There was a student film night at my college, and they brought back all the success stories that had graduated; and they were a guy who shot TV commercials for all the used car dealerships, this guy named Paul Kyriazi, who made kung fu movies for drive-ins, and Jim and Artie Mitchell, who made pornos. They were the notorious Mitchell brothers, who actually went there and took that same film class as their only instruction. Jim was the only one who showed up. Anyway, they show my film, and I had the best one because mine actually had a story. Afterwards, the used car guy came up and said, "I really like your work, and I'm looking for somebody to carry equipment for me and intern for me. Would you be interested in doing that?" I thought, "Gee, no money to do all the slave labor?" I said no. Jim Mitchell came up and told me they were always looking for new talent, but I didn't take the job with the Mitchell brothers because I said, "What if my mom sees a porno film that I directed?" and then I thought, *What is my mom doing watching porno?* It ruined my life. Then Paul Kyriazi came up and said, "Hey, pretty good film." I had this script, so I asked him to read it, and he read the script. A year later, he called me up and said, "Bill, I got a job for you." I thought, *This is awesome, I'm going to write a script for a movie!* He said, "Yeah, we're shooting this film in Diamond Mines Park, and we need someone to show up at five in the morning and create this bikers camp, and then stay there all night when the crew leaves to clean up the bikers camp. We need you to do it for three weekends." I said, "Hollywood, here I come!" The movie's called *Weapons of Death* (1981), so you know it's good. I worked on that for no pay, but I got to watch them shoot a 35mm Panavision film, and I got to hang with the crew and become good friends with them.

Jose: Not exactly the auspicious screenwriter debut you imagined.

William: Paul called me up a year or two later and said, "Bill, I got another project." I said, "Ok, where's the park? How fucking early do I have to get up?" He goes "No, it's not that at all. Here's the thing, we have this script, we have a cast, and we have locations, but the script is not as good as it could be. I need someone to punch up the script to make it work, and if you can write a better script than what we have in two weeks, we'll shoot it." I was working at Safeway, but I had vacation time, so I took two weeks off and pounded out this script that used almost nothing from the original.

Jose: Did you have any restrictions?

William: Oh yeah, we had the locations and the cast, so everything had to be written around what we had, including props. The thing I learned about Paul is that he would make a list of all the shit he had access to and say, "That's in the movie." The original film was called *The Falcon's Claw*, and it was about hypnotized dockworkers that work for free. I don't know how that's a movie, but Sid Campbell, even though he didn't write a great script, was absolutely great about not bitching about the changes to his script. My version was about two guys who join a woman's self-defense class to pick up girls. They witness this mob hit, and the mob guys have a contract with ninjas, so from that point on, it's these two morons fighting an army of ninjas. We called it *Ninja Busters*.

Jose: Even with a better script, it wasn't smooth sailing from what I hear.

William: I wrote the script, and what happened was that Paul had to fire the first director, who was his best friend, because after two weeks of shooting he had blown the budget, and shot nothing. For example, there was a scene in a nightclub that was probably a minute long, and we shot there for eight days. The film collapsed. They went out to raise money and a year later they came back with another director, shot some more footage starring the world-famous Oakland Raiders, and that went south. I think they thought that once they had the Raiders on set, people would put in money, and it didn't happen. Everything went back into boxes for a while, until they found another investor who said, "My son has to star in this movie." So, a complete re-write happened, not involving me, and probably not involving any writer, because I think they made it all up as they went along, and that ended up being cut into the movie. The movie stinks.

Jose: Is it hard to love something like that?

William: You have to love the movies you're making, or find the way to love them. I call it the 'doorway.' If there's no doorway into a story for me, I don't take the assignment, and most of the time I try to pitch my own project instead of doing their project, if possible.

Jose: Speaking of loving the movies you work on, let's talk about your erotic thriller *Victim of Desire* (1995).

William: *Victim of Desire* was a spec script that got me meetings all over town at studios. It was originally called *The Victim's Wife*, and this was one of those scripts that with no agent and no manager that I was getting meetings at Warner Bros. with, but nothing ever happened with it. I think the problem was I had no closer, no one to close any deal. So, I did Blockbuster research, which you can't do anymore, because there aren't any Blockbuster video stores. I went to Blockbuster, took a basket, and put every erotic thriller in the basket. I flipped them all over, found out who the producers were, and the name that popped up again and again was Ashok Amritraj. This guy was making the kind of movies I was writing. I called his company, and the guy I got on the phone said, "Dude, I can't help you. I'm not even the guy who answers the phone here. I'm the temp guy." I tell him my story anyway, I give him the three-sentence pitch, and he says, "You know, that sounds like all the posters on the walls here." So, I sent him the script, and he read it. Now, the center of any business is the person who answers the phone, because everyone, including the president of the company, will go to them and ask, "Do I have any messages?" So, the message was, "I read this script, and it's awesome," and so somebody covered it, and it got great coverage. They set up a meeting with me and I went in and they said, "We want to buy your script."

Jose: A dream moment for any writer. Are you happy with the results?

William: The budget went from being a good budget to being a shitty budget, which means you get the shitty cast and the shitty director. Jim Wynorski, whom I hate, and by the way he'd say the same thing about me, although we have a truce now I think, was the last person I'd hire to direct this thing. I have a cool story about Marc Singer, who I think is the fucking greatest actor in the world as far as I'm concerned. We're out on set, somebody knocks a glass off of a table and it breaks. Jim, being Jim, yells, "Some asshole get up and clean that up right away! I'm not going to have broken glass on my set!" Marc Singer goes over, grabs a broom and a dustpan, and starts to clean it up. Jim goes, "Not you, Marc! You're the star!" Marc turns him and goes, "But I was standing next to the broom." That guy is gold.

Jose: Let's talk more about working with Wynorski, who has a ton of credits, most of them quickie films, so I imagine he's very set in his ways of doing things.

William: Jim is a screamer. For instance, on *Victim of Desire*, we had a sound man quit because Jim yelled at him. The producer ended up on set for three or four days just to try to get people not to quit. Jim and I had so many disagreements on that film. He was trying to make a movie in twelve days, and do as little as possible, which is one of his things.

Jose: How do you write the sex scenes, are you vague, or are you descriptive?

William: It's not like I write "Sex Scene #3," it's all totally there on the page, and you can't tell from the movie, but in the script every sex scene has a critical decision for the lead character to make, and those scenes are so much a part of the movie that you can't cut them out. But you basically, in non-pornographic lingo, describe what happens. Writers aren't there when they shoot the sex scenes. Writers aren't there when they shoot the *movie* half the time. On *Grid Runners,* I show up on set one day and the director goes, "Bill, I'm so glad you're here!" I go, "Holy fuck, what went wrong?" Sure enough, something went wrong and they needed act three rewritten overnight. At six o'clock in the morning, they were going to start shooting and they needed pages.

Jose: *Grid Runners* **was released as** *Virtual Combat* **(1995), which was directed by Andrew Stevens, who is primarily an actor, so how did you guys meet up?**

William: *Grid Runners* was the working title, and it exists that way everywhere else except for the U.S. and South America. Andrew was, and for all I know still is, Ashok Amritraj's on-again off-again producing partner. Andrew had been involved with *Victim of Desire,* and he had been the producer who was trying to get people not to quit on set. The thing with Andrew as a director is that he's an actor, and he comes from a different perspective than someone who is visually oriented like a director, so when you come from a strict acting background, the visual side of the story sometimes gets nothing. This movie had dialog scenes, action scenes, and special effects scenes. We had some fucking awesome special effects, but the problem with Andrew was that we'd go out to shoot and he would shoot all the dialog scenes first, and in the last couple of hours he'd say, "Ok, we got an hour left for action scenes and special effects." They would shoot the fast-ass action scene, but there'd be no time or money left for the special effects. He prioritized the acting first, and for me if I go to see an action movie, I don't care about the acting. The cool part about the pitch was that you can attract the action crowd and the science fiction crowd, but the science fiction got cut out, and the action got cut down.

Jose: Let's talk writing action, which is similar to a sex scene. Are you specific when you write action beats?

William: Absolutely, it's an action movie; the action is the story. If you don't write the action, it's like writing a comedy and saying, "Oh, we'll just cast somebody to come up with the jokes." One of things that always pisses me off is the Chuck Norris type scene where he is surrounded by an army of ninjas and they take their turn getting their asses kicked one by one. I didn't want to do that, so I sat down, did stick figure storyboards, and figured out how one man could fight a group of people surrounding him. Of course, if might all change when it gets to set, but you want people to read awesome action scenes. I learned how to write action from Walter Hill, by reading his screenplays. I got the script for *48 Hrs.* (1982) and read it, and said, "Man, this guy can freaking write action scenes!" So, my action scripts read like Walter Hill scripts because that's my big influence. Later on I read Shane Black's scripts and said, "This guy can write action scenes!" Later, when I met him, I said, "Dude, you can write action scenes!" and he goes, "Learned everything from reading Walter Hill scripts."

Jose: You bring up a good point about how things change between page and set. What can probably be amazing in a script, could end up remarkably shitty, and that's usually due to the harsh realities of making a movie. I'm curious if you and Don "The Dragon" Wilson had any input regarding the action scenes?

William: Yes, and input in ways I didn't like it. What I wanted to do was Jackie Chan scenes, and so that's what I wrote. Don comes out and says, "I don't know how to do any of that stuff, but I know how to kick a guy in the head." So, all the scenes got changed into 'kick a guy in the head.' There's this one scene where Don is surrounded by an army of bad guys, and the fight coordinator comes out and he goes, "You know what I was thinking? Instead of this thing where they all fight him at once, it would be so much simpler if he fights them one at a time." So, that's what happens in the movie, and it went from being this awesome scene to this other scene that I was trying to avoid. Don is the star, and when Don is the star, he dictates. On that movie, Don controlled everything except the time for action scenes, which needed more time.

Jose: You send him vampire hunting with your next project together, *Night Hunter*. Was this your first horror script?

William: I had written horror scripts before, but what happened was that *Grid Runners* had been an HBO world premiere, and they told Ashok that they wanted more Don movies, so he called me in to pitch. I had this treatment called *The Last of the Van Helsings*, and that's what I pitched and it turned out to be the one. And again when I wrote it I wanted to mix two genres, so now not only does Don have the people following for the martial arts stuff, but he also gets the horror people. This whole thing was written to go extreme. I said, "Man, we are going to get right up to edge of NC-17 with this shit. We're going to do stuff that people have never seen in a horror movie before." But none of that stuff ended up in the movie, all the effects got cut, except for the vampire teeth. All the horror stuff got cut, which was shitty. We didn't have any of the cool fight scenes I had written, because Don just wanted to kick people in the head. So, it ended up being that "Oh, wooden stakes is a myth, you have to kick them in the head to kill them."

Jose: He fetishizes head kicks, I guess, and yet you work with him one more time, right?

William: That was a nightmare. It was again a spec script, called *Soft Target*, which got me studio meetings all over the place. I was taking my low-budget skills and adapting them into a bigger budget story. I wanted to do a movie that was limited locations and limited cast, but was balls to the wall action so when a studio picks it up that lead actor is a movie star; it's George Clooney, not Don "The Dragon" Wilson. Except it ended up being Don "The Dragon" Wilson. You know, it was a post 9/11 script, inspired by the movie *Narrow Margin* (1990), but no one makes it, and it just ends up on this list of movies that I have. So, Don's looking for a movie and I send him the list, and then I said, "Fuck, I should have taken that one off." Sure enough, Don says, "I want to do that one." His producer guy goes, "Look Bill, I promise you we're not going to change a word of your script. We love the script." Afterwards, they've changed every single word. There is not a single word that's the same. The film bears no resemblance to the script at all, but that was a valuable lesson.

Jose: Every writer learns that lesson at some point. What we write is expendable to everyone else.

William: Sometimes it's stuff that makes no sense. The example I always use is that I had this script that was very similar to Heat (1995), before Heat was made, about a group of bank robbers. This producer at MGM read it and a loved it, and they actually optioned it for some money with three zeros behind it. It was a real money option. But the producer's first note was, "What if they're cowboys?" I go, "What do you mean, like make this a western?" He says, "No, they're wearing boots, and chaps, and carry six-guns, and they're on horseback." So, now the Village People are robbing banks? Somewhere there is a draft of this script that is the Village-People-rob-banks draft. But those kind of questions are the ones I get all the time. What if they're cowboys? Where the fuck did that come from? I get script killer notes, too. The one I keep getting is, "Why do the hero and the villain have to keep fighting? Why can't they just be friends and get along? We can just show them being friends." Where does that stuff come from? There's no movie there.

Jose: And all the stupid shit that happens in the movie is blamed on us, too. We weren't responsible, but since it all appeared to have originated with us, we get pinned with the Scarlet Letter.

William: Exactly. You get blamed for all the shit that you fought like hell against, but it ends up in the film, and you're the screenwriter, so they think you did it. But no, those were all the things I thought were the stupidest ideas ever and I battled.

Jose: I had similar issues with a film I wrote called *Hansel and Gretel* (2013), which I won't go into here, but I got to work with Dee Wallace on that film, who's a really sweet lady. You and I have her in common, because she was in your film *Invisible Mom*. That must have been a nice change for you, working on a family film.

William: It was. I wrote *Night Hunter* for Ashok, and *Invisible Mom* for Andrew, back to back. It was for Andrew's new company, and he wanted to have five films for AFM, and have one in production. The stuff that was hot back then on video were babysitter movies, which are movies that mom pops in the VCR for the kids to watch while the mom does whatever it is moms do. I went in and pitched him family films, and when I pitched *Invisible Mom*, he said, "Yes!" I asked, "Don't you want to hear what it's about?" He said, "No, I love the title, let's just do it." So, I write the script, and they hire Fred Olen Ray, one of my favorite directors. Fred has this reputation for being a hack; he does a lot of movies under his own name, and if you look at his pseudonyms, he does even more movies. Here's what I like about Fred, he has a rule that every five shots is a cool shot. For a low-budget movie, ninety-five percent of it is you put it on sticks and you shoot the two-shot of people talking, and then close ups, and then you're out of there. Fred's thing is once he does that he will try and get a cool shot, even if the budget is incredibly small. Fred's films aren't great, and they're shot in about the same amount of time as this conversation we're having, but when you watch one of his films every once in a while you'll say, "Hey, that was a cool shot!" On top of that, they cast Dee, and she was a huge get.

Jose: Yeah, she had just been on *The Frighteners* (1996) previously.

William: Yeah, she was not doing anything low-budget. They cast Dee, but then I was cursed. I call it the Curse of Good Casting. Part of my pitch was, you cast someone to play the mom and she's on set for three days, everything else is her doing voice over. The minute they cast Dee, Andrew asks her if they can get an extra day. She says, "I love this script, so you can have as many days with me as you want. You have me for the whole shooting schedule." Andrew says to me, "Write her into as many visible scenes as you can." The movie is called *Invisible Mom*, how do I do that? Fred says, and probably one of the reasons that I love Fred, "That doesn't work. We've got a script here that works, why are we going to fuck with it at the last minute? Do you want her to be invisible at the end? Because that won't work. Or do you want her invisible, but with stuff on her face so we can see her?" Andrew says, "The stuff on her face is good, as long as we can tell that it's Dee." So, a ludicrous rewrite occurs where Dee becomes the lead character, not her son, and she has to figure out how to get herself visible again. But I was jazzed that Dee was in my stupid little movie, and that movie sold awesome.

Jose: I remember watching that back in the day, it was a fun flick. I know someone else wrote the sequel, but were you involved at any point?

William: Andrew calls me up and says, "We're making *Invisible Mom 2* and *3*. Come in and pitch." I came in and was using *Honey, I Shrunk the Kids* (1989) as a model. In the second one the kids don't shrink again, they blow up the baby. The thing that I loved the most was an idea called *Gunslinger Mom*, which is basically *Back to the Future III* (1990), which involves a time machine and Dee Stone rescuing her son by becoming the fastest, baddest gunslinger in the world. Andrew said, "No, she's got to be invisible again." What the fuck, you can't have that, she's just invisible again? I pitched a whole bunch of cool ideas, and different possibilities, but he said no, so I said, "I can't write it." So, somebody else wrote it. Now what happened was that Andrew double sold it at AFM. He said, "This is the hottest film we've got." It was so popular that when two companies from the UK wanted to buy the sequel, he sold it to both. Then he had to make a second *Invisible Mom 2*. So, there's *Invisible Mom 2* (1999) and then *Mom's Outta Sight* (1998). Then Andrew said, "We're still selling *Invisible Mom* stuff, but Dee's not coming back, so now it's *Invisible Dad*, so can you come in and pitch on that?" I said,

"WHY IS HE INVISIBLE?" I didn't really want to write that, so somebody else wrote part one and two of that. There were four sequels, and I made no money off of those. No story credit either.

Jose: Are you disappointed that you didn't credit on those?

William: No, no, no. There was a point during the making of the film *Treacherous* (1993) that they sent me the director's re-written script and asked me if I wanted to fight for credit. I said, "Nah, I'll just take 'story by' man. I'm not fighting for credit on this." I wish I would have, because I think I would have gotten some residual money off that, but *Treacherous* sucked. *Invisible Mom* was ok, but not nearly the script it could have been.

Jose: You seem to work with the same people multiple times, is that on purpose or purely accidental?

William: It's by accident. And there's a shitload of people in between, where the movie didn't happen; a lot of bigger stuff where the film didn't happen. I came to town off a script called *Courting Death* that I sold from my hometown. It got picked up by a company on the Paramount lot, and for five years it was in the trades once year when they were announcing their projects, but it just never got made. That would have been huge. David Fincher was the first director signed on to it. The funny part is when they told me that back then, I didn't know who that was. They said, "He directed the Madonna 'Vogue' video." I said, "A music video director? What the fuck does he know?" Now I look back, and I can't believe it, but he ended up ditching that job to shoot *Alien 3* (1992).

Jose: And that sale was done all by your lonesome? No reps?

William: Yeah. I don't have representation. I've had an agent, and I've had a manager; neither one of them sold a damn thing for me, and the last manager I had ruined my career. He told me, "You are no longer writing direct-to-video movies." Original Films, who do the *Fast and Furious* movies, read a couple of my scripts and loved them. They had me in and said, "We love your writing and want to work with you. Here's the thing, we are a doing a series of *I Know What You Did Last Summer* direct-to-video movies, and we'd like to try you out in one, and if we work well together, we'll do other stuff." I thought that was awesome and I handed it over to my manager to negotiate, who then said, "Bill's not doing those movies anymore." It ended up being a bunch of those things.

Jose: I suppose he thought he was being protective, but detrimentally so. Most assignments aren't worth the trouble, but it depends on your financial status and how hungry you are.

William: My friend Terry ended up getting a gig for a treasure diver for sunken Spanish galleons stuff for Robert Downey Jr.'s company. Steve McQueen, while he was alive, commissioned a 1,700-page treatment on this subject. Somebody found it in a box and Robert Downey Jr.'s company bought it and now my buddy got hired to write it.

Jose: That sounds like a fun, but daunting task, much like seeking out representation that works.

William: I am on a soft manager search. The thing that always gets me is that the hoops I have to jump through to get a manager are much more difficult than the hoops I have to jump through to get a meeting with Joel Silver's company. Why is it more difficult for me to find a manager who will represent me than to be sitting across from the giant crocodile in Arnold Kopelson's reception area? You get all these meetings based on nothing! I call it the pass-around script, where somebody reads a script and thinks it's pretty good. They hand it to somebody else who thinks it's pretty good, and then the phone rings, and it's someone who wants to meet with you on a studio lot, and you say, "Where the fuck did you get my script?"

The High-Concept Massacre

Jose: I've asked this to all the writers, but why do you think it is that writers get crapped on the most despite the fact that we are the most integral to the existence of a movie.

William: Part of it is that we're first on, to some degree. The Director's Guild says that the 'a film by' credit is open for anybody to grab. I can take 'a film by.' The problem is when they're negotiating to buy my script they say, "I'm not going to give him 'a film by' because then how are we going to get a director?" So, you're first on, and because you're a first you get shit in. When you're first on they can say, "Oh, we don't have the budget yet to do the film, so can you do us twenty-five re-writes for free while we try to clean it up to get the budget?" It would be one thing if after all that loyal, hard work you got repaid for it, but no. It sucks.

Jose: After you're done doing all the heavy lifting, you're left high and dry. But let's talk about the finished product now. Is there one movie you can point to as an example of perfect screenwriting?

William: Absolutely: *Notorious* (1946), the Hitchcock film. It's one of my top five. That's one of those movies that I love, and that I can watch again and again. *Notorious* is just such a sad story, and the movie does things that make you feel sorry for the villain at times. It has so many different things going on in it. It's almost a hard movie to watch. How did that film get made in 1946? Again, great writing. *Notorious* is a script that I've ripped off a couple of times. I was up for *Whore 2,* and I went in and pitched a version that was like *Notorious,* but nothing happened. They never even ended up making that sequel. The other film, my number one favorite film, is *Point Blank* (1967) with Lee Marvin. The thing that I love about that movie is that every time I see that movie it's a different movie. This movie is dense. There are so many small clues planted that you didn't see before, and when you see them they make you question it. What if he *is* dead? What if this *really* is a gay love story? That movie has so many little things planted in it. That movie is so densely packed with information that I can watch it a million times and notice new things. Movies that have a lot of information in them are interesting to me.

Jose: Which one of your films are you most happy with?

William: My favorite is a film called *Hard Evidence* (1995), which was made for the USA Network, and it is different from the script, but not that much different, which is why I like it. What happened was I had the spec for *Hard Evidence* and it got to them twice, once through me and then through a line producer. The development person I got it to didn't like it. The line producer got it straight to production and they said, "This film is ready to shoot tomorrow." The script was written that the hero lives in Los Angeles and goes to Mexico. They say, "Well, we're shooting this in Vancouver. So, you need to do a re-write where instead of them going south of the border, they go north." There was a line in there that said, "I can't be in a Mexican prison for the rest of my life," which I had to change to "I can't be in a Canadian prison for the rest of my life," which makes it sound like the worst that could happen is that they might not deliver tea on time. The producer here shipped it to production in Canada with a note that said, "This is the writer's final draft," meaning that they had used all of my contracted re-writes. The Vancouver production company didn't realize what it meant, they thought it meant they couldn't change the script, so they shot that script, except for two things I didn't know about. One was that they wanted to start the movie with some action, so they had a dirt bike race scene, but that didn't offend me at all. The other thing was that at that time movies that were showing on USA were PG to PG-13, but there was an after-market on VHS, so I didn't realize that they were going to take my movie, which was written so it could be shown on television, and take it to the next level so it's re-rated R. The director went wild. There were extended sex scenes that were not written by me, and I don't really mind that much, except for one moment where there are three of them in a row and I'm thinking, "This is getting really porny here." My entire family watched that, so now they think I'm writing porn.

Jose: What's one assignment that you got paid for, and never materialized, but you wish it had?

William: I wrote the remake of *House,* which never got made, or hasn't been made at this point in time. It's sitting on a shelf, and I love that script. I wish something would happen with it, but we hit bad timing at Lionsgate. Lionsgate had been doing a zillion 1980s movies remakes, and then they stopped making money, and they said, "We're going to do something else." There's always like fifteen things that go wrong with a project, and once things get a little shaky, it all falls apart.

Jose: What do you say to people who consider screenwriting not real writing?

William: It is real writing! It's totally real writing! That ends up being the biggest problem, because there are people out there that say, "I'm not a good enough writer to write a novel, so I'll write a screenplay." Look, a novel has like a thousand fucking pages if you're Stephen King. A screenplay has ninety pages sometimes, and those ninety pages have to work as a story. Once you shrink it down and you don't have the time to fuck around, that means every word has to completely count. I think that's the thing that fucks up a lot of wannabe screenwriters, that they think it isn't writing; it's haiku, it's poetry. People don't get that. They think it's going to be easy, and it's harder. By the way, Stephen King is the perfect example of a guy who may have never gotten that lesson. If you look at stuff taken from his work, like *Stand By Me* not the crappy stuff, and then you look at the scripts that he's written himself: he *don't* get it. He *don't* get it.

Jose: How does somebody become a screenwriter nowadays?

William: Write a bunch of scripts. It always comes down to that. It's always the writing, right? Everything else happens because there's writing that exists. I think the thing that I did right was that I wrote a lot. Just write. Have a stack of scripts. First of all, every time you write a new script hopefully you get better, but you also build up an inventory. What happens is that when you're looking for a manager you're sending out cold queries or trying to get referrals, and when you go out once with that script it's polluted, it's used, it's toilet paper. A script is like toilet paper. Once a script goes out, once it's used, no one wants the used toilet paper. So, it's dead and that means you have to have another script. If you have a stack at least you can rotate through them and hopefully something snags. If you get close enough that they say, "We really liked this, but it wasn't right for us," then you say, "You know, I got this," and you can keep shoveling shit through the door until something sticks or maybe they've read enough of your stuff that they like your writing and bring you in for an assignment.

Jose: Now you've switched to nonfiction screenwriting books, so what would you say is the biggest mistake most first-time writers make with their script?

William: It ends up being that they don't take it far enough; it's not dramatic enough. The emotional stakes aren't high enough. They don't take it to the limit, and a lot of that ends up being because a lot of people watch television, and they think television shows are what a movie is, and it's not. A movie is what gets you off your ass to turn off the television, and go pay twelve bucks to see it. People write TV scripts. They don't take their story to the limit, or their emotional thing to the limit, or their story to the limit. In my book on action, I wrote a chapter called "You Can't Do That In A Movie." *Taken* (2008) is my new example because *Taken* keeps doing that. There are scenes that sell the script. The biggest problem with beginning people is that they have an idea, but it's the TV idea, it's a small idea and not a big idea. You need to have the great idea. After that, it's the execution, and they have the crappy execution, the plain execution. It's missing the thing that takes it right to the line so that the reader, and the audience goes, "Holy crap, I've got to tell my friend about that, you're not going to believe what just happened in this movie." I want to write those scenes. People always write the script where they disarm the bomb, but what if the bomb went off? Now what happens?

John Penney, pickin' and grinnin' at the keyboard.
Photo courtesy of John Penney

John Penney

The Kindred (1987)
Return of the Living Dead III (1993)
Hellgate (2011)

Jose: I always like to break the ice with this question, which I think is the all-important one: so how did you discover screenwriting?

John: You know, it's funny, my biological mother, Raylyn Moore was a writer; she wrote novels and short stories. My stepfather was Ward Moore, who was a science fiction writer in the 1950s. We had a very dysfunctional writer family, but luckily my stepmother came along and gave me some semblance of a real, structured life. So, the first thing I said was that I don't want to be a regular writer, because besides the chaos and insecurity, it looks so incredibly boring, just sitting there by yourself and drinking wine. But I grew up in a world where film and television were the cheesy, bastard cousins that you would never want to work for as a "real" writer. We didn't have a TV, and when my parents got divorced, my father would take us to the movies every week. So, I was aware of movies and loved them far more than reading, or anything like that. I lived in Carmel, and, at that time, Clint Eastwood came through town and was filming a movie called *The Eiger Sanction* (1975), so I ditched school and started following the production around. I got to see what making movies was like through hanging out on this set, and this was pre-9/11, there was no security. I would just stand in the corner and watch scenes being shot. It was pretty amazing, and I became aware that this was something possible.

The High-Concept Massacre

Jose: What was the first script you leafed through?

John: We had a close family friend, Alan Marcus, and in the 1960s, he wrote a TV show called *Here Come the Brides*. It was a big sensation. I got a copy of a script from him, because they were trying to get my stepfather to write an episode for them, but he would have nothing to do with it. He would say, "This is garbage and trash. I'm not going to write garbage and trash." So, I got the script for the hour-long show, and I said, "Wow, this is really amazing!" I never saw the show; I saw the script, but it kind of opened up this whole world of Hollywood. But I still didn't quite put it all together until *Butch Cassidy and the Sundance Kid* (1969). I always thought that the actors made it all up. I had no idea, but then I found a copy of William Goldman's script and I read it over and over and over until the pages were falling out. Holy crap, somebody wrote this movie! I thought they just popped into being. So, I started to become aware of Hollywood creatively. The third thing that lead me down the path was Fred MacMurray. He was shooting a commercial across the street from my house, so I ran over because I was fascinated by it. One of the guys said I could talk to him, so I knocked on his trailer, and he brought me inside and sat me down and we talked for what must have been an hour. He asked me, "What do you want to do?" and I said, "I think I want to write movies." He said, "I'll send you some scripts for examples." This is before Internet and all that, so I didn't realize you could get a hold of this stuff. I thought I'd never hear from him again, but a few weeks later I get this package in the mail with a hand-written note from Fred saying, "John, good luck on your journey. Here are some scripts." I still have that note. So, basically, Hollywood came to my town and that's how I became aware that you could go make movies. I thought that was great, because I didn't have to compete with the family business. I was far more interested in movies, so I could just go and write those.

John with literary alchemist, Ray Bradbury, on WGA picket line in 1988.
Photo courtesy of John Penney

Jose: You commit to screenwriting. When did you decide to move to Hollywood and consummate the relationship?

John: I decided to come down to L.A. and write movies, and my mom says, "I'll call Ray for you," and she calls her friend, Ray Bradbury. He wrote the Introduction to one of my mother's books and they had been friends for ages, and he was even the roommate of my stepfather up in Topanga Canyon in the 1950s. He tells me, "I'll meet you at the Daisy," which was this restaurant in Beverly Hills, and he was very proud that they had a sandwich named after him. He was a nice guy and he really helped a lot of young writers. He asked me what I wanted to do, and I said I wanted to write movies. He says, "If you want to be a real writer, don't write movies." I was taken aback, but he continues "Yeah, no, no, no. Look, write short stories, or novels. Don't write movies. Stay away from them." He told me the whole story about John Huston and *Moby Dick* (1956), and how Huston took credit, but he didn't write a freaking word on it. He starts bashing the whole Hollywood system. He says, "If you write a short story, there is nothing between you and the audience. You're connecting with them through that page. You write a script, and it's a blueprint that's going to be interpreted. You've got the poetry of the dialog, of course, but it's a blueprint that an actor is going to interpret, a director is going to interpret, and on and on and on." I left there completely confused, and I fell into editing. I came out of UCLA and worked on *The Dorm That Dripped Blood* (1982), which I was Assistant Editor on, and I continued editing for a while and writing on the side. Ten years later, Ray was shooting a movie on one stage, and I wrote and produced a movie on the other stage. Somebody told me that Ray Bradbury was outside, and I go over and say hi, and we're chatting about the same old stories of my stepfather and mother. Then I tell him, "You know, ten years ago you told me not to write movies if I wanted to be a writer," and then he looked at me and said, "You know what John, but it's the most relevant art form now, isn't it?" I thought, *Oh great, thanks for sending me out into the wilderness for ten years!* Obviously, a lot of his stuff got made into movies and he had bad experiences, but I learned that you have to really consider your source when people give you advice.

Jose: Absolutely, and much to Ray's dismay, who is one of my writing idols, you did become a screenwriter and your first credit was on the film *The Power* (1984), so let's discuss the birthing process there.

John: It was sort of a gang of us from UCLA and USC, Jeffrey Obrow and the guys that did *The Dorm That Dripped Blood*. It wasn't like a closed system, so if you had an idea, you could bring it. I worked on the story, and I got a story credit for *The Power*. I edited the movie, as well. Ed Montoro, from Film Ventures International, watched the movie and said, "Nah, you don't have a big enough opening, you need a punchier ending, and you need more genre stuff." He paid for some re-shoots, and we went in and wrote and shot a whole bunch of stuff. The move was released in theaters and it was great; it was fantastic. Later, Ed went missing. They think he took all the money from his company and disappeared, but a lot of people think he was killed; he had mob connections, but we weren't ever sure about that. Anyway, what I learned from that experience as a screenwriter was sitting in the audience in Culver City while that movie was playing. Everything was happening to the lead actress, she wasn't driving the plot, and you'd start to see people leaving the theater or yelling at the screen. Once you go through that experience as a writer, you don't want to repeat it. It seared in my brain when I saw that. You've got to have your protagonist active in the story; you can't have them be passive.

Jose: Character is crucial in a movie; it's really the bones of the whole thing.

John: It was a real lesson. My biological dad, who was a journalist, used to say, "Character is story, and story is character." It meant nothing to me, until I realized at that moment watching *The Power* in the theater that a specific character is going to turn a story a specific way; they need to drive the story, if not, things just happen to them and the thing is generic. In *Jaws,* how do they get isolated? Quint smashes the freaking radio, because of who he was. All of that started coming together for me. You see that in front of you and you can't deny it.

Jose: You put all that newfound knowledge into your next film, *The Kindred,* I imagine?

John: Yeah, that was the first screenplay credit I had. It was the same group of guys. Jeff Obrow was cleaning out his aunt's kitchen and he had this idea about what if she passed away and they found something. So, me and my roommate, Earl Ghaffari, went home and made up all these cards of a story for *The Kindred.* We pitched it to Jeff, but it was terrible. He said, "You know, there's something there, so why don't you work with Steve Carpenter," who was Jeff's partner, and they used to direct everything together. So, Earl, Steve, and myself sat around with a Dictaphone and we wrote the rough draft of *The Kindred* into that Dictaphone. Then, Jeff came in, and that was the team. What is really interesting about that film was that Earl and I were the editors on it, too. It was a weird combination, but we got to tell it the first time in the script form and tell it the last time in the editing room. Right toward the end we brought in Joe Stefano, who wrote *Psycho*. We were in awe of this guy; he was just the sweetest, nicest guy. This guy was such an inspiration; he was so enthusiastic. He did a draft of our script, and he ended up coming onto the credits, so now it's like an army of writers on this thing. But the great thing was to watch Rod Steiger take dialog that was not great and play it like a jazz musician, then watch it come out the other side and believe everything he said. Joe would come into the editing room and watch stuff with us, and he would say, "John, isn't this like Christmas morning? It's like opening presents." I'll never forget how enthusiastic he was. This is a guy who did all these great things, like *Outer Limits* and *Psycho,* but he still had that enthusiasm. In terms of developing as a writer, it was really huge to see it on the page, and then all the footage ended up in my lap, and I had to cut it and tell the story a final time, so it was a really fun experience.

Jose: What lessons would you say you took away first and foremost?

John: Well, editing is a storytelling tool, and what it did was it started my mind really thinking about what you had to work with as a screenwriter. You've got anything you can see and anything you can hear, that's it. It's flexible, of course, but really that's all you've got; you learn you can't fake something on a page. I've always had this production point of view in my writing career, and I think that's served me well, because all these people are going to interpret it. So, I started thinking about what the main things were that are always picked on, and I realized it was generally always story and structure. Those are the ones they always give you notes on. I figured if I could get those down, I'd be fine. I was never a great dialog writer, I wasn't a natural; I really worked hard on that. I felt that was more the poetry of the screenplay, but if my story and structure were solid, then I could get a little bit further, and I really focused on that after *Kindred*.

Jose: That's a very good perspective to have, because in the editing you really know what you need and don't need in terms of writing. You really learn how to interpret movie language, which will affect story and structure positively because you know what you need to do more or less of the next time around.

John: Exactly. You got a real sense of what a screenplay is, how important that structure is, to make sure your conflicts are clear and clean, and your characters are well defined and moving the story forward. I don't want to have that experience again. Editing is writing, essentially. It's the same pacing and gut instinct. I learned a lot about storytelling through editing. But *The Kindred* was the big break for me. First full screenplay credit, released in theaters, and it was a big trip to see the ads on TV. At that point, because I had been working in such a group situation I really wanted to go out on my own. From then on I decided that I was just going to write by myself, and that was sort of a turning point.

Jose: Was that difficult to part from the group?

John: Very. It wasn't so much about the group, but you start to realize that if you're a writer, you've got to write every day. It was very hard because I was used to working within that group dynamic. The minute I start working with someone else, I find I take less creative responsibility. I feel I don't really commit, unless I'm alone, so if I was really going to be a writer, I knew I had to do my own thing by myself, so that's what I did.

Jose: How'd that work out?

John: I wrote a bunch of stuff, and one of the things I wrote was bought by Warner Bros. So, that was great, and I got into the Writer's Guild, and

The High-Concept Massacre

got to go to the Warner Bros. lot for notes. I worked with David Heyman, who ended up producing the *Harry Potter* movies, those are his babies, and he's one of the most brilliant development executives I've ever been with. That guy was so accurate with his notes and descriptions. This was for an action movie that dealt with racism in the Pacific Northwest, and Jeff Dowd, who gave the Coen brothers the inspiration for the Dude, was my executive producer. We got the deal at Warners with on big note that was: "This is great, but we just want to change the antagonists. We're not crazy about them being White supremacists." We say, "Oh yeah, no problem. We can do anything. It's going to be great. We can make the same story work." You know, you just want that deal at Warner Bros. So, we all went through this process. We wondered, "Can we change the antagonist without ruining the plot?" Well, it turns out you can't, but for a year they just kept paying us tons of money. "Oh, you turned in that draft. Here's your check." Of course, I was young and I was blowing all the money as soon as I got it. I thought this was going to last forever. We kept trying different antagonists and none of them really worked, because you needed a racist antagonist, and the head of the studio, which was Bruce Berman at the time said, "I'm not going to make any movie that glorifies White supremacists." Well, they were the antagonists not the heroes, but he just didn't want to promote their agenda at all. So, finally, we get a call that this other nameless executive has solved everything and he invites us to this meeting. We all go out to Warner Bros., and he says, "Here's what we're going to do. They're going to be South African White supremacists. It'll be great!" I get home and thirty hours later I get another call saying, "Umm, the White supremacists are the antagonists in *Lethal Weapon 2* (1989)," which was coming out that that summer from Warner Bros. So, this other executive had just taken the antagonists from that movie and plopped it into ours, and of course that was sort of the end of our project. That was a huge experience for me. Studios pay you a lot of money, but they don't always make your movie.

Jose: That seems to be the consensus among writers who've toiled on both sides of the screenwriting world. You may sell a spec, but I doubt it'll ever get made.

John: At that period in time, the industry was driven a lot by spec scripts, and it was great. It established me as a solo screenwriter, and it also gave me a real perspective. But it got so crazy there that one time during Christmas I got this big check, and I called my agent and told him they didn't owe us any money. He called us back ten minutes later and said, "Merry Christmas, it's yours." They just didn't even care! It was just too much trouble to go through and figure out why. It was great in that regard, but they just didn't make the movies. After the glow is gone and after the big Warner Bros. deal was over I lose my agent, and I'm all alone out there as a writer, working on spec stuff. Then I got a call from my friend Scott Alexander, who co-wrote *Ed Wood* (1994), and he said, "Hey, my agent's assistant just got a gig as an agent at H.N. Swanson's and he is looking for clients." No one's ever done that for me; that was really amazing. I went over, he loved my scripts, and he became my first solo agent. Sandy Weinberg was his name.

Jose: So, you have a new agent and you're trying to attack the town. Are you going about it with a new strategy?

John: Well, the first specs I had didn't sell. I was trying to do comedy, but it just didn't jell. I feel at a certain point your voice as a writer starts to get clearer in your head, and I realized that I worked better on the dark end of the spectrum. Be true to who you are as a writer. I mean, you should always push yourself as a writer, but play to your strengths rather than push in a direction that you're less than capable in.

Jose: Around this time, *Return of the Living Dead III* drops into your lap, correct?

John: Sandy, my agent, calls me up one afternoon and says, "John, they're looking for a sequel for *Return of the Living Dead*." I sit up and say, "Oh, I know that movie." He says, "I know you do. You were an editor on the first one. You have to show up in two days and pitch an idea." I was thrilled, ecstatic.

Jose: I worked with both Linnea Quigley and Don Calfa on my second film, *Corpses Are Forever*, so *Return of the Living Dead* has a special place in my heart. You were an editor on that picture?

John: For the first one, I was an Assistant Editor, and our editing room was right there where they were shooting, so I ate lunch with everyone. I was there during production and I remember seeing the dailies and going, "What the hell kind of movie is this? Is this a comedy?" After a while, I left for another movie, but I came back for the cast and crew screening and I said, "Oh, my God, this is brilliant." It all came together. Everything about it, whether intentional or not on Dan O'Bannon's part, worked like gangbusters. It was that EC Comics pulpy, scary fun, and I was very proud to have my name on that movie, albeit as an editor.

Jose: And then you get the chance to take the reins and shape the next installment in a more direct way.

John: When I get this call, I already knew this world intimately. Two of the things that stuck out to me are the half-corpse that's on the table and they ask her what it's like to be dead, and she says, "It hurts." I've never seen anything like that. I've also never seen anything like the scene where James Karen and Thom Mathews are slowly dying and rigor mortis is setting in. To me those were the genius moments of the first one; it was taking zombies and going to places that I'd never seen before. Now my father had passed away fairly recently, and I was dealing with a lot of emotional stuff about letting go of someone that I loved so deeply. So, I thought *Return of the Living Dead III* would use this world where you can communicate with the zombies and that mythology that Dan invented, and I'm going to tell the story about a father and son. The father dies and the son won't let go of him, because that's what happened with me. Then I sat there for about twenty seconds and said,

"Nah, that's not going to work. It's got to be a girlfriend who dies, and a boy who won't let go of her." I put that together and went to my meeting. I told them, "This is *Romeo and Juliet*, this is *Sid & Nancy*, she's dead, he's alive."

Jose: Obviously you nail the pitch and land the gig, so how does the writing process go for you, equally as smooth?

John: One of the best experiences I've ever had in my entire career as a screenwriter was on *Return of the Living Dead III*. First of all, Trimark didn't care a whole lot about what we did; they were selling the title. Basically, I was contracted to do treatments, and once we got the green light we'd go to drafts. So, I'm working on an outline and I get a call from Brian Yuzna and he says, "Why don't you come over tonight to my house and tell me what you're doing?" So, we started this great relationship, I'd show up every night to work on it with him. The big decision was that we could let go of the tone. If I hadn't worked on it with Brian, I'd have made it far more like the first one, tone-wise, but Brian said, "No, no, why do we have to do that? Let's liberate ourselves. Let's go to the dark places. Let's not do the comedy thing." It was really Brian's incredible insight, because like it or not, the movie stands alone. It does use the mythology, and time's been very good to that movie. It's pulpy, but it holds together, and I think the thing that works best is the love story, people always gravitate toward that, but it still delivered on a genre level. I went through all the drafts, no one replaced me, and Brian says that it's the only script he's ever been involved with where he never wrote anything, and he gave me big credit for that. Now, I was collaborating constantly, but he never had to sit down and type anything. I held on to that script. It began a friendship that lasts to this day; it was a writer's dream.

Jose: That's wonderful. Give me a few examples of the collaboration process.

John: He felt we were part of a team, so he included me in everything. I kept rewriting during production. If there was a problem, I'd fix it. We both knew that story intimately. Brian came up with all the piercing stuff, and it was my job as the writer to motivate that emotionally. Brian has a great knack for the big ideas. Trimark didn't bother us much at all, there were some little notes, but I've never had an experience as a writer that pure. It was unbelievably perfect. As I writer, the one thing you dream about is that the emotional idea gets through and you connect with it. I also felt that what I wanted to do with genre movies was to add a human dimension to it, which is usually missing. That's the rainbow I've been chasing ever since; to do genre movies that have an internal human component to them that swims with the genre, instead of trying to fight it.

Jose: I'm a big fan of that film; I was blown away by it when it came out. What was the critical reception for it like?

John: Trimark dumped the movie; they didn't promote it. They didn't commit to it. It got mixed reviews at the time, but since then it has really taken hold, and it's proven to have a long-lasting effect. For me, it was one of those dream projects, and it was nice to not have that frustration of getting into a project that you're not just getting a paycheck, but you're getting a full movie at the end of it. It was just a great experience. I came from a place where I expected to be treated like a battered wife, so when you work with a director that you can team with, it's great stuff.

Jose: So, you have the amazing experience with *Return III* under your belt. How does that shake out for work?

John: There were a chunk of movies I was offered after *Return III*. They offered me *Leprechaun 2*, and my take was that a witch was capturing these children and that the leprechaun was kind of the hero, saving the kids, but the head of the studio said, "No, the leprechaun just wants his gold." That was the first time I ever quit a project, because I was so full of myself after *Return III*. In hindsight, I think they were right and I was wrong; of course that's what the leprechaun wants!

Jose: You did *Past Perfect* (1996), which was your first sci-fi film, right?

John: Yeah, I did that one for Avi Lerner, who went on to do *The Expendables* (2010). This is the classic story of a genre writer's demise. I worked on a spec called *Past Perfect*, which was basically *Minority Report* (2002) before that was a movie. I was very proud of the script; I think it was one of my better scripts. No one was biting. I changed agents and he said, "Hey, these guys want to make your movie." So, I go over and meet the director and the producers and it's fantastic. They say we have to make it on a lower budget, but that's fine, and we go over to Canada to shoot it. We go through this process of making the movie, and I'm thinking it looks a little less expensive around the edges than I'd hoped. The way it was produced I felt was not fantastic, but at the end of the day I thought it was solid. We get back and we get called into Avi Lerner's office; he's a very warm, enthusiastic guy. He says, "Your movie is too short. It's eighty-something minutes and in order to sell it to Japan it's got to be ninety-four minutes," or whatever it was. Then, he goes and puts on the TV and says, "John, I want to show you something." He shows me this stunt of a car flipping upside down and exploding. He says, "I need another ten minutes of movie, use this stunt, and write some stuff that will put this in there." He just wants shooting and stuff. So, we ended up adding this entire thread to the movie that had nothing to do with what was cool about the movie, and it was very heartbreaking because I don't think the movie works the way it should and unnecessary action derails it. It's one of those things where you want to climb up there and say, "No, that car stunt was never in there. I know it doesn't make any sense!" That's the nightmare story you always worry about, them building a sequence around a stunt they have.

Jose: Producers are known for being intrusive, but I wonder if you've had any actors approach you in regards to changing their dialog?

John: I have a lot of stories about that. *Contaminated Man* (2000) was another script that I was really proud of. We cast William Hurt, and the great thing about an actor like him is that he knows what the big story is and he also knows what his role is inside the bigger picture, so he knows what's required to tell the bigger story. Not all actors are like that. Not all actors have the ability to hold both perspectives. Another actor I was involved with didn't see that and wouldn't play the antagonist the way it was written, so the middle of the movie collapses because you don't have a real antagonist. Maybe that actor was right, but I just know on the page it worked great, and the way he played it didn't serve the bigger story. It was a big lesson, because I thought it was right on the page, but he didn't see it that way. If you're lucky enough to get a movie made, you know constantly these variables keep coming into play. Most of the time it's that the narrative and structure aren't clear enough, it's muddy, and there are problems. You can sometimes point to the page, but sometimes it's not there.

John with William Hurt on the set of *Hellgate.* **Photo courtesy of John Penney**

Jose: In this business, you never stop learning lessons.

John: At that point in my career I realized that to be satisfied it's not about the end product; it's about the process of writing. If you love that process, then you'll be happy as a screenwriter. You start attaching to outcome too much and you're always going to be disappointed on some level.

Jose: Next up for you is writing the movie version of the Desmond Bagley novel *The Enemy* (2001). Was adapting a novel trickier than you imagined?

John: Desmond Bagley was sort of a poor man's Alistair MacLean. The book was an espionage thriller, a kind of James Bond-y, post-cold war kind of thing. It had been written in the 1960s, and it was super sexist, and it was very British in that basically all the action takes place off camera and then they just sit around talking about it. I said, "No, no, you have to make this American. In American action movies you see everything." I jumped in there and worked on it, but it still felt archaic. The producers said, "John, do whatever you have to do." So, I just gender flipped the roles. The CIA agent became female and the scientist became male. That book just needed to be gender-flipped to make it modern day.

Jose: Now when do you make the decision to become a writer-director?

John: Right around that time my manager said, "You know John, you should be directing your own stuff." I had thought about it, but I had gotten so deep into my writing and I was producing, so I had never gotten cut out of the process. It was kind of a weird place for me because once I left the studios suddenly I was a bigger fish in a smaller pond. But I did feel that there was a breakdown between the finished movies and what I had on the page. In my humble opinion, *Past Perfect* and *Contaminated Man* were great scripts, and I don't think they came out the way they should have. So, when my manager said that, I decided to switch gears into directing, but only on stuff I wrote.

Jose: Your first film as writer-director was *Zyzzyx Rd* (2006)?

John: Yeah, *Zyzzyx Rd,* that was when I finally played my card. There is a wild story with this movie, I'll tell you the whole thing, and it's really a funny story. I went to meet this guy named Leo Grillo, he was looking to do a thriller, and I pitched this story about a guy who goes to the desert with his girlfriend with the body of her ex-lover in the trunk and they're going to bury the body, that's how the movie starts. He said, "I want to do that one!" I said, "Ok, but I want to direct it." He thought about it for about thirty seconds and then said, "Ok." All I had was a treatment, so I went off to write it, and had a great time writing it. Everyone responded to the script. We cast Tom Sizemore, who at the time was using, claims he wasn't, but I saw things that made me believe that he was using at the time. We also cast Katherine Heigl, and by the way, she was so nice and so accommodating and effortless to work with that I can't say enough nice things about her. She has this rep now for being difficult, and she had that rep from a previous show, so it could be that she was on her best behavior to get over some bad word of mouth, but at the time she was fantastic. I could not have made the movie without her doing her job the way she did it. In fact, when the movie wrapped, she did an interview in *Co-Ed* magazine and said that it was one of the most creative, and fulfilling experiences she'd ever had. At the end of the day, I think it all turned out great and the movie was pretty damn good. We finish the movie and we sell it internationally, but we hold back domestic rights. It was shot under the SAG low budget agreement and you have to prove it played in theaters before selling it to ancillary markets. Regent, the distributor, says, "We can help you qualify for the SAG screening," because for SAG you have to screen it to get that theatrical requirement down. They say, "We own theaters in Texas, and we'll just throw it in there for a screening and that will qualify it." I'll buy a ticket and then we can prove that it was a theatrical release, everyone does this. Then you sell it to TV, which was a whole other contract with SAG. So, a DVD of the movie goes down there, that's the last I hear of it. I'm up in Carmel, where I make wine with my brother-in-law, and I get this call from Joe Gutowski the editor, "John, have you been reading anything? This movie is blowing up all over the place. It is now considered the lowest grossing movie in U.S. box office history." I don't know what he's talking about, the movie hasn't come out. He says, "No, the cashier from the theater box office had recorded the receipts and turned them in to the national box office reporting organization." It was like $30! A website picked it up and wrote a story, and then Variety picked it up and published the story. It just becomes this great, clickable headline: The Lowest-Grossing Box Office Movie In History Made $30. *Time* magazine wrote an article called "The new *Ishtar* (1987)?" I mean this is the first movie I ever directed. It just took on this whole life of its own, and of course no one had seen the movie, but everyone starts bashing it. The Internet vitriol kicks in. I washed my hands of the whole thing, but the movie did come out, and it still is known as the lowest-grossing movie in box office history. That was my directing debut, but I stand by it. I think the movie works. People know that the "release" was for contractual reasons and was never promoted or meant to be a real release, because the truth came out in an article in Entertainment Weekly, but every once in a while it will pop up on a list. James Cameron and John Penney, one end of the spectrum to the other.

Jose: How does that weird situation affect you professionally?

John: It didn't affect me one way or the other, people working in the business knew that the film wasn't meant for a theatrical release and they knew how things worked with the low budget SAG agreement deal at the time so I kept writing. I moved on to *Hellgate*, which was an amazing, fantastic experience.

The High-Concept Massacre

Jose: Yeah, let's talk about *Hellgate*, which I was really impressed by. It's a very expansive-looking horror film in terms of scope. How did that one come about?

John: I had this idea about this guy who loses his family and he's got this weird connection to the other side. It's a similar theme to *Return III*, but done as a supernatural thriller. I pitched the story and I was hired to write and direct. Ryuhei Kitamura came on as my producer to help with the visuals. I wrote the part with William Hurt in mind, and he ended up coming on board, and then we cast Cary Elwes as the other lead. We shot the whole thing in Thailand and it was called *Shadows*. You know, when you're the director you just have to fight as hard as you can to get what you want. There were some things that we couldn't accomplish because of budget constraints, so the ending wasn't as spectacular as I'd hoped it would be, and I had some problems with the makeup effects that didn't deliver on what I wanted, but overall the movie is good. I did the film festival circuit, and we won Best Picture at the Bram Stoker International Film Festival, and in Italy we won at the Fantasy Horror Awards. That movie put me back on a

John directing Cary Elwes on the set of *Hellgate*. Photo courtesy of John Penney

good footing; in the genre world anyway. Then we got our distribution with IFC Midnight, and they say, "We don't like the title. It's too soft." So, now we have to find another title and I'm wracking my brain and can't come up with anything. I was with Brian Yuzna and he was describing what the movie was, "Yeah and then they go through this sort of hellgate and then they . . . oh, that's an idea. Hellgate!" I felt it wasn't really what the movie was about, but that's the title that IFC used to release the movie. Of course, it misleads the audience, but I stand by the movie. I'm happy with it. And I'm about to do a new movie, actually, based on a novel I wrote called *Truck Stop*, a supernatural thriller.

Jose: Oh great, so you finally decided to do some real writing like Ray instructed. How precious are you with your writing?

John: You know, when you're on set, if your characters and structure are true, then in terms of details there is going to be a give and take, and I'm ok with that. I think I can now see the clarity of narrative, so that it's monkey-proof, and if someone offers a suggestion that's not right, I can explain why that idea doesn't fall in line. The real goal is to do a great job on a script, get people interested, build the momentum, build the project, and once you do, start introducing the actors and make sure they're heading in the same direction. For me, as a writer, it's kind of sad once it's shot because you realize it's now locked in stone. I love the idea of continuing to tinker with it right up until we're shooting. It's kind of a Zen thing. You can't be attached to the outcome; you have to really enjoy the time you're spending on it.

Jose: And when you spend that time, what's your process like?

John: For me, if I can hook into a premise and see it blossom into three acts, it happens rather quickly as I hammer it out from there. I do believe in doing a beat outline and working it into a treatment. For me, if I jump into the script too soon, I lose sight of the overall flow, or I lose sight of the more important elements that I'm trying to pull through like the character's journey in the story. So, I am a big believer in being turned free by a nice treatment that is clear and makes sense. It is absolutely liberating, so I don't have to worry. I can just go along and listen to the characters talk to me, and I can have fun and relax. I never ever worry about the first draft, because no one has to see it. You put on your editing hat for the second pass. Just give yourself that freedom, like a kid throwing clay on a wheel. It may turn out to be a lopsided pot the first time, but then you can go back and shape it and get the form going. For me, outlining is about liberating yourself, not locking yourself into something. I tend to do a treatment, and then re-do it, because it's faster to write a treatment than it is to write a script.

Jose: What's the worst advice you've ever received as screenwriter?

John: The one thing that happened that probably ruined my writing the worst was Robert McKee's seminar. I was doing my movie at Warner Bros., and Jeff Dowd said, "Guys, you're going to go take this class by Robert McKee." I didn't know who the hell that was. I go there and my mind was blown, but I didn't know what to do with what he was telling me. All I saw was the pattern, and I felt I had to figure out a way of constructing my idea into this pre-formed mold. And I realized that he's not really saying that. You have to organically be able to get there; you can't use it like a checklist to just plug your idea into. I didn't know that, I thought I had this checklist that I had to address, so the writing was the worst writing I had ever done. It was so dead and dry. I realize now that it was about integrating that without consciously doing it. Knowing structure, it should come out of you naturally. It all comes down to a beginning, a middle, and an end. Any good story has those.

Jose: Any good pitch also has a solid beginning, middle, and end, so as someone who has pitched successfully, what advice would you offer to someone who is stepping into the lion's den to sell their screenplay?

John: I think what was hard for me at first was to take an idea that seemed so special and amazing and distill it into three or four sentences. But to force yourself to do that will actually help you focus the idea in a positive way. It will always show you where you're lacking. I think it's very important to do that, to be able to articulate it verbally. In those three or four sentences you have to show us who the protagonist is, who the antagonist is, and the complication. You don't have to tell the resolution, just march them up to the third act, and they can imagine how it's all going to play out, unless it's something specific. Anything that turns the story or the characters is all you mention, avoid the little details like the color of a character's tie. Then, if they're interested, they'll start asking you questions and then you can draw them in by fleshing it out. I don't like to talk a lot about what I'm writing, but I do think it's important to distill it on the page. So, unless I'm required to pitch it, I don't usually pitch stuff just to hear the sound of it.

Jose: The business has changed a lot, but what advice would you give someone who wants to join the league of movie scribes?

John: When I started, the path seemed clearer, but the odds were astronomical that you'd ever get there. The odds of ever selling something were maybe one in twenty-five people. Most of the people that I knew then, only a handful are still in the business, because it's always been difficult and competitive. Now, with the means of production in anyone's hand, you may consider making a piece that may put you in a place that is better than just having a script. Also Amazon, Apple, Netflix, all those people rushing into content is lighting a fire under the traditional studios so the opportunities are getting greater, but I think you really have to know your stuff. However, there is no substitute to just writing and writing and writing. If your writing is strong, it will find its way. It's still about storytelling, it really is. At the end of the day, if you're going to write, you just have to make sure that what's on the page is in your voice, and something interesting. I think the biggest mistake people make is to write down to the genre. There are too many of us that love it so much that we can smell a poser a mile away. Don't just say, "I'm going to take genre conventions and spin out a story." That's bullshit. It's harder to construct a screenplay than say a short story because the form is very demanding, and you still have to push to get something interesting and different, but you don't want to lose what came before you. If you can tell a story on paper, there will always be a need for that. Often times it's not about good or bad, it's if you can solve a problem. If your script comes across someone's desk and they say, "Oh we were looking for a creature movie. This is great!" That's where you get your movement, you're solving a need, and if you have the ability to do it, you will do well. My litmus test for any new writer is that I ask them to tell me what their favorite movies are. If you tell me movies that you have gone to a theater and paid to see the kind of film you want to write, then your arena of movies is one in which you can get paid. Whereas if you tell me your favorite movies are very off the beaten path and not in a world where there are people paying money to see them, then it will be much more difficult for you with your own voice, because I don't think you can fake it. You have to have a passion for the genre to write it. If you say *Jaws* was your favorite, well that movie made a shitload of money, so you have that sensibility, and that's a sign that I think you can really make a living doing it.

Doug Richardson discussing life, liberty, and the pursuit of *Die Hard* with Bruce Willis on the set of *Hostage*. Photo courtesy of Doug Richardson

Doug Richardson

Die Hard 2 (1990)
Bad Boys (1995)
Hostage (2005)

Jose: Doug, before we start talking all things Bruce Willis, let's go back to the beginning. How did you discover screenwriting?

Doug: I didn't discover screenwriting; it discovered me. I don't know what that means; it just sounded good. I was a very vanilla film nerd, loved movies, did everything I could to see movies, and wanted to make movies. I got into film school, and afterwards I realized that being in film school didn't qualify you to do anything, or get you anywhere. A lot of the directors I admired thought very highly of writers, or had written, and I thought that writing my way into the business was going to be the best way to get myself in the door as a director. It became a means to an end, and then I realized, *Oh, I like this. I really prefer to do this. This directing stuff is really kind of stupid in many ways.* That's how I started, as simple as that.

Jose: So, did that work? Did you break the doors down through writing?

Doug: I had a very interesting way into the industry. I wrote some specs like everyone else did, I got an agent, and I was sent out to do some pitches. I pitched to Robert Shapiro, who was a former president of Warner Bros., who had just left and had gotten a very nice production deal. He wanted a puppy writer at his disposal, under an old studio contract. I may have been one of the last writers to have a weekly studio screenwriting paycheck deal. There weren't any specific projects involved. I was assigned to that producer, and I was given a broom closet to work in and a parking pass. Looking back on those things I wrote then, were they even close to being a makeable movie? No. They showed a lot of gumption, and that could get you in the door then. I don't think it works now. I think you need to be more bulletproof. So, he hired me. I was the kid. He got really busy making some movies, and I got the weekly paycheck, and I got to develop whatever I wanted.

Jose: All your ideas or his?

Doug: My ideas. I mean, I had to run them by him, but he would say, "Great, go on. The studio's paying you." I went from dirt poor to making a $1,000 a week. How hard is that? I would just walk in and work with the development people. I developed a bunch of different scripts while I was there. Over the course of a couple of years that I was there, I wrote three or four scripts that I worked on various drafts of. The last one was one that he decided to hold out from the deal, because he did not want to do it at Warner Bros., he wanted to do it elsewhere. So, he held it out, as if I hadn't written it, and let my deal lapse, which allowed him to say, "Oh look, I have the this spec script. Now we're going to go make it over at New World," which I made even more money on. We were in prep on that movie for two years with four different directors, and it ended up not happening.

Jose: That happens a lot, and I know for a fact that it's the most frustrating thing about this business, especially when you feel you're so close. It's like screenwriting blue balls.

Doug: If you've never had a movie made, it's probably the most frustrating, because you're just hoping, hoping, hoping you get off the schneid. You're an unproduced screenwriter, and an unproduced screenwriter back then could make a pretty good living. Hell, I bought my first house before I ever had a movie made. I was a very well-paid unproduced screenwriter. But you always end up in that conversation with people who ask, "What do you do?" So, you tell them you're a screenwriter and they say, "Oh really, what have you written?" You tell them you haven't had anything produced, and then they ask, "Oh really, so what do you do for a living?" It was this cyclical thing, so I actually invented these lies of what I did for a living so I wouldn't be caught in that cycle. But once you get a movie, you're not that guy pretending to be a screenwriter anymore. It was very frustrating. The money kept moving, or the money kept going away. Directors kept falling out. One director got so sick in Mexico, looking for locations, he blamed the movie and quit. It was crazy. The last director on it was Abel Ferrara, and he'd never directed anything like it.

Jose: Abel's a real indie guy, what's working with him like?

Doug: It was Australian money, and we were going to be making half of it in Sydney and half of it on an island in Tahiti. Abel would come to L.A., he'd go to the Chateau Marmont, I'd meet him there and we'd talk about the script. He said, "I really feel like you know what you're doing on this, so I trust you," and then he'd leave. It got to the point where he'd call me from New York and say, "There's a production designer in L.A. You know what these sets look like, why don't you sit down and talk to him." Then they were going to build these exteriors on the island in Tahiti that we were going to be spending eight weeks on. He called me up and said, "You know what these things look like. I don't want to go to Tahiti right now. I'm a New York guy. I'd just like to sort of show up and shoot it as best I can. Can you go to Tahiti and supervise the sets?" I got my passport and got my plane ticket. Three days before I was supposed to go, the producer called and said, "The bottom fell out of the bag, there's no money. The studio's folding." It was terrible. That was the last gasp. It never got made.

Jose: Now, you're set adrift. Do you ready some pitches? Is that something you consider yourself good at?

Doug: A certain style of pitching, yes. The kind of pitching that they do now, I don't think I'm very good at. Standing up and doing three full acts and somewhat of a performance, that's kind of what they want now. They want to see storyboards and everything. I was around at the time when Dale Launer went in and famously sold *Blind Date* with, "She's blond, she's beautiful . . . just don't get her drunk." That was it, that was the pitch, and they bought it for a lot of money because he was Dale Launer and he wrote a certain kind of thing. I was very good at a certain style of pitching where they didn't want to know everything. They wanted it to be teased. They wanted a trailer. They wanted that feeling of expectation. They weren't so scared and fear-based that they had to know every tiny, little thing. Which I think is a terrible thing to put a screenwriter through, because by the time you deliver it, their expectations could be in an entirely different place and you lose the opportunity as a writer of entertaining and surprising somebody. You don't get that call from somebody saying, "Oh my God, it blew me away!" It creates bizarre expectations that go sideways. They want that pre-digest thing, and it's hard to pitch that. I found it difficult. I was back in the time when the point was to tell them the first act, hook them, and turn it into a conversation. Once it's a discussion then it's a deal, because they're now involved and they want to make it.

Jose: I had a meeting at a studio, which shall remain nameless, and they had enjoyed my script, but wanted to bounce ideas off of me. They wanted to make a movie based on the game "Twister" of all things, and they wanted me to come up with ideas for them.

Doug: Oh yeah, and not only do they want you to come pitch them a whole movie based on the "Twister" concept, but everything that you bring to the meeting belongs to them. From a development standpoint, it's very unfortunate. But there is still a world out there, if you want to risk and attach talent and find money. You can still make really interesting things.

Jose: Let's talk about the first film you actually get produced, *Die Hard 2*. I'm a big fan of that film, and I consider it one of the best sequels ever made.

Doug: *Die Hard 2* is brilliant in its invention, and Larry Gordon gets all the credit in the world for it. *Die Hard* (1988) was in theaters for only three weeks, and I was already a big fan of it, because I had never seen anything that was this kind of hyperbolic type of action. My agent calls me up and says, "Do you want to go meet Larry Gordon on this project?" I go in and meet with him, and the project is *Die Hard 2*, but here's the deal: the movie has only been in theaters three weeks and Fox didn't order sequels well in advance back then. They waited for the movie to get bigger. Larry said, "I know the studio is going to want a sequel. They're not ready to develop one yet, and even if they were, it creates all kinds of problems for me." Now it's a known fact that Larry and Joel Silver didn't like each other. Larry brought Joel in to manage the making of *Die Hard*, because he was busy with the making of *Field of Dreams* (1989) or something like that. The minute someone said, "*Die Hard 2*," Joel was involved and as Chuck Gordon said once, "My brother's had one heart attack. He doesn't need another by working with Joel again." There're a whole lot of reasons not to develop *Die Hard 2*, this is all being explained to me. So, Larry said, "It's real simple. I have this book called *58 Minutes*. I'm Larry Gordon. I have enough juice at this studio to hire a baby writer, for not a lot of money to adapt what could be a really cool action film. That's what we're going to do. I'm going to hire you to adapt and write *58 Minutes*, but you and I know we're doing *Die Hard*. By the time you get done with it, they're going to be saying, "Where's *Die Hard 2*? We need *Die Hard 2*." And if it's not the *Die Hard 2* they want to make, I might have a really great script I can make elsewhere. That was his plan. He knows all the moving parts, and I'm just slack-jawed. He was a genius. I was blown away.

The High-Concept Massacre

Jose: So, you adapt this book, which is basically the concept of *Die Hard 2*, but with a slant towards making it more John McClane-friendly?

Doug: I get hired to adapt *58 Minutes*, but I'm writing *Die Hard*. There were a few cases, in case the studio looked out, that there were a few name changes and sex changes, it was a big deal. But they were all in there, Thornburg and Holly, in different forms. Holly was his daughter on the airplane, but the dialog was easily changed. It was all real simple. Then Joe Roth became the head of Fox and I swear that the week I delivered the script his first order of business was, "We need a *Die Hard 2*." Larry said, "Funny you should ask that." It was that simple. Practically slid it across the table to him, and it was green lit like that from my first draft, which I had probably worked on for about twelve weeks. Then here's the bad news for me. Chuck Gordon took me out to lunch and gave me the "My brother's had one heart attack" line, and now that *Die Hard 2* is green lit it means that Joel is involved. On *Die Hard*, the minute he got hired, Joel's first order of business was to fire Jeb Stuart and bring in Steve de Souza. Chuck said, "That's what's going to happen. Joel's going to repeat himself. He's going to fire you and bring in Steve de Souza. My brother is not going to tangle with Joel." And that's exactly what happened.

Jose: And that effectively ended your involvement with the movie.

Doug: I mean, the Larry Gordon people kept me involved. I got a cool crew jacket and some hats. I got updated on all the production nightmares, because I was writing something else for them.

Jose: How close is the finished film to what you wrote?

Doug: I always say up until the snowmobiles and the blanks, up until it turned into a James Bond movie, it was mine. The end with the plane and the "Yippee Ki Yay" moment, that was mine. He reversed it, but that's still how they got the landing lights.

Jose: Did that burn you to be shunted aside, or had you made peace with it as just part of the game?

Doug: It's part of the game. I understood it very well by then. I had been working as a writer for a while by then. I knew. But you see your name on a one-sheet and suddenly you say, "God, I don't have to lie anymore!"

Jose: Did Bruce have any involvement with the script?

Doug: Oh no, Bruce had no involvement at that point. I didn't even know Bruce until I wrote a version of *Die Hard 3*. Everyone wrote a version of *Die Hard 3*. Everyone wrote a version of *Die Hard 4!*

Jose: Tell me about your involvement on *Die Hard: With a Vengeance* (1995) then, because I've got to be honest, it's not one of my favorites.

Doug: Andy Vajna had bought the rights from Fox, which was idiotic, one of the worst deals they ever made. Bruce was the big 800lb gorilla and he kept saying, "I don't want to make *Die Hard 3*. I do want to make *Die Hard 3*. I want to be an actor. I want to be a movie star." He was in that weird kind of place. So, we all got on a plane and flew to Ketchum and I had to pitch him my version of the movie, which was pretty weird. The only thing in *Die Hard 3* that I brought to the party was the robbing of the gold from the treasury. That was New York, but mine was the opening of the L.A. subway and it was the downtown Federal Reserve, and they were going to use the initial ride of the train to rob it. It was set in the subway, and it was not Hans Gruber's brother, it was a bunch of cops. My third act of *Die Hard 3* was the third act of *Speed*, which Fox owned.

The High-Concept Massacre

Doug Richardson, in sunglasses, on the set of *Hostage*.
Photo courtesy of Doug Richardson

Jose: That sounds like a way better movie. I'm curious how they ended up going with the version that became *With a Vengeance,* because to me it feels very low key and dour compared to the first two.

Doug: Andy Vajna would say, "I make any movie for $75 million with Bruce Willis and call it *Die Hard 3*, and I'm in profit before I roll the first frame of film." In foreign presales, that's the way his business was set. That's where he and Mario Kassar made all their money, foreign pre-sales. I don't know if they invented it, but they sure perfected it. What happened was that while I was developing my version, he'd hired John Fusco or John Fasano, I get those two mixed up, to write another version quietly, because someone told him you can't have a bake-off. It violated Writer's Guild rules, and I was publicly the guy who was writing *Die Hard 3* at that time. As I discovered years later, when Bruce and I became friends, the week I was delivering my script, someone in the other writer's agency decided to put out a release that said they were writing *Die Hard 3*, and that's how Andy got caught. Bruce had developed a few *Die*

Hards in the past, and then had said, "I changed my mind." Andy was covering his bases, his plan was to slip two *Die Hards* to Bruce and say, "Make a *Die Hard*, any *Die Hard*." Bruce had just unfortunately made *Color of Night* with Andy, and knew it was a dog, and because he knew it was a dog, when the guy comes to him and says that he says, "You know what, I'll make no *Die Hard*." Bruce backed out, and Andy was screwed. He'd spent a million bucks developing two scripts. Someone found the *Simon Says* script by Jonathan Hensleigh, and they were able to give that script to Bruce and say, "Let's turn this into *Die Hard*," and Bruce was willing to say yes to that. I think bringing McTiernan on was big, too. Bruce was happy that McTiernan was going to make the film and not Andy, so that's how that got made. The Fed Reserve stuff got fed into it eventually at one point and that was my only contribution, but I got paid.

Jose: Is that enough compensation? Obviously at that level you get paid well, but is that satisfying enough to you as writer?

Doug: When you don't get credit for the work that's on the screen, that's unsatisfying, but the work that was on the screen wasn't mine. I would have liked to have been the guy who delivered *Die Hard 3*, but once you see the big picture, you realize that you're in this funny situation with a Hungarian who is trying to cover his bases because he knows he made this dog of a film with Bruce. I think my *Die Hard*, if it had been made, I think it would have been really cool. The subplot was that it was Al Powell's last night on the job, so what Al wanted to do for his last night was get he and McClane in uniform to do an 11 p.m. to 7 a.m. shift. They weren't planning on getting in trouble, or do any bad things, it was just to remember what it was like, and that's how they get into it and it was all contained in the subway.

Jose: Damn, that sounds like a great three-quel. I'm kind of sad now that you told me how cool it could have been, but let's push on. You mentioned not doing anything "bad," which provides me with a great segue way into your next produced script, *Bad Boys*.

Doug: A guy named Lucas Foster, who has since gone on to produce a bunch of movies, was developing stuff for Don Simpson and Jerry Bruckheimer at the time. I had thrown my back out at little league practice, pitching to my nephew, and I was driving home to grab an ice pack, and I get a call from Lucas. He says, "Where are you? Are you available and can you come to Disney right now?" And I said, "If there's an ice pack waiting for me." So, I get to Bruckheimer's office. Don's not there, but Jerry is, and they lay it out for me, "We got Martin and Will, who both have hit TV shows on hiatus. We've got this hotdog shooter named Michael Bay, who shoots these great videos and commercials. We've got this window, and we've got not even half a script." Apparently, seven months earlier, this script had been a green light with Michael Bay attached, with Jon Lovitz and Dana Carvey, seriously. Bay was going to direct Lovitz and Carvey in a movie that was originally titled *Bulletproof Hearts* that George Gallo had written ten years earlier, that was this farce that involved two police officers and a witness that was a complete comedy. That was the movie they were essentially going to make. Martin and Will wanted to do an action movie. They had this farce at the center of it, two cops and witness, and that's all they had. They had this eight or nine week window that they could get out of their hiatus, and they had four weeks before they had to start photography. There is a line in the movie where Joey Pants says to the guys, "Do what you do, only faster." That's what Jerry said to me that day. I'm sure I'm not the first guy that Jerry said that to, but I'm the first guy to ever put that in a movie. That's how that adventure started.

Jose: You're given four weeks to turn a comedy into an action movie?

Doug: Four weeks. I had half a script that was written by Jim Mulholland and Michael Barrie, who were these *Tonight Show* writers, and it was just jokes. It wasn't even an action movie at that point. Lucas and I sat down and talked out what was essentially this 80s, *Miami Vice* drug thing. Michael wasn't at all adept in developing, at that time, so the process of sitting down with me and Lucas drove him out of his mind. So, he flew to Miami to start doing stuff, but it turns out the movie's not even green lit. They're not giving us the money yet. The studio wants an outline and a pitch of the movie we want to make, but I've only got so many weeks to write this crap. I remember putting together a bad outline and a pitch that we had pasted together from the pages of some of the other scripts. I think it was really confusing for the studio, and if it weren't Simpson/Bruckheimer they would have kicked us out. Jerry calls Lucas and I and says, "I think you guys need to go to Miami, because Michael's got nothing to do down there. There's no script, but we've got a crew. So, if you go there maybe you could start forming the movie." Jerry was in prep on *Crimson Tide* (1995) and *Dangerous Minds* (1995). Don is in the Canyon Ranch in Arizona, getting slim and fit and clean of all the chemicals that he was known for consuming. So, Jerry is juggling, he is a genius. I will just tell you right now. He did so many genius things on that movie that I got to see first-hand where a lot of their success comes from. Don was like the front man, full of all kinds of great ideas, but the mechanics of what those guys did was all Jerry. He's brilliant.

Jose: You don't stay in this business by being dumb, so I assume sending you to Miami, my hometown, was the right decision?

Doug: We got on a plane and flew to Miami, and start dealing with it. It was green lit. It started at $20 million, then it was $19 million, and then it was $18 million; they kept removing money. Weeks turned into days, as we rushed toward the start date. There was no shooting script, per se. I had an office and

The High-Concept Massacre

I hung up these manila envelopes with scene names on them. I had a board with a rough outline of the movie. Every day, I would write one scene; how they string together we're not sure yet, but we have kind of a rough outline, and the manila envelopes. So, instead of blue pages and green pages and whatever going out to various departments, they would come into my office and pull out one of those envelopes; that was the only way we could organize it, because it wasn't finished yet. Don, a week before production starts, shows up. We had a table read in front of him, four days before we started photography, with whomever we had there at that point. We had just gotten Tea Leoni, who was willing to do it, but the studio didn't want to cast her because she was a White girl and they thought they were making an ethnic, urban action movie. Martin had said, "I'm not doing any love scenes with any White girl," and was insisting. It was really tense. Tea was the most competent actress who was willing to say yes without having seen the full script. Anyway, we do the table read for Don and he says, "Great, it's awesome. I know what I like, and I know what I don't like." Then the re-writing began.

Jose: This is four days out from a multi-million dollar movie?

Doug: Like half the script was thrown out three days before we started shooting. So, for the first few weeks, it was write it on Monday, shoot it on Wednesday. There was a lot of that. The movie turned out really well, considering. Movies aren't supposed to be made like that. Usually movies made like that suck, but everyone had their oars in the water going in the same direction, and I credit Jerry for holding it together for many different reasons.

Jose: With a track record like Jerry's, he's got to have some magic.

Doug: He's got some magic. We'd look at dailies and Michael Bay maybe didn't get the scene at least as funny as it could have been, or whatever, and sparks would be shooting out of Don's head. Jerry would say, "There's enough there. I can fix it." The next day you'd look at the scene cut together, and it worked. He pulled it off. There's lots of magic. He's a post-production genius. He can look at scenes in dailies, or snippets of moments, and know that there's enough to build a scene and make it work. He knows what he can leave out, and he knows how to go back and fight with the studio to get the extra money to get that one single that you need.

Jose: Scripting-wise, how does a White guy write a film for two Black leads? Obviously there would be some improving from Martin and Will, but how do you shape these characters and do you worry about it ethnically at all?

Doug: It wasn't hard to do because I had Martin and Will in rehearsals for a few days. We had only half a script, so I would toss out an idea for a scene where the characters do this or that and they would start going back and forth. They were both brilliant. It was nice to see Martin's stand-up ability to kind of riff on stuff. I got some great stuff out of that. I tried to get it all down, and for a while I was the highest paid transcription person in all of Florida. There was some improv on set, but sometimes improv means that some of the scenes didn't get finished if they went off the page. There were some days where I would go to Michael in the morning and say, "They can go off the page, but if this line and this line and this line aren't in the scene, there is no next scene." Sometimes they would go off the page and the line wouldn't be there, and those are some of the things that Jerry fixed. Michael was a crazy genius shooter. I mean that movie doesn't look like it cost a total of $18 million, even for the time. It looks dynamic. He was busy really making it look great, and we were busy trying to make it work. It's funny how many people thought I was Black after *Bad Boys*, because my last name is Richardson and there's a significant number of members of the African-American race that are named Richardson.

Jose: Despite playing catch-up with the script, were there are any other issues with the making of the film, script-wise?

Doug: The only really big issue was Martin, and it was all before the movie got made. I remember being in Miami and getting calls from him saying, "I'm not doing no love scenes with no White girls, and I'm not shooting no brothers or Mexicans." I wondered why no Mexicans and he said, "Because my audience for *Martin* has a strong ethnic base of African-Americans and Hispanics and I don't want to alienate them." So, I said, "What you're asking me to do is make sure that your character only shoots White people?" But as soon as he showed up and realized that we had barely a script, a first time director, a diminishing budget, only eight weeks to shoot it and all these obstacles in front of us, he said, "Oh, ok we're all in the same boat. Let's do it." He couldn't have been cooler or better or harder working.

Jose: You don't even get story or character credit on the sequel, so were you even considered for *Bad Boys 2*?

Doug: Yes, and no. I was involved very briefly with the second one. Will and Jerry brought me in, and that was before Michael Bay had signed on. Once Michael Bay had signed on, everyone knew I was out, because he and I didn't get along. Michael doesn't like me very much.

Jose: Well, you were busy with your next project *Money Train* (1995).

Doug: They were actually prepping *Money Train* while I was doing *Bad Boys*. Same studio. *Money Train* came about because somebody told me about the actual train that picks up the money from the Kiosks in New York, and I had the movie instantly. It's *The Great Train Robbery* in the New York subway system. I wanted a director on board, and we got Tony Scott. He was involved with the development of it for a while, which was wonderful; one of the best experiences of my life. Tony was just amazing for so many different reasons.

He and I spent days in the New York subway system, seeing stuff that nobody would ever get to see and figuring out how to shoot it. Then, Jon Peters came on board, and that's one of the reasons that Tony wanted to get out. Tony had said to me, "I've made movies for Ray Stark, I've made movies for Joel Silver, and I've made movies for Don Simpson. I don't need to add Jon Peters to that list." Tony left right when I finished the script, and once Jon Peters came on board they wanted to make *White Men Can't Ride The Subway*. They had Woody and Wesley, and they loved my script, which was much grittier, but they had to service the Woody and Wesley relationship. So, I was in Miami while they were servicing the Woody and Wesley relationship. There are two scenes in *Money Train* that are direct lifts from *Bad Boys*, I'm not sure who the writer was at that point, and the movie is a lobotomy.

Jose: You weren't involved whatsoever in the production?

Doug: No, no. Columbia loved me from *Bad Boys*, and they were ruining *Money Train* at the same time. But they kept saying, "It's going to be a hit movie. No matter what, you're going to thank us. As the writer, if you hate the movie, but it's a hit movie and your name's on it, it's still going to do something for you." That was their apology. It's funny, a lot of people think that was a hit movie, but it was not. It opened up against *GoldenEye*, (1995) and I remember Columbia saying over and over again, "James Bond is dead. We're going to kill the opening." I was friends with Barbara Broccoli at the time, and I wanted to write a James Bond, and I was saying, "That's not how they see it. They think they're making the right moves." I remember the weekend it opened. I walked into one theater and *Money Train* was playing to a house that was half-full, and then I walked into another theater showing *GoldenEye* and it was packed. I was hoping for a hit, because I hated the movie.

Jose: That was Wesley and Woody's last pairing, right?

Doug: Wesley had more to do with that than *Money Train*, I think. That had to do with substance abuse and all that other stuff that comes with it.

Jose: How does a failure affect a writer's career?

Doug: It hurts you worse now. You're only as good as your last hit. Back then writers didn't actually get blamed for failures on movies. For example, everyone who had read my version of *Money Train* kept saying, "They should have made your movie." At the premiere, one of the executives, I won't say which one, came up to me and said, "I wish I had had the balls to make your movie." It would have been a really cool Tony Scott movie.

Jose: You team up with Bruce Willis again for *Hostage*, which has *Die Hard* elements. Was this from your original concept?

Doug: No. Bruce was developing this movie and it was based on this Robert Crais book. They had a script that they and Bruce really liked. David Wally, who worked for Bruce, sent me the script and said, "What do you think?" I was working a lot with Bruce, developing stuff for him, so I was really high on Bruce's list. I read it and said, "It could be really cool, but it needs style. If it doesn't have a lot of style, this kind of movie can feel stale." He said, "We might come to you for a little polish. Would you just do us that favor?" I was busy, but they were like my number one client, so if Bruce wanted me to do this polish I'll do it. I sat down with Florent, the director, and within a couple of hours of talking, we realized we both saw the same movie, and it wasn't the script that was on the page.

Jose: How different was the original material from what you guys wanted to make with *Hostage*?

Doug: He wanted to do something much darker, and so did I. The original was much more in Bruce's wheelhouse. It was much more *Die Hard*, and I

Doug Richardson and Bruce Willis having a powwow on the set of *Hostage*.
Photo courtesy of Doug Richardson

kind of wanted to make the anti-*Die Hard*. We had some talks with everybody and they said, "Sure, go try, because we have the money in place, and if it sucks, we can always fire you guys and make the movie with somebody else." So, I locked myself in a room with Florent and his artistic director and his assistant. They showed up at my house every morning at 9 a.m. and left every day at 5 p.m., and four weeks later, we had a script. It was the only time I ever wrote with somebody in the room. It was great because Florent didn't want to write the movie; he just wanted to talk about it and he would let me write. I would write and then I would give him the scenes and we'd talk about them, and we'd move on. We'd hang out and talk and it was great, we became really good friends. We finished the script, and we knew it was very different, so we gave it to Bruce to read it first. Bruce said, "Thank you, this is the movie I wanted to make." Once the 800-lb. gorilla said that, everyone else was on board.

The High-Concept Massacre

Jose: Was that it for you as far as involvement or were you on set at all seeing as you're friendly with both the lead and the director now?

Doug: I was supposed to quit. I was supposed to finish the script and go right back to another project called *True Believers*, that was going to be directed by Hideo Nakata, but there were some issues with that between MGM and Hideo. But it became clear early on with *Hostage* that Bruce and Florent, as much as they liked each other, had a hard time talking to each other. Well, Florent was afraid to talk to Bruce, let me put it that way. I was only supposed to be on set for the first three days, but it never happened. I never left. I was there every day, and then in the edit room, and through the tests.

Jose: Hideo Nakata has made some very stylish films, how was it working with him, and why didn't *True Believers* happen?

Doug: MGM put him through hell. He was the one the nicest, sweetest human beings I've ever worked with in my life. Hideo Nakata is great. I loved every second with him. We had such a cool movie we were going to make, and MGM just ran roughshod over him. He spent a year in L.A., having MGM kick him every which way. They thought I was like his puppeteer, but I was more like his translator. I was the biggest Hideo Nakata fan, but he's very shy. He would actually say, "I'm considered shy in Japan. So, now that I'm not using my first language, I'm really shy." MGM would think it was me that didn't want to screw up my script, not what Hideo wanted. In the end, MGM got stuck in this fight with Dimension over the *Amityville* remake. If you recall, there were two remakes going on at the same time, and suddenly there was only one they were going to do. Bob Weinstein said, "I want the Hideo Nakata movie," and MGM traded the movie to Dimension. We got traded like a ball player. They came up with a brilliant way to get rid of me and they fired me. Hideo said, "If Doug's not around, I'm not around." That was it. He left and went back to Japan, briefly. Then he came back and he unfortunately made the remake of his own remake and it was a terrible experience for him. He didn't want to leave L.A. without making his American movie, so he made a bad American movie. He called it his American dream.

Jose: That's terrible that the Hollywood dream factory seems to be so good at chewing up dreams sometimes.

Doug: MGM was horrible to him, and Dimension was horrible to him. Why would you hire Hideo Nakata to do weird, crazy stuff, and you don't let him do that? Part of it was racist, one of the heads of the studio admitted to that. They made him take English classes at UCLA. His English was fine. No one had a problem communicating with him. They beat the crap out of him.

Jose: I don't understand why people in those positions think they can abuse writers and directors the way they do.

Doug: Because they think they're smarter. That's all it is. They actually do think they're smarter than you, or me, or anybody else. It's as simple as that. They think, "I'm in this job to give my opinion and my opinion is more important than yours, otherwise I wouldn't have the keys to the bank vault." You talk to the old guys, who are some of the great producers and executives and they say, "Most of our job is knowing only when to step in, and the rest of the time just letting it happen." Robert Evans, crazy as he was, he knew how to let it happen and he knew when to step in. Studios actually looked at what writers and directors did as kind of magic, but now with the marketing people, they think they know what they're doing and what will sell and what's not going to sell. I can't tell you how many times I'll see a big movie, and I look at the director, and I'll say, "Who?" I've been in meetings, and I won't say which executive said this, but they said, "We want a director we can control. We want a director that we can manipulate. We don't want a director who thinks he's an artist. We'll give him the 'film by' credit, but we don't want anyone with final cut. We want them to bring it in the way we want it."

Jose: It's crazy to me that it's become such a cold, calculating thing, when those who made it, not just the fans, originally considered movies a transcendent art form.

Doug: Yeah, sort of. I remember I had a meeting at Warner Bros. It was a general meeting with the senior VP and he said to me, "I just want the high concept." I come from the school where the high concept is great, but it's all about the execution. He goes, "I've got all the execution I need. I can hire as much execution as I want." And I wanted to say, "That's why your movies suck." Yes, they're successful because they're pre-digested marketing things. I don't go to the movies to see something that's pre-digested. I want to be moved. I want to be surprised. That's kind of lost. What do all the top ten movies of this year have in common? They're not movies, they're all a marketing scheme. I had to learn the hard way on *Die Hard 4*.

Jose: You worked on *Live Free Or Die Hard* (2007)?

Doug: I got involved with *Die Hard 4*. Bruce dragged me in, kicking and screaming, and the only reason I did it was because out of my ass I came up with a part four that I wanted to see and that I thought was relevant and fun. I was the only one who wasn't cynical. I was trying to make a really good movie, and I had Bruce behind him, until *16 Blocks* went in the toilet and he needed a *Die Hard*, and the studio wanted to make the movie they always wanted to make which was the Mark Bomback script. They studio said, "We want to make *The Day After Tomorrow* (2004) with John McClane, because we know we can sell it, because we sold *The Day After Tomorrow*." They wanted that movie, but that's not what I did. I put my heart and soul in that script. I spent eight months on that script, just beating the crap out of myself. Bruce was really difficult to work with and I actually fired myself off of the movie. For me it's never a cynical endeavor. That was it for me and sequels.

Jose: *Hostage* was the last thing you've been credited on, what have you been up to since then?

Doug: Right now I'm not even writing movies. I was trying to develop television for a while. I mean for movies you either have to go spec or go independent if it's going to be interesting. Really love it, live it and kill it until it's there, that you make that kind of movie you want to make. Or you work on the inside, which is terrible. Or you work in TV, which is interesting and really cool. I would much rather watch any premium TV show, because the writing is fantastic.

Jose: Was it all worth it? Are you happy you hung on for the ride, as bumpy as it was?

Doug: Yeah. I went to a Writer's Guild meeting very early in my career and they were doing these small meetings with twenty or so writers so I got to see the old, cynical screenwriter up close, and I did not like what I saw. But I didn't lose myself; I'm still not cynical. I know a lot of people who did it and it beat them up and they became cynical. Would I do it again? Look at me, I've never had a job in my life, I've never worked for anybody. I've always been an independent contractor. For a living, I've been able to make crap up in my head. I'm very, very blessed. Could I have had a better career? Yeah, sure, it's been full of ups and downs, but I am very lucky. It's also something you'll learn with your kids. They help you see things through their eyes and not be so jaded.

Jose: It's interesting you say that, because most of the screenwriters I've met that are heavily embittered don't have kids.

Doug: An executive sat down with me one night, a friend of mine who had just gotten out of a very short and bad marriage, and he said, "Everyone I know who has kids isn't happy. I'm happy." And I said, "You may be happy, but you will never know joy."

Jose: Absolutely, well said. And how do you go about attaining joy in a screenwriting career, in terms of breaking in?

Doug: The answer is real simple: be really good at what you do and stand out. Figure out how to stand out, because it is a business filled with competitive, noisy individuals. First thing I ask new writers when they're talking about their script is, "Is it awesome?" There's no step 2 until it's really, really awesome, and it's unavoidable that it stands out and makes someone go, "Whoa!" That's all you need to do. Be awesome.

Screenwriter and former optimist, Chris Watson.
Photo courtesy of Chris Watson

Chris Watson

Zombiegeddon (2003)
Slaughter Party (2006)
Dahmer vs. Gacy (2010)

Jose: What lead you down the path to screenwriting?

Chris: I was working with David Lawson on a couple different magazines. We worked on one for the UK, and we started our own; our idea was a small *MAD* magazine-type thing. We started talking and decided to do a short film. We showed it around to people at our respective colleges, and the reaction was so positive that we got carried away and decided to write a feature; and then we got carried away and decided to make it ourselves.

Jose: It wasn't exactly out of the blue, though, because I know you and I know you're a big movie fan, so how did that love of cinema begin for you?

Chris: I grew up in that time period when HBO was kind of new, and you were getting the same movies over and over. They were looking for anything they could get; any content they could show, so you would see these really crappy movies, and I fell in love instantly with the crappy ones more than the big-budget ones. There was something special about those crappy ones. As the VHS boom came along and progressed, there was a plentiful amount of crap. I was a bit obsessive, I lived in the middle of nowhere, so that's how I spent my time. You either go hunting and play with your cousin, or you watch a lot of TV. I chose TV.

The High-Concept Massacre

Jose: Is there one film in particular that you credit with your career choice, or was it just a collection of influences that shaped your decision?

Chris: I think it was a collection of the cheesy B-movies. I remember watching stuff like *Hard to Die* (1990) on late night, and loving that, *Sorority Babes in the Slimeball Bowl-o-Rama* (1988), too. Stuff like that, I could watch over and over again, and it was mindless entertainment. Those were the types of things that seemed like they were within reach. When we did *Mob Daze* (2002), even though it doesn't feel like a Troma movie, our goal was to make a Troma movie. Even though a lot of people trash Troma movies, that was our goal. That was the high point that we wanted to get to.

Jose: It's funny because a lot of screenwriters claim they were inspired by stuff like *Chinatown*, but you and I are cut from the same cloth, because for me Full Moon was the tops, back in the day. It's interesting to me that you were inspired by the low-budget stuff, not just because it was entertaining, but it felt attainable.

Chris: And it's not like either one of us don't watch those great movies and enjoy them, but there's something different about the crappy ones. I remember going into a bank, and during a conversation it came up that I had made films, and when they asked me what I had made, I told them I made crappy movies. The guy said, "Oh, I love crappy movies." I asked him what he thought was a crappy movie, and he said *They Live* (1988). Worst comment ever because he actually put this classic, wonderful movie in the crappy category. It is cheesy, but it's great.

Jose: Well, you wade into those treacherous classic versus crappy waters by putting it all on the line for your first film *Mob Daze*. Let's talk about the process of jumping into making your own movie.

Chris: On every movie, you learn something, but *Mob Daze* was an extreme crash course in filmmaking. Of course, at that point, I was still oblivious to the difference between micro movies and reality, so shooting on video didn't seem like a big deal to me. The thing you don't ever think about, and learn the hard way, especially on your first one, is that we're shooting locally in Kansas, and we were using mostly local actors. They weren't getting paid, so they started dropping off like flies. The movie is about six college friends, then one of them dies, and the others go and get vengeance. There's one guy we hired, who's one of the main characters, we go to the airport to pick him up and he decided while he's at the airport that he doesn't want to be involved with the movie. He flies back home, and then that character either has to be written out or we replace the actor. So, we're re-casting at the last minute, and cutting out this one character all the way through, divvying up the lines, trying to make it all work even though we wrote each character with a certain personality and when you yank him out, it sort of puts everything off balance a little bit. Everyone had to memorize new lines, and of course most of them couldn't remember their lines because most of them are local, so you end up on set cutting out dialog, and jokes that were great on the page, but all of a sudden just don't work. On that one, we had a lot of problems, where the people just weren't very happy with the director and we had to shoot around all this kind of nonsense of people not showing up, or having to replace people at the last minute, or whatever the silly scenario was. Locations would pull out, once we showed up, or the owners didn't show up when they were supposed to. They weren't used to it, they weren't getting paid for it, so they didn't care about us. Those are the things you learn as the downside when it comes to making a film in Kansas. There was a lot of re-writing on that one, because of how unreliable people were. It hurt because I think that was one of the better scripts that we wrote. You watch the movie and you can't see the script in that at all. Throw on top of all that the fact that we had no budget and it's a little bit ridiculous that we attempted it.

Jose: Why did you decide to make your first film something that was seemingly action-heavy, and by genre conventions, a bit more complicated?

Chris: It was more of a college comedy, but then we threw in the mob part, which meant that guns would have to be involved. The college part brought in the gross-out comedy aspect, and then the mob part brought in violence and guns, and it was a combination that we thought would sell. Even though it wasn't your typical Troma movie, we saw it as close enough that they might have picked it up at the time. Then you throw in a few of the B-movie stars, and I think it definitely could have been a Troma product if it had been a little better made.

Jose: Most people get their script torn apart by producers or studio executives with bizarre notes, but you guys had to slash your own script and cut and paste it into some kind of shape just to get it made on your own. Was that difficult to keep the plot together, much less the character motivations and whatnot?

Chris: The re-writes that we had to do didn't hurt the plot as much as characterization. It hurt some jokes, that sort of stuff. What ended up hurting the plot was the directing. It was my first experience where you couldn't leave the set, because if you did, they would tear out pages and try to cut corners; do what they can to speed things up. They just wanted to go back and hang out, that's what it was. Every time I left the set, I'd come back and hear about that. That's something I faced a lot on my next one, *Zombiegeddon*. I had a couple of the actors ripping out pages and saying, "Ahh, we don't need this." They just wanted to get back to their hotel and go to sleep.

Jose: Wow, real professionals.

Chris: Yeah, and sadly, those were the ones that we had paid.

Jose: You directed *Zombiegeddon*, so I'm wondering why you didn't take the reins on *Mob Daze*.

Chris: At that time, and rightfully so, I thought I didn't have the experience and knowhow to do it. I tried to hire guys that were going to college for it, and we would go on a location scout, and after one scouting, they'd be too tired to do stuff, so I threw them away one by one. But we had this guy from the UK, who was willing to put his money where his mouth was and flew out. He was going to AD it first, but we just bumped him up to director, because he had a little bit of experience. It seemed like a good decision at the time, but you live and you learn.

Jose: What was post like on *Mob Daze*?

Chris: The editing took over ten years, and the guy who finally did it took like two weeks. It went from one person to another. There was a guy who kept the tapes for a long time and claimed to be in Africa. We had to send people to his door to get the tapes back. There was one guy, who I made a deal with, where I would produce his movie, in exchange for him editing mine. I produced his movie, which he never edited, and then he never edited *Mob Daze*. Eventually, it got to a guy, who put it together in two weeks, which was the most frustrating thing ever. It probably could have gotten a tiny release when it was originally made, but nowadays I couldn't do anything with it. It's sad because it's a waste of my money and time, and a waste of a lot of people's time, but it was definitely an experience.

Jose: Did you go to film school?

Chris: No, that's why I didn't want to direct it, because I felt I didn't have the experience and knowhow. I learned a lot on *Mob Daze* though, so that's why I felt comfortable directing *Zombiegeddon*.

Jose: I went to film school, but I feel I learned more making a movie than taking classes. I always tell people to skip film school and use that tuition money to make a movie, if you can convince your parents, because you learn so much by doing that.

Chris: Right, make a couple of no-budget movies and throw them away.

Jose: Let's talk about your official coming out party, *Zombiegeddon*. This is a great, big hodgepodge of micro movie. After what happened on *Mob Daze*, why make another one?

Chris: Originally, we were going to make a *Dumb and Dumber* style comedy called *American 'Tards*. We had a script, which I co-wrote with a novelist friend. It was a road trip movie, and I was going to make it, because it made sense to me. I started attaching people, you know, whoever I could get to come and do it for pocket change, and it ended up that the only people who were saying yes were the cult horror movie people. It was the weirdest thing because the script was done, and people seemed to like it, but for some reason I wasn't happy with it. I was going to make this crappy, no-budget horror movie with Ari Bavel, because he had been in a ton of these crappy, no-budget horror movies. I said, "You know what, I'll just make this $500 horror movie and bring in all these people who had agreed to do this comedy, shoot them as cameos, and put their names at the top of the box. Easy." Then it kind of expanded. People were so positive about joining up that it just grew and grew.

Jose: All still within the $500 budget?

Chris: The movie was shot for under $1,000, but then all the actor costs and crap ballooned it to about $10,000, at least. Originally it was just supposed to be Ari Bavel and some locals, but since the locals were so unreliable, as I had learned, I just started casting the parts with some B-movie people and then I got some modeling agency to come and fill in the gaps.

Chris signing DVDs of *Zombiegeddon* at an event.
Photo courtesy of Chris Watson

Jose: I started in micro movies, so I have my own tricks when it comes to casting folks, but how does casting actually work on a Chris Watson joint?

Chris: Well, I had started out with Joe Estevez and Robert Z'dar, who I worked with on *Mob Daze*. Robert I had met through a photographer, and Joe I met through Robert. Then Joe introduced me to William Smith. So, I made sure that I had parts for them in it, and I made sure that the parts were something I could shoot in a day. In those days, it was a little bit harder to get a hold of the people. They weren't all on Facebook or had e-mails readily available, or whatever, so I actually had to do some detective work to find them. People think I got them all from conventions, but I only got a couple of people from there like Edwin Neal, and I think Conrad Brooks, too. I was in the middle-of-nowhere Kansas, so you're kind of at the mercy of where you're at. Most of them were through e-mails and I always tried to tell them upfront what they were getting into.

Jose: So, you were able to get all these folks, cover their flight and hotel, and still keep it at $10,000?

Chris: Yeah, there were some that I found trick ways around. We did a convention in Cleveland, which wasn't far from me at the time, and I had a radio station set up ahead of time, so I got Conrad Brooks and Brinke Stevens' part for the film there. Tom Savini was at the convention, but couldn't remember me, so Brinke ended up intervening and got him in it. Linnea Quigley was in Kansas doing another movie, so I got really lucky and contacted her the day before she left. We benefited from having the time. We only had to fly in Lloyd Kaufman, Z'dar, Felissa Rose, and Edwin Neal. At that time, there was an airline called Vanguard, where you could get flights for around a $100. It was really nice. Coincidentally, the week after we stopped filming, they went bankrupt. I guess you can see why.

Jose: Let's talk scripting. Since you are working on it piecemeal, what kind of script did you have, or was it sort of an outline more than anything?

Chris: The script for *Zombiegeddon* was kind of rushed. People were getting upset with me because I told them it was written in three days, but, yeah, the majority of it was written in three days. I don't want to say that a lot of it was improvised, but in some cases they would forget their lines and make it up. In some cases, they would do a good job of getting the point across, but not saying the words exactly. We had one actor who had Alzheimer's, so we weren't getting anything out of him. You're relying on these actors to dance around him and get his points across in addition to getting their points across.

Jose: How did that make you feel having actors rip out pages of your script. That would piss me off to no end. That's got to be a major wound.

Chris: Honestly, I didn't know about it until after. It wasn't because of the content; it was just because they were lazy. They had no interest in continuing the film, and that was their way of cutting their hours on set.

Jose: Do you even have a complete movie by the end of all this, or are there large patches of stuff missing because of all these headaches?

Chris: Yeah, I feel with that one more than any other, we had to patch things up. The Brinke Stevens character was added to patch things up, to make things work story-wise. It helped that she stuck with the script a little better.

Jose: And now, you finally have your Troma movie.

Chris: We didn't know that at the time. We didn't know until after *Slaughter Party* was released. My first L.A. meeting was with this B-movie producer, reasonably well-known, and he offered me $500 to make *Slaughter Party*. That was kind of not what I was expecting, number-wise. I turned him down and I was so annoyed, because I had this script and I had everything ready and packaged, that I ended up offering it to Lloyd at Troma, who offered a couple times to finance something, and he offered me a whopping $1,500 to go make it. So, we went out and made *Slaughter Party*.

Jose: What are your thoughts on working for Troma?

Chris: I was actually surprised by the release they gave that movie. We had so many problems on it and it's not a very good movie, and they were still able to give it a pretty good release and it was very successful, despite the fact that it was made for a lot less than the $1,500. Other than the fact that it's a bad movie, it's easily the most successful movie I've ever had. It's still doing very well. *Slaughter Party* kind of got thrown together, and there was added pressure because it was someone else's money, and I was footing the money because we didn't get our check until we turned it in.

Jose: Who wrote this movie, because I know you worked on the script, but it's credited to Fred Rosenberg, who also directed, but is he a real guy or what?

Chris: In reality, I was one of about five writers on it. Fred was a real guy, but the credit is fake. Fred was a friend of ours, but he wasn't the director or anything. He was actually excited to have the credit on the movie, and at that time I had another script, *Dead in Love* (2009), with a big producer, so I was dumb and I thought I was going to be making bigger movies and more money, and I didn't really want that credit. It was kind of a win-win at the time. But I've had several instances where I've tried to get away from horror movies, because that's how you get pigeonholed, and I worked on a lot of dramas and comedies. Directors love to have you work on their script for free, and I was looking for credit, but I've had numerous gigs where they took full credit, because they love to have that "written and directed by" title.

Jose: You have to spill the beans on a few instances.

Chris: The first one I had it happen on was a student film, which is something you would think you'd be able to get credit on. A friend of mine needed help writing a script and she had only done two pages, but she had to shoot in two days. So, I sat down and cranked out fifteen pages, and I even ended up being cast in the film. Then when I sat down to watch it, I saw the "written and directed by" credit was all her, and I said, "Wait a second...."

Jose: You never know what some people are capable of when it comes to fame, even student film-wise.

Chris: You end up trusting people, and this is a lesson I've learned over and over again, but I keep making the same mistake. The biggest mistake you can make in filmmaking is trusting people. I have this bad habit of getting excited when a deal's going to happen, and I'll go over and say, "Hey friend, I got this great deal happening. He's got my script and he's taking it to his agency and we're doing all this stuff." Later, you'll be taking to the producer, and he'll say how everyone you've told that to has been bombarding him, wanting him to produce their movie, and all of a sudden, you start getting all these different interferences. Then, the deal falls apart, because either he ends up liking another idea better, or he gets annoyed with all the people harassing him. I had the same sort of thing happen to me recently. It's a fresh wound. I reconnected with this actor friend. He wanted me to write something for him, and he's even going to put in his own money, so it looks like it might happen. I got very excited about it, and I told a filmmaker friend of mine about it. I even told him some of my ideas, the ones I was bouncing off of; that was the main conversation. A few days later, on my birthday, I get all these text messages from the actor telling me that my friend has contacted him and that he has taken over the project, and will be writing the script for him. Obviously I was a little upset, and I confronted my filmmaker friend, and he plays a little game about it. Later on, I'm talking to the actor, and he keeps telling me that the guy is still contacting him, trying to get the deal to happen. I don't know what's happening on either end of that right now. I'm supposed to reconnect with the actor soon. It's not even that great of a gig, but for me not having anything else to do, and not being connected to that world anymore, any opportunity and is a good opportunity, especially if there's a little bit of money there.

Jose: We digressed a bit, but I think it was worth the journey. Let's get back to the state of *Zombiegeddon*, which rests on *Slaughter Party*.

Chris: The original editor was kind of heading down that same *Mob Daze* route. I always tell the story about how he was always finished and I went to his house to stay for the weekend thinking that my annoying presence would force him to finish it. Instead, he went out with his wife and had dinner and all this stuff, and didn't do any work on the movie while I was there. That was the trend of the type of editors I had working for me, until I started editing myself, unfortunately, too late. We fell into a problem with *Zombiegeddon*. Somebody who had come to help the movie, actually messed it up more and combined the audio, so we couldn't do any non-English speaking sales, so the only people I could get to take it at that point was Troma, because almost every other company required that track separation. That's where the big money was at that time in micro horror, overseas. That's where most of them made their money.

Jose: That's crazy to me. There was a market for micro stuff overseas?

Chris: Oh yeah. They're out there. An actress told me that one of mine was playing illegally on Japanese TV. They probably know they can bootleg it, and I'll be excited about it, instead of suing them. I can dream of young, beautiful Asian women watching my movies.

Jose: There you go thinking positively again, good for you! Now, at what point did you move out to L.A., because I know *Slaughter Party* was an L.A. movie, right?

Chris: Right. I wrote *Slaughter Party* right away, about a month after I moved out there, so around 2005. Obviously, it's a huge culture shock. Kansas has a lot of hillbillies, and L.A. has a lot of crack heads. You're just trading one novelty for another, but there's more to do and better weather out there. At first, *Slaughter Party* was just something to do, to learn stuff and meet people, which I thought would be a positive thing. But I was shopping around an action movie too, which still hasn't gotten made. And I had *Dead In Love*, which right off the bat had James Merendino, the director of *SLC Punk* (1998), shopping it around. There were a ton of things going on, and *Slaughter Party* was just kind of this small thing that happened out of nowhere.

Jose: You hit the town and have two specs in the main vein of the industry already, which isn't an easy feat, so how did you accomplish that?

Chris: Both of them were not the natural ways to do it. The action movie was called *Die Slow,* and we put together a lower-level *Expendables*-type cast, some of them even ended up being in the *Expendables* movies, and we started to shop it around. It never really got anywhere. We had meetings and stuff, but it was all minor. There was talking from some people who thought they could get money and then you'd never hear from them again. Some people will meet with you twenty times, and then it's slowly revealed that they have no money. I have no idea what their motivation is. I got a lot of that. But eventually a movie came out that was similar enough that it killed that project. We were going to make *Dead in Love* ourselves, because it was very no-budget friendly. It was very play-like and would be easy to do. Much like with *Zombiegeddon,* I started casting people that I wanted to work with, and one of them as James Merendino. I contacted him, and he was very nice. He seemed hesitant at first, and then he read the script and he really liked it, and went to shop it to his agency. He wanted Owen Wilson and Vince Vaughn and Jack Black for the main characters. That kept looking good and looking good, and at some point James got a divorce, and that's the last I ever heard about it. It's just one of those things where you're about to get the big deal you need and some random thing happens and kills it. That's when I decided that I want to try and make anything happen that I could and that's when *Evil Ever After* (2006) ended up happening.

Jose: Let's talk about *Evil Ever After,* directed by your friend and mine, Brad Paulson. This movie is incredibly sick and twisted and some parts are incredibly difficult to watch. Let me phrase this question as politely as I can, what the fuck were you thinking when you made this movie?

Chris: That one was a lot of fun to make, script-wise, because it was the first time I worked with someone in person, so we were able to hang out and bounce ideas off each other. We knew we had to cast certain people, so we tried to work everybody in, and figure out how to shoot them out fast. We still had that aspect, but not the degree that we had in the past. We had met Randal, so we knew we had this great character already ready for us, but casting was very difficult, because like you said the film was very insane. You had to have people that were going to go all the freaking way with you. You know, we wanted to something a little bit crazy, a little bit fairy tale, and a little bit *I Spit on Your Grave* (1978). That was all the stuff that we were interested in and we wanted to try to pull it off without a budget.

Jose: How quickly did that script come together?

Chris: We were actually writing a lot of that on set. We were filming before the script was done. The original script was extremely long. The majority of it was Brad's script and we worked on the story together. We were both cut-

Chris flanked by frequent collaborators, *Evil Ever After* co-writer and director Brad Paulson and actress Rebekah Brandes from *Slaughter Party* and *Evil Ever After*. Photo courtesy of Chris Watson

ting and rewriting on set. We even filmed a scene with Lloyd Kaufman before we had any script at all, but when he's in town you've got to take advantage of it, and we did that with everybody. With *Zombiegeddon,* we shot the majority of it within eight days, but with this one we spread it out, and it was probably too long because I think the actors got tired of us. We would shoot it when we were all available, which I think was actually a lot more fun to do.

Jose: It definitely has this fun, anything-goes attitude, despite some of the subject matter. It did look like it was a blast to make, and it comes off like Troma film, even though it isn't. Was that something you always wanted to have come across, that freewheeling aspect?

Chris: Yeah, the kind of no-holds-barred, push the limits type stuff, which is funny because both me and Brad have tamed down since doing that movie, and I don't think either of us would do that type of movie ever again. It was fun at the time but we're old. That was a "for hire" job for a UK company, which is the reason it was kind of rushed, because they gave us a timeframe.

Jose: I assume there was no dragging your feet during post?

Chris: Yeah, we didn't feel the time crunch that much until post, because we had been going at this relaxed pace, and then suddenly we have this producer who wants it spit out quick because he wants to make money off it, and you can't blame him. We definitely rushed that one in post, and I think it could have looked a little bit better than it did. We worked on a movie since then that looked a lot more polished, and just from post and not anything else. We could have definitely used a few more months on post with that one.

Jose: Then you switch gears by writing and directing a romantic comedy, of all things, called *Dead in Love*, which I consider in all sincerity your *Citizen Kane*. How soon after the madness of *Evil Ever After* did that happen?

Chris: We shot *Dead in Love* pretty soon after that one. We shot it the same way we shot *Evil Ever After*, where it was based on everyone's availability. It was a script that was sitting around for years, and it was low-budget, so it was very easily done, and it was a script I was excited about that was not horror. The obliviousness to micro movies was still there that I thought it might have a chance of doing something. It felt like it was time to do something different.

Jose: *Dead In Love* is very much a Woody Allen-type of movie, very character driven and dialog heavy, so I assume the script was better respected this time?

Chris: We put a lot of time into it, too. While we were waiting for *Mob Daze* to shoot, David and I sat down and wrote *Dead in Love*. I cranked out the first draft and he punched it up. He was trying to be a comedian at the time, so the additions were all funny stuff. We were talking about actually filming it back then, but we just didn't have the time or money.

Jose: What's the biggest lesson you learned from making *dead in Love*?

Chris: The biggest lesson I learned was that you can't get anybody to watch a straight-laced movie. It could have been the best freaking movie in the world, but nobody's going to watch it. I can't even tell you how many DVDs I sent out and then hear from those people that they haven't even watched it yet. Years later, people are saying, "Oh yeah, it's sitting on my shelf. I'll get to it eventually." We never got any reviews from any place, either. If I had put a knife with a naked girl on the cover they would have watched it.

Jose: The *Dead in Love* script was the closest you came to really blowing up with something, right?

Chris: Yeah, probably. There were so many people mentioned for roles, that I always wonder what could have been if some of those people were cast in the movie. When James was shopping it around to the bigger agents and their clients, it was very strange. They try to wine and dine you to get their clients into your movie. It's so weird to go from that to the set of *Slaughter Party* with $500 bucks in your pocket, instead of hanging out with Owen Wilson and Vince Vaughn.

Jose: So, you've been wined and dined, but you've never been signed?

Chris: No. There was talk of it, and they had me bring in demo reels and stuff. They always claimed to like them, and they were still buying me food and drinks, so I assumed that things were going well. I checked in on the project one day, and he told me he was getting a divorce, and then a week later, his contact info was bad, and I wasn't able to track him down until years later, when I returned to Kansas. I sent him a message, and I never heard back from him.

Jose: Did you ever attempt to take on the studios yourself?

Chris: I never went that route because I was looking to be another Fred Olen Ray. If I would have had a career like Fred's, I would have been very happy. I was hoping that *Dead in Love* would lead to better gigs, at least writing-wise, but when that dried up it was back to hitting the B-movie grind and pitching.

Jose: Are you good at pitching?

Chris: I think it's a mixed bag. A lot of the pitches I made in L.A. were forced, because I was so desperate. If I heard anybody wanted something I would try to throw some stupid idea at them to see if it would stick. Sometimes it did, and I would get some small-paying jobs out of some stupid idea that never should have been written, or thought of in the first place. There are so many crappy idea scripts that are so ridiculous you can smell the desperation off of them. But when it's more constructed, like the *Dead in Love* pitch which I had worked on for a while, those are much more professional. When you're working with a *Dahmer vs. Gacy*-type of idea, everyone wants to make that because they know it's simple and that shitty idea isn't out there yet. The title definitely got an instant reaction from people.

Jose: You're the king of segues. Let's talk about your super smack down movie, *Dahmer Vs Gacy*.

Chris: Andrew Rausch was the main writer on that one. Originally, I had this silly, no-budget idea of serial killers going against each other, and then the cheeseball idea of having it be Dahmer and Gacy came into my head. I don't know why those particular two; it was just names that I knew, because I don't know many of them. I called Rausch and told him my idea, and he was excited about it, so it started there. It spent a few years being shopped around to minor producers until we found someone we were happy with.

Jose: Was there much tweaking on set, or did you guys stay close to the script?

Chris: Parts of it were close. One of my personal favorite scenes is the back and forth between Ford Austin as Dahmer and Ethan Phillips, which those two guys completely improvised. I thought that was one of the best parts of the movie. Sometimes an actor doing his or her own thing is a positive. Not very often, but in this case, it worked.

Chris flanked by Dahmer and Gacy, Randal Malone and Ford Austin, in the glasses. Photo courtesy of Chris Watson

Jose: Now let's talk about the realities of not only working in Hollywood, but living here, and the difficulties inherent. You ended up moving back to Kansas after a brief time in L.A. Let's talk about what caused the move back home.

Chris: The last couple years I was in L.A., I was working two to three jobs. I was taking these small writing jobs and rushing these scripts out for people, that you'd be happy to get $250 bucks for. In reality, writing a good script takes time, and it is very evident when you rush something out, but if you're working three jobs and you have to pay rent and any other bills you have, and you're only getting paid $250 bucks for a script, you kind of have to work fast. You have to do as many of those as you can, but you have to maintain your regular day jobs, too, and I found myself staying up twenty-four hours trying to crank out scripts and keeping my jobs, and trying to find this balance with everything. I got constant low-level film work, but I still found myself unable to pay the bills. Compared to most of my friends, I was actually considered successful because I was getting paid work. But I didn't want credit on any of them, so there are a lot of movies out there that I pasted a fake name on. The big thing I learned when I was interviewing filmmakers that I consider successful, as I started writing for magazines and books, I noticed that these filmmakers, if they didn't come from some financial background that could support them, were living in poverty. You find the same thing with actors. Although they were a little bit better set up, but they complain more.

Jose: That's the incredibly frustrating truth about this career. You may have work, but it may not sustain financially.

Chris: You don't see any sort of light at the end of the tunnel. It's the same thing for filmmakers. You make a movie for say $10,000 or $500, even better. It gets out everywhere and you do all this, but instead of someone saying, "Wow, he did all this stuff with so little money, let's see what he can do with more," you go into a meeting and they offer you $250 for you to do the same thing, so they can make a little bit more money.

Jose: If you can, take me back to that moment when you finally realized you had to move back.

Chris: It was weird, because I knew it was God-awful in L.A., but at the same time it was ripping my heart having to lose it, and it wasn't so much because of the industry, but more because of the friends. The food is better there than someplace like Kansas, where you're basically exiled. The flipside of that as far as industry goes is that I feel like I've accomplished more in Kansas than I ever did in L.A. My best writing jobs came after I left L.A.

Jose: So, from your experience, it isn't crucial to live in L.A. and still be a screenwriter?

Chris: Even more so now. I'm very happy to be away from all that. When you get to the point where you're really desperate for work and you're willing to do some really stupid crap to make a buck, you know it's time to go. As far as the industry goes, I was more than ok with leaving. I miss the people, but I don't miss all the movie industry junk.

Jose: Keeping all that in mind, do you have any final words of wisdom for the future screenwriter reading this?

Chris: Yeah, don't do it.

Worm wrangler and robot romanticist, S.S. Wilson. Photo courtesy of S.S. Wilson

S. S. Wilson

Short Circuit 1 & 2 (1986 & 1988)
**batteries not included* (1987)
Tremors 1, 2, 3 & 4 (1990, 1996, 2001, 2004)

Jose: How did you come to discover show business, S.S.?

S.S.: The answer to that is that my dad pushed me into the business; the opposite of most people's experience. I was one of those kids with an 8mm camera, and my Uncle was the one who showed me how animation worked. Somewhere around the same time, I discovered Ray Harryhausen, and put together how stop-motion works. I could never sculpt or anything like that, but I did make a clay dinosaur. Ray's stuff was just so distinctive; it wasn't just a lizard with a fin glued on. But, yeah, from age ten or twelve on, I was doing movies in the back yard, that kind of thing. When I went to college in Pennsylvania, my dad came down the first week or two I was there and he asks, "What are you taking?" I say, "Well, you're a psychologist, so I signed up for pre-psych." He does this double take and says, "You've been making movies since you were twelve years old! What the hell are you doing?" That's true. He went to my advisor and said, "My kid is an idiot. He signed up for pre-psych, and we need to change his whole thing. Do you have anything about movies?" Well, way back then they didn't really, but they did have a TV production course and a rudimentary film course and something else, so they worked my Bachelors Degree around the three things that they had.

My advisor was really cool. He was an ex-CBS guy, and he got me a job at the local PBS station. I did some films for them, and I kind of never looked back. I got drafted, spent some time in the army, but I even ended up doing some animation in the army. I was really lucky, because the Vietnam War was still going. It was winding down, but they were still drafting people. They took advantage that I knew how to do this stuff so they sent me up to do some movies for the cadets at Westpoint. Then, my Commanding Officer there said, "Gee, you should go to USC. I went to USC." So, I got a letter of recommendation from my CO to go to USC, and that's how I ended up there and that's where I met Brent Maddock, my writing partner.

Jose: During this formative period, beyond Harryhausen, what else fueled your creative fire?

S.S.: The influences for me were comic books and science fiction; the hot guys in the 1950s: Robert Heinlein, Theodore Sturgeon, Burroughs. That was the stuff that I was really interested in. It was that kind of storytelling that got me excited. I loved movies, and my dad would take me to these things, like *The Beast from 20,000 Fathoms* (1953), which had a monster eating a roller coaster, the two greatest things in the world. It could not get better than that. The 1950s monster movies were a big influence, and that's what *Tremors* grew out of.

Jose: Was screenwriting something you always had in mind, or was animation more the direction you were leaning towards?

S.S.: Good question. No, I fell into it. I assumed I was going to be an animator, that's what I was shooting for. At USC I did *Recorded Live* (1975), which was my big thing and it was an animation tour de force. My friend Ron Underwood, who was a much better businessman than me and Brent, immediately got a job making these short films for schools and libraries. He had seen some of the animation stuff I had submitted to USC to get in, and my running joke is that I could have skipped USC altogether if I realized that Ron was going to hire me from the first day I was there. Ron calls me up as soon as we all graduate and says, "Hey, I'd love to put some of your animation in these low-budget movies for schools, because they don't have anything like that." We talked about it and we came up with some ideas. Brent wrote the first one we did, Ron produced it, and we made this talking dictionary movie, and it was a huge hit in that market. The company was really happy and we did quite a few of those. I ended up writing the animation sequences, because the company would come up with an idea that wasn't doable in my garage budget, so I would say, "Let me design the animation sequences that would fit into your budget." It would be like $500 a week, and I would have to figure it out. I'd say, "Ok, if I can shoot this out in three weeks, I can live and I can pay my rent." We did that for about ten years, and we did pretty well at that. I would write more and more and it got to the point where they'd say, "Steve, why don't you just write the whole thing." That was great for me because now I was getting a check for writing, too. Brent and I kept doing a spec every so often. I say we wrote seven specs, but Brent doesn't remember. We would try it every so often, and one of the specs was *Short Circuit*. The others were bad, they really were.

Jose: *Short Circuit* **is a much-beloved film. I consider it one of my all time favorites, and I'm not alone with that assessment. Where did the inspiration for that spec originate?**

S.S.: *Short Circuit* was based on one of the short films we did, and it had a stop-motion robot. Again, it was a huge hit, the kids loved the robot, and we go, "Wow, that should be our next spec." Our thinking was, since we had been unable to get an agent, unable to interest anybody in our specs, unable to get any traction in the mainstream, we were going to do it ourselves. I would do the animation, Ron would direct, and Brent and I would write it. So, we wrote the script, and of course it is not doable on any kind of budget that we could get. The big step was Brent was at a screenwriting workshop and it was the classic Hollywood thing: kid in the workshop knew a kid whose dad was a producer that was looking for any script with a robot. It was really overnight. I was at the grocery store, and keep in mind this was before cell phones, and my wife knew where I was, so she called there, and this box boy tracked me down and said, "Your wife says you need to go to MGM right now." So, I did. It was that weird. We met with David Foster at MGM, who's still out there doing stuff; he's the classic cigar-chomping producer character. He says, "I like this robot picture you guys got. I want to do it. I want to buy it from you." We called everyone we know and said, "We don't have an agent, but we need an agent, because we have no idea how to make this deal!" So, then we got an agent; our agent of twenty-five years, Nancy Roberts. That was the big sale. Front page of *Variety* and away we went.

Jose: That's amazing that it went down that way, because it's sounds so apocryphal. That experience is what every writer dreams of.

S.S.: Yeah. John Badham came on board, and we were in production in three months. It was insane. The lady who ran the screenwriting workshop said, "This will never happen again," and she was absolutely right. It was harder every time since then.

Jose: I don't write with a partner, so I'm always curious how a writing partnership works. What makes you and Brent click so that you guys can work so well together?

S.S.: Well, we were roommates first of all. He came to USC the same time I did, and the point of being at USC was to try to meet people and network. We were always trying to develop projects with one person or another, and Brent and I, for whatever reason, hit it off together writing-wise, and we never lost that. We've known big mainstream writer teams that have imploded. They just couldn't keep working with each other. Brent and I have gotten better. We used to get into screaming fights, and now we're like this old married couple, we just mumble at each other. We both tried writing separately and not done as well at it. We've come to accept what we both bring to the table. I'm kind of the story guy, and Brent is the guy who comes up with the wacky twists and turns, the unexpected lines. He's always pushing for the truly different.

Jose: Speaking of different, the design of Johnny-Five in *Short Circuit* is very unique. I've always wondered if any of those details were in your script.

S.S.: It's a funny story. We thought we were going to make this movie, so we hired an artist to help us design the robot, and we had a sheet of his designs, so the one that we liked the best we put on the front of the script. People were telling us not to do that, that it was a bad idea. We didn't care, because we couldn't get anyone to read anything. Again, we thought we could raise the money and make it ourselves. In the script, it describes him to some extent, also. But that all went out the window as soon as it became this big movie. John Badham hired Syd Mead, the futurist, and he was big in Hollywood then. He was the guy you went to for anything sci-fi and weird looking. He was really out there, and he came in with some wacky stuff. I was at one of the meetings where John got mad and said, "Damn it, this thing has to be relatable." It ended up looking a lot like our original, little sketch, but they went all over the map before they came back to that.

Jose: Whatever happened to the Johnny-Fives? Did you get to keep one of those?

S.S.: David Foster had one of the full-scale ones in his living room, because he had a house big enough for that to fit in. I never lived anywhere big enough where I could fit a Johnny-Five. They were massive. They weighed several hundred pounds. The effects guy, Eric Allard, kept them somewhere for a long, long time, and I think he put one up on eBay, a few years ago.

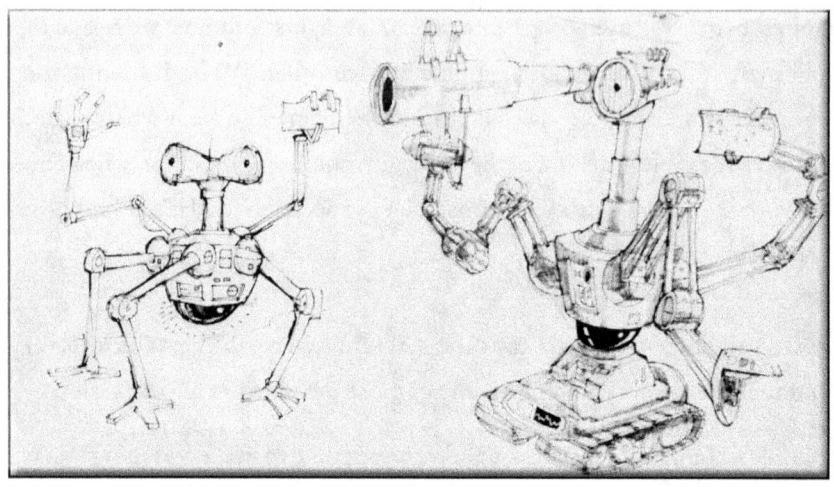

The "original, little sketch" for Johnny-Five. Photo courtesy of S.S. Wilson

Jose: So, your first script just got sold, but does it get gutted like so much spec material does nowadays?

S.S.: Half of the answer is no, the script didn't change very much. John, in retrospect, was really good to us, compared to what can happen. But first, because of the high profile of the sale, we get a call from Steven Spielberg, and he said, "Yeah, I missed out on Short Circuit, but I want you guys to come in and consider some projects that I have." We went to Amblin, which is on the Universal lot, and ended up working there almost a year, on a bunch of things. We were extremely busy, went from zero to sixty. So, Short Circuit is rolling forward, it's in pre-production, and this was our introduction to the fact that writers, for the most part, are forgotten when the movie goes into production. At that time, we were working for Matthew Robbins on *batteries not included, which was being done at Amblin, and John hires a comedy writer to punch up the script. It freaked us out. We were furious. The punchline is: no, the script changed hardly at all, and Badham kept us on to cut it. We were really lucky that our first script was with him. The biggest change, and the funniest thing, was with the character of Ben, who was just an ordinary sidekick in our version, but it became more slapstick than we intended. We get credit for the thing that freaked us out and we hated the most. Our feeling was then, and is now, that you have one fantasy thing going on in your script, if you do what we do, and everything else should be played straight. We really wanted the security guys to be scary, and our biggest argument with John was that he turned them into the Keystone Cops.

Jose: *batteries not included* had light moments, but nothing as broad as that. You mentioned you were working on that while all the *Short Circuit* stuff was happening, so let's backtrack and talk about how you landed that project.

S.S.: Brad Bird and Matthew Robbins had done a script, adapted from a story by Mick Garris. Brent and I had gone to Amblin and were asked to work on *Ghost Dad* (1990), or *Ghost Boy*, it was called at the time. That's what Steven brought us in there for. At that time, Amblin was like the coolest place in the universe to be in the movie business. It was the best part of our lives. It was awesome. Steven ran everything the way I fantasize Walt Disney ran everything. He was in every meeting, on every decision, and everything going through Amblin. Steven came over and said, "Matthew's script is too big. They're in pre-production, he's never going to be able to re-write this stuff, and Brad is off doing something else already." So, we met with them and our job became shortening the script, and as a result of that we started coming up with ideas; you can't help it, you're a writer. I can't even begin to tell you what is our stuff per se, because there's a lot of stuff from Steven in there, a lot of stuff from their first draft, and Mick's basic story. It was a pure collaboration, on a racing train. The pressure on us was to get the pages out, take out gags, and figure stuff out, but Matthew and Brad laid all the groundwork.

The High-Concept Massacre

Jose: After working on two movies with robots, were you worried about being pigeonholed as the robot guys?

S.S.: We did think it was funny that that happened. But our agent was more concerned that we said yes to *Ghost Boy*. Steven had said, "I've got this script called *Ghost Boy*, and I'd like you guys to consider re-writing it." We went to Nancy and told her this and she says, "You just sold a spec screenplay for a lot of money that instantly went into production with a big director. You can't do a re-writer. Big time writers don't do re-writes." Then we said, "But it's Steven Spielberg!" It really was an issue, believe it or not, but now it's completely changed. You can't do anything *but* re-writes and re-makes. It is an odd thing. Part of what has hurt Brent and I lately is that we keep coming up with original ideas, and they're a really hard sell. A few years ago we were at Fox pitching an idea that I deeply love that I eventually turned into a book called "Fraidy Cats." The guy said to us, "Oh God, I love this!" and we were relieved, it was a breath of fresh air. "Can't touch it," he says. "It's not based on anything, and I'll never get this past marketing." That was what he said. Great idea, can't touch it.

Jose: Let's talk *Short Circuit 2*, which came about a year or so after **batteries not included*. Obviously, the first one was a big hit, and a sequel becomes imminent. How did the conversation for that begin?

S.S.: I guess, in a way, it was the beginning of that thinking where you just keep making them until you've killed them. We had a million ideas we left out of the first one, so we were happy to come back and do it. Our agent Nancy wasn't happy. Back then you didn't write sequels. Hacks wrote sequels. What helped there was that John Badham wanted to come back, he was willing to do it, and they wouldn't wait for him. He's a busy guy. He was at the level where you got to schedule things, and they wouldn't do it. I don't know why they wanted to go so fast, but they did.

S.S. Wilson, in glasses, flanking Johnny-Five with co-writer Brent Maddock on left, with Producer David Foster all smiles. Photo courtesy of S.S. Wilson

Jose: They always seem to be in a hurry, even if it's to their detriment.

S.S.: Yeah, once they make up their mind, suddenly they have to be in a hurry.

Jose: Was it tricky to concoct a story for the second one?

S.S.: Not for us. I'm pretty sure it was David Foster who said, "Oh, Number Five just has to go to the big city. It's great! He goes to New York!" Brent and I saw endless possibilities there so we said, "Sure." It wasn't hard to come up with the basic story, but we never nailed the script for that movie, and we didn't have time. We were the ones who wanted to cut and shorten it, because we had learned from Badham, but for whatever reason director Kenneth Johnson didn't want to cut anything, and once the director is calling the shots, no one is listening to the writer.

Jose: Did you guys work well with Kenneth Johnson?

S.S.: Kenny came out of TV, like John Badham, and I never quite understood him. He would say weird things like, "Don't worry about this, I shoot fifty seconds a page." Maybe he does, I don't know, but the first cut was like two and a half hours long. *Short Circuit 2* sort of hangs together, but there was some drastic editing to make the story work. It was a pretty rocky production. People weren't getting along. Kenny was mad that they made him shoot Toronto for New York, because he really wanted to work in New York. He was furious. He made me go into the script and change all the location slug lines to the real streets in Toronto. I will say Kenny nailed the beating up of Johnny-Five scene; it is hard to watch, but it's awesome. Kenny went for it.

Jose: Was it always the plan to use Ben as the hero, because it's an interesting direction to take to use the sidekick as the lead?

S.S.: You make a good point, but yeah, it was always Ben as the hero, and I don't know what all the internal discussions were, when that decisions was made, or by whom. By then we loved the character and we loved writing for him. He's so un-PC now, and there was a huge discussion about that while we were working on the remake. This is at Dimension, where it was set up, and you'd have thought they would have wanted to be edgy, but they were really scared about it. One idea was to start on the farm where they took him at the end, but it went by the wayside for some reason. The heart of it for us was the world accepting that he is alive. That was the key to us as writers.

Jose: Why no part three?

S.S.: It kept coming up over the years. David always wanted to do it. Every five years, David would call up and say, "What about part three?" We would have loved to do a part three. There was even talk of a TV series, because it seemed like a character that you could do that with.

Jose: Let's touch on the remake, since you've brought it up. How do you remake your own movie?

S.S.: It was a great challenge. We really enjoyed getting into it. We butted heads with Dimension over the central issue, which was that they wanted to have a kid be the star, and we thought that was insane, frankly. They go, "We've had a lot of success with *Spy Kids* (2001)." Of course that's not a correct comparison. I told them, "If you put Johnny-Five on a poster, you cannot keep kids out of the theater. Your problem is teenagers, that's what you should be worried about." We couldn't win that argument and we actually did a draft for them that had a kid in it that we did not like and they did not like, because it fights with Johnny-Five. He's the lead, and you can't have this kid in there also being naive. Then, we did another draft, and we told them, "Here is what we think the movie should be," and it was really fun re-inventing the movie with all the technology we have now. But they didn't like either draft, and I've lost track of it now because they went to other writers for some time. This was years ago. But as far as I know, it isn't happening.

Jose: One film series of yours that had multiple sequels and allowed you to have a firmer grip on is the *Tremors* series. I consider *Tremors* a masterwork, so tell me about its inception.

S.S.: *Tremors* came from our frustration of realizing that writers are not part of the filmmaking process after they write the script, because we came out of this world where we had done everything and we felt we had a lot to say about how things should be done. We would complain to Nancy periodically, and she would say, "You're not talking about writing; you're talking about producing. So, you guys need to think about a project that you're going to control and not just hand off." That's what *Tremors* was. First we pitched it all over town, and couldn't sell it. We couldn't convince people of what it was, but Brent and I are bad pitchers anyway. Then we wrote a twenty-five-page treatment, which explained in great detail what it was, but

The High-Concept Massacre

we still couldn't sell it, so we broke down and decided to just spec the script. We did seven drafts, and we had worked very closely with Ron Underwood, who had remained in the short film world after pulling out of *Short Circuit*. When it became apparent that *Short Circuit* was going to sell, Ron called us up and said, "I'm pulling out. You won't be able to sell it with me attached." So, he pulled out and Badham moved in. Of course, he was right. We didn't understand any of this. This time around with *Tremors* we said, "It ain't happening, because Ron hired us to do our first movies." So, we were going to give this to Ron to direct. It was an additional rock to get up the hill for Nancy, because she had to figure out how to position Ron, but by then we were known and we could get the right meetings.

Jose: You had some clout to help open the doors.

S.S.: Well, she involved Gale Anne Hurd early on, because she knew we were going to need support, because even the really smart studio people don't really know filmmaking. Nancy really produced it, in the sense of orchestrating all of this, and the next *Tremors* films as well. Eventually she got credit, but in this case she was just the agent. Gale looked at Ron's films and went to universal and said, "Look, this guy can direct. Trust me, it's okay." She was working on *The Abyss* (1989) at the time, with Jim Cameron, and she was involved at key moments all the way through the process as our Godmother. Then the other key piece, in order for us to control all of this, was getting support at Universal and that came with Jim Jacks. He was the kind of executive that no longer exists, somebody who would find cool material and go to their bosses and say, "This would make a good movie." Now, the marketing department makes all the decisions. Jim got it immediately, "Oh great, 1950s monster movie with a twist. It's different. Let's do this!" He was notorious for screaming at other executives, "You idiots, make this movie!" So, we had his unwavering support, and that was great, because it was a weird movie, it was this odd blend. Even in script form it wasn't clear if it was really scary or really funny. Eventually we got a low budget, and off we went.

Jose: Any studio tampering with the script?

S.S.: Once we nailed the comedy thing, which was hard, the script never changed, other than being adjusted up and down for budget. Those first seven drafts were about figuring out who Val and Earl were and how funny the townsfolk were, and it went from more funny to less funny. We found that gags at the expense of the monsters didn't play. We were applying our rule. We have underground monsters. That's really weird. Everything else has to be as real as possible. I swear, every once in a while movies come together like a Las Vegas poker run or something. That was a movie where everything fell in line.

S.S. Wilson with gun nut Burt Gummer himself, Michael Gross.
Photo courtesy of S.S. Wilson

Jose: Tell me how Michael Gross, who became synonymous with the series as Burt Gummer, got on to the picture.

S.S.: The cast was great. Things that we thought were crazy at the time, were perfect, like them telling us, "You have to read Michael Gross for Burt." They said, "A big TV star, that helps you!" And I said, "Yes, but he's *Family Ties*, he's not a survivalist." He was on his last season of *Family Ties*, and Michael was surprised; he couldn't understand why he was being offered this part either. He went from shooting the last episode of the show right to our set, within hours. He is a wonderful actor, and it is funny that he became the centerpiece of that franchise.

Jose: What about the rest of the gang?

S.S.: Universal said yes, but now they're doing everything they can to shore this movie up, which is their job. They wanted to get some names into it, and Kevin Bacon came up as available, after a lot of weird things were considered, and Ron was sent off to convince Kevin to do it. Thank God Kevin said yes, because that was a key thing. I mean he couldn't have been better to us, or more professional, but you know Kevin didn't like the movie for a long time. He did not like it. He's brilliant in the movie, but it's taken him decades to realize it.

Jose: Similar to my question on Johnny-Five, did you guys describe the Graboids at all in the script, or did you keep it vague?

S.S.: We did, but it was very limited. The spines on the sides are there, and there's a line in there something to the effect of, "The mouth opens like a grotesque flower." That's pretty much it, and with that tiny phrase Tom Woodruff Jr. and Alec Gillis came up with the Graboid. The first drawing they held up was pretty much the monster. I remember saying, "Oh my God, there it is!"

Jose: How does the movie fair when it meets the big, bad world?

S.S.: It did not do great, it did okay. I think it broke even, technically. The studio was disappointed. They knew from the beginning that it was a marketing difficulty, and unlike today when marketing makes all the decisions before a movie gets green lit, back then the studio green lit the movie and somewhere along the process they said, "Hey marketing, here's this movie coming along, you better figure something out." In post, we would go to marketing meetings, and they would say, "This is really weird. It's kind of funny and kind of scary. What do we do?" They felt that they never got it right. But it has been blessed for its whole existence, this movie.

Jose: It's got four sequels now, three of which you were involved with, and a TV series, so I would say it went on to some kind of success.

S.S.: That was the beginning of the VHS revolution, and like other studios, Universal created a division. I don't remember how many years later *Tremors 2* was. We hadn't been thinking about it at all, we were just kind of sad. We knew the studio viewed it as flop, but we liked it, and it was huge fun to make. Then one day, we get this call out of the blue from the video division, "We've really got to have a *Tremors* sequel. You wouldn't believe what *Tremors* is doing on video!"

Jose: One element that separates the *Tremors* franchise from other monster films is the idea that the Graboids mutate in each picture, so where did that idea come from?

S.S.: That came specifically from knowledge of 1950s sci-fi, but we were struggling with it, because the video division was really bugging us and they were saying, "We're going to make this whether you guys work on it or not." As a kid I always had the idea that a lot of little things could be creepy, and it's not a totally original idea, but for some reason it just popped into my head,

"What if the Graboids just fragmented into something small?" We kept kicking that around and around, and we started involving Tom and Alec, because they are just wonderful creators of things, and they work the way we do, they work from reality. The Ass Blasters from *Tremors 3* were a pure Tom and Alec idea, and there is a bug that does exactly what the Ass Blaster does. It's called the Bombardier beetle, and it mixes chemicals in its butt, and it makes an explosion from its butt. It makes a sound like a firecracker.

Jose: Did you originally intend to have Val and Earl together again?

S.S.: The original draft is Kevin and Fred, because it didn't occur to us that he wouldn't do it. So, we went and begged Kevin to be in the movie, and he never ever gave us the slightest hint that he was unhappy, but all he ever said to us was, "You know guys, I'm really taking a different course with my career right now." Which he did, he started doing all these weird character roles. He was concerned about being a leading man. I mean the studio thought it was a flop, and that was very painful for him. He'd also had a couple of other movies not do great, and he was in a very dark place in his career. But he said to us very politely, "Well guys, you know I appreciate that you really want me to do this, but when people talk to me about that movie they never say 'you're so great' they say 'those worms are so cool.'" Which is ironic, because he is so great and the worms only work because he is so committed to that character. I mean, as every actor does, Kevin worried all the way through the movie. I remember him saying often, "I never know how scared to be. Am I most scared now or am I only halfway scared? Where's the point where I'm really, really scared?" It was really bugging him.

Jose: *Tremors 2* was your first time directing a feature, so were you precious with your material, or did you put on your director hat and treat it like a doormat like some directors?

S.S.: Oh no, it was utterly delightful directing my own script. The buck stops with you, so if you screw it up, you screw it up yourself. It was great fun, and we always had the best teams all the way through every *Tremors* experience. It was hard work, and we never got paid anything more than minimum because everything went toward the movie, so we weren't making a fortune, but we were doing what we had set out to do, making movies the way we used to.

Jose: *Tremors 2* does well enough that you guys get to go back to perfection with *Tremors 3*.

S.S.: Oh, yes. In those days, it took a long time to decide whether you'd been successful or not, because video is not a first weekend business, it's a word of mouth business. They do very little advertising in that world. They did do advertising for *Tremors 2*, but they didn't do any for three or four. Whenever they decided that it was working, and they did their numbers, they said to us, "We've got to have *Tremors 3*." So, yeah, we loved doing these things. I had directed *Tremors 2*, so Brent directed *Tremors 3*. One of the negatives that we heard about the sequel was that audiences missed the townsfolk, so it was an easy decision to bring it back to Perfection. It was great, because everybody was still available and wanted to do it. And it seemed natural that Burt, whether he got rich or not from the monster stuff, he's a survivalist so he's going to come back to his hometown. We tried really hard to make all the rules work. It was very important to us, because we had a fan base that we were hearing from all the time. We had lists and piles of gags that we hadn't used so it was great fun to sit and brainstorm. And when Tom and Alec said, "What about an exploding butt monster?" We said, "Oh absolutely, we've got to have that."

Jose: And you were able to retro-evolve them one more time with *Tremors 4*, which was a prequel, but also a western.

S.S.: The funny thing about *Tremors 4* is that Universal said, "Three is going to be the right number. We understand our market very well, and this will close the loop." So, we asked, "Ok, so we can finish this whole thing up and say this is the complete lifecycle of the monsters?" They responded, "Oh, absolutely. We're never going to do another one." *Tremors 3* had not been out for more than a few months when they said to us, "We've got to have *Tremors 4! Right now!*" We said, "Guys, you're screwing us up, we're trying to serve the fans here."

Jose: What about the TV series, when did that come into play?

S.S.: That was at the same time as part four, almost. Sci-Fi Channel came to us and asked if we wanted to put together a series, and we had talked about it years ago, but we couldn't interest anybody despite the fact that we pitched it all over town. We said yes to Sci-Fi, and they gave us a twelve-episode buy, or whatever it was, which was cool, and we plunged into that. Sci-Fi Channel is owned by Universal at this point, and Universal home video comes and says, "We need *Tremors 4* and we won't wait for you to finish the series." That was odd, we thought, and it put tremendous pressure on everyone. We did the story for four and we hired a really great guy named Scott Buck to write the script, while we're in production on the series, which is the most insane kind of production that there is. It is just relentlessly non-stop. We were working with writers, trying to get them up to speed on how the *Tremors* comedy works, and we had good people, but they come into *Tremors* thinking it's a comedy, so there was a huge learning curve, and Brent and I were frantically re-writing people's scripts. They were upset, of course, because they couldn't see what was wrong. *Tremors* isn't a comedy, there was a fine line there, but they got it eventually, and by the end we didn't have to re-write anyone, but we were losing control in other ways. We got pushed off of the show because we were being perfectionists and doing what TV executives are supposed to do, but Sci-Fi was on the fence about whether they were going to pick it up for season two, and ultimately they didn't pick it. But I actually left before the end, because Universal would not wait three weeks for the show to finish shooting and they pulled Michael out of the show and we went into production on *Tremors 4* before the show even finished. Brent and Nancy were there alone trying to keep the ship together.

Jose: What prompted that decision to make it a prequel?

S.S.: I like to say that it was my idea. Universal stuck us with this problem, because we had closed the loop. Yeah, we could cheat and maybe come up with a new monster, but it would be weird. I said, sort of offhandedly, to one of the executives, "What about something completely crazy like re-telling the story as a Western?" They said, "I don't care. As long as it says *Tremors 4.*" That's how that world works. One of the backhanded compliments we got from the video division early on was, "We could sell an empty box called *Tremors*." I'm not sure that's a good thing, but that's what they think. So, when they said yes to the Western, we were all excited.

Jose: *Tremors 4* is the end of an era as far as your involvement with the franchise, but you got to direct it, so I hope it was at least a fond farewell.

S.S.: It was super fun to do a Western. It was very hard, of course, and everything was so much more complicated. The weather was ghastly, raining all the time. There are fans that liked the movie a lot, but there are others that wondered where Burt went, but Michael had a ball because he got to play this slightly effeminate, strange character. Also, in spite of what we had said, we really felt we had to deliver something new monster-wise. We did say that Ass Blasters lay eggs, so to be true to that concept, maybe there could be baby Graboids and we can squeeze those in, and that's what we did. It was sort of cheating, but that was the new monster. In the end, we tried to make it all fit geologically, story-wise, and character-wise. But there is a big mistake in either *Tremors* 2 or 3, I don't remember which one that the fans caught us on. Somebody says the number of Shriekers that come out of a Graboid and then it's completely wrong in the next one. We completely forgot what it was.

Jose: Let's briefly touch on what happened with *Tremors 5*, which I have to say I didn't actually hate. How did that film happen without you and Brent?

S.S.: I hated it. You know, I actually like the monsters, though I thought the idea that the tentacles separate from the creatures was ridiculous. It breaks all the rules; all the rules that we established are broken in *Tremors 5*, without exception. The comedy is slapstick, the deaths don't mean anything; I mean people die and you don't even know who they are. There is no sense of reality. I can go on and on.

Jose: Speaking of stuff people hated, let's backtrack a bit, get off the *Tremors* train, and talk about your involvement with the bizarre Will Smith and Kevin Kline pairing *Wild Wild West* (1999).

S.S.: Some producers who knew us came to us and said, "We've got the rights to the *Wild Wild West* TV show, and we'd like you guys to pitch a version." That's a show that I loved as a kid. But they had some rules like no atom bombs, no dirigibles, and no hot air balloons; weird rules like that. We re-watched the show, we got in touch with the fan club that still existed, I mean I knew the show pretty well, but we got really in touch with it, and we did a draft that we really liked. It didn't go anywhere, I didn't hear about it and forgot it. They never even triggered our next draft, because we were contracted for two drafts, and within the Writer's Guild, they have to trigger certain things within a certain amount of time. We went off to do other stuff, maybe another *Tremors* thing, but then, out of the blue, they call and say, "Hey, it might go forward. We need your other draft now." We were busy,

S.S. Wilson bids adieu to the Graboid on *Tremors 4*. **Photo courtesy of S.S. Wilson**

but we caught up with what was going on and we turned it in. Somewhere along that process, Barry Sonnenfeld, Will Smith, and Kevin Kline said yes, and now it was a giant movie. The two producers who brought us on got pushed aside because Warner Bros. wanted a big producer to go with their big movie, and they brought in Jon Peters. I was out of town doing something, and Brent goes to this first meeting with Jon, and it was just so comical because he did not know the show and he did not know it was a Western. He said to Brent, "You keep talking about horses. Why are you talking about horses all the time?" Brent would say, "Because it's the 1880s and it's the Wild West." Jon replies, "Oh God, that's boring! No motorcycles or anything in this thing?" Of course there wasn't, not then, and that's why the Nitro-Cycle is in there. Also, our original script had this giant walking spider in it, because I love Steampunk stuff, and I knew where CG was at the time and they could just nail this thing in a way you couldn't back in the day, but Peters' people hated it immediately. They said, "It has to be a stealth bomber." And we said, "You don't mean a real stealth bomber, do you?" "Oh yeah,"

The High-Concept Massacre

they said. "You ever seen a stealth bomber? They're scary." They wouldn't budge on this, and we said, "Can we at least say that it had rivets and stuff on it?" And they said, "Well maybe, as long as it's a stealth bomber." So, the next few drafts had this giant flying machine in it, and Brent and I really pushed it; we kept describing gears and things on it so it was really Steampunk. That was the draft that Barry Sonnenfeld said yes to. Then, late in the process, there was a giant meeting with everyone and Brent and I are in the back of the room. It's a big movie, so everybody wants to be present when the big decisions are made, so there are executives we'd never heard of in this room; there are like thirty people in this room. Eventually, Sonnenfeld says, "You know, I really don't like this big flying machine thing. I don't want the whole end of my movie to be up in the air. I'm going to be on a blue screen stage for weeks, and I'm not going to know where I am." Finally, I raise my hand and say, "Mister Sonnenfeld, there was a version with a giant walking machine." And he says, "Now that's interesting, I'd like to see that." Then another executive stands up, true story, and says, "I really support that idea, Mister Sonnenfeld." I don't know who the guy was, but the spider was back in. We handed in our last draft, and never heard from anybody ever again. I was told that there were nine writers after that.

Jose: That movie always played like it was such a bizarre nut to crack. Did the casting inform any of your re-writing when you had your hands on it?

S.S.: In my opinion the other writers always struggled with a key ingredient. Will Smith is an absolutely brilliant actor, and at the time I totally respected the idea that we were going to cast a Black actor and we weren't going to say anything. The problem was, in my opinion, Will Smith is the funny guy. We had written *Wild Wild West* the way it was, and the Will Smith character was not funny, but the Kevin Kline character was. You know, every draft we wrote we thought it would be so cool if they got Kevin Kline for this, we never said this to anybody, and son of a gun we almost fell over when they got Kevin to play Artemus. It couldn't be better. And I can't even say that we thought at the time that it was going to be bad for Will to not be funny, but when it got to previews it was bad. That's when all the frantic re-writing and re-shooting began. The funny thing, and even funnier than all of the other stories, is that it is widely viewed as this monster flop and it wasn't. It did ok. It wasn't a monster flop like some other Hollywood movies, but at the time Brent and I caught a lot of flak for that because we got credit on it. We were surprised we got credit, other than the giant spider, there's probably not more than ten lines of dialog from our script in that movie. I mean, it's okay, it doesn't exactly work and it's overblown and confusing, but it's not the show. That made us mad. We always thought it was disingenuous and insulting to take a property and just take its name, which is how the marketing world works. And if *Tremors 5* does super well, then it will prove the point even more.

Jose: Did you guys ever work on a version of *Tremors 5*?

S.S.: They were going to make *Tremors 4* and *5* back to back. Everything changed. They used to make them really fast, so they said, "Yes, write *Tremors 5* right now!" So, we wrote it with Burt in Australia, and it was supposed to be a handoff movie. It was going to be Burt handing the reins over to a young guy. Our version included some of the elements that appear in *Tremors 5*, not many. They did start with our script, but they hired John Whelpley, who wrote *Tremors 3*, to revise it and to make it fit their budget. It was a much lower-budget than the ones we worked on. You know, for the longest time, I tried to make my peace with it. I've had fans tell me for so long, "Please, why don't you make *Tremors 5*?" They were so hungry for it. So, when I watched it I said, "Ok, ok, I'm fifteen years old and I've seen all the *Tremors* movies, and there hasn't been one since I was five years old. I'm going to watch this movie and I'm going to give it every break possible, and I'm going to enjoy whatever I enjoy of it," but no. I've had people e-mail me, hardcore fans, saying, "I could not watch this, it was so terrible. I'm so horrified and I feel so bad for you."

Jose: Why do you think writers get the short end of the stick all the time?

S.S.: It goes back to the beginning of Hollywood. It goes back to some very smart business guys who ran the studios, way back in the day, who figured out they needed to buy the rights to things outright. This does not happen anywhere else in the writing universe. You write a play, you own it, and they can't change a word of your play unless you agree to it. Hollywood said, "No, we have a better idea, we'll just buy all the rights forever." That's the beginning of what happened to writing in Hollywood whenever those bigwigs, whoever they were, said, "What we need to do is buy the rights to this stuff forever and never have writers bother us again." That was a deliberate thing and it got set in stone and it's never changed. It's sad that the writer has become just a step in the process. They sense that they need writers, but they don't really like them around, and particularly don't like them around during production, bugging them about stuff, and that's still true. Some directors are open to writers and understand that they need writers, like John Badham, and even though he changed *Short Circuit* in ways that we didn't like at the time, in retrospect he was really respectful compared to other people. There are probably three or four people who have ever had the power to fight back because they want the material so badly that they will bend their rules a little bit. There are other rules they won't bend. They don't want you to share in the profits ever, and the Writer's Guild has had to fight tooth and nail to get half a cent or whatever we get on DVDs and that kind of stuff. It's a business, as everyone says over and over.

Jose: With that in mind, and looking back on a career that is filled with wonderful, memorable films, what have you learned that you can pass on to the next generation of screenwriters?

S.S.: Part of it is the old Ray Bradbury joke, "You've got bad screenplays to write, start writing them." Also, don't get hung up on one script. Brent and I did that a few times, probably clung to things more than we should. Just write one, hand it out, get notes, and listen to the notes. If three people tell you the same thing about your script, no matter how horrible it is to hear, it's probably true. That's a rule we apply to scripts as a whole, and to gags. If you're going to be a screenwriter, you've got to be able to take notes. Don't reject notes. You may disagree with their notes, but look behind the note. They say they hate a character, but you love it, so look behind the note. Why are they saying what they're saying? Be true to your vision, but be open to notes. Also, write a lot. More than anything, you learn from writing, and in Hollywood writing is re-writing. You've got to be open to the process that is filmmaking to be a film writer. It's funny, I thought I wanted to be an animator; I did not seek out writing or directing. The biggest advice is to write, because the worst thing that can happen is that you find out you don't want to do it.

Fade Out: A Re-appraisal of the Typist

"The wise screen writer is he who wears his second-best suit, artistically speaking, and doesn't take things too much to heart. He should have a touch of cynicism, but only a touch. The complete cynic is as useless to Hollywood as he is to himself. He should do the best he can without straining at it. He should be scrupulously honest about his work, but he should not expect scrupulous honesty in return. He won't get it. And when he has had enough, he should say goodbye with a smile, because for all he knows he may want to go back."

~Raymond Chandler

The High-Concept Massacre

I know why I write.

I know why I love movies and making movies.

The answer is the same for each: because I have to. I am compelled to. I can't think of anything I would rather do, or that would bring me as much joy. Yes, there is quite a bit of heartache attached to it all, but in the end it's worth it.

The funny thing is, almost every screenwriter I interviewed for this book said the exact same thing. There was no option left to them but to write. There was no Plan B, because Plan B meant death, and they weren't ready to give up the fight. And there is no end to that fight, whether you wrote *batteries not included or Zombiegeddon.

Much advice is given in these pages, but the one that should stick for good is: just write. Yes, that spec may never sell. I've written a hundred scripts that never will. To be a screenwriter, in my opinion, is to first be a writer. To be a writer, you must write, and not for practice, but for love. You must be passionately enthralled and overcome by the act of opening your mind, letting the universe pour in nonsense, and letting your fingers batter the keys. Without that all-encompassing lust, there can never truly be writing.

Sometimes I've felt like a typist, just bashing out bullshit for someone else to turn into a movie. I've felt no better appreciated than one of those monkeys trying to figure out Shakespeare.

Do this, but don't do that!

Change that, but keep all these things I like!

Less dialog, but more scenes of people arguing!

More action, but keep it within the budget!

At one point or another you, the screenwriter that is reading this, the person this book is for, will feel like a typist. It happens to all of us. The truth is, sometimes we are typists, but what you must always remember and you must never, ever forget is that writing is a super power. It is an art, and nobody can write the movie or the novel that you can write, because your mojo is different from my mojo.

My advice, which may be at odds with some of my fellow screenwriters in this book, is to write for love, not for money. There's nothing wrong with taking assignments, I'm not saying that, but remember what *you* can do, and don't ever let them take that away from you with their notes and their frowns and their disapproving head shakes. You are a fucking writer. You weave the magic that can place any thought or image into someone else's head. You can move mountains. All you have to do is type it, and mean it when you type it, to make it so.

Ray Bradbury is mentioned a few times throughout this book. He is absolutely my favorite writer. I feel a kinship to him, because he speaks to my soul. He was a very wise man, a fellow dreamer, who was full of universal-knowledge. I got to meet him briefly once and I shook his hand, the one he used to create words out of thin air, and I said, "Thank you." He was old, a year out from his death, so all he could do was smile and nod, but the look in his eyes told me he understood what the "thank you" was for. He was known for his books, but he was a screenwriter for film and TV, as well, whether he thought it was slumming or not, so I think it would be very apropos to end here with a few words from the man that reminds me to this day that words, whether in film or just on paper, have life.

> "You must stay drunk on writing so reality cannot destroy you . . .
> You can't try to do things. You simply must do them . . .
> You fail only if you stop writing."
>
> ~Ray Bradbury

P.S.: Good luck. Go get'em.

~ Jose Prendes, February 201

www.ingramcontent.com/pod-product-compliance
Lightning Source LLC
Chambersburg PA
CBHW050335230426
43663CB00010B/1870